The Highlights Book of

Things to DO

Highlights

The Highlights Book of
Things to
DO

DISCOVER,
EXPLORE, CREATE,
AND DO
GREAT THINGS

HIGHLIGHTS PRESS
HONESDALE, PENNSYLVANIA

Parents and Caregivers,

For your child's safety, we have carefully developed the activities in this book so they can be performed and enjoyed by children age seven years or older. The activities specify when children should ask an adult for help.

However, since children develop at different levels, only a parent or close adult can judge the abilities of a particular child. Please review individual activities to ensure they are appropriate for your child.

The Editors

For information about permission to reprint selections from this book, please contact permissions@highlights.com.

Published by Highlights Press
815 Church Street
Honesdale, Pennsylvania 18431
ISBN: 978-1-68437-642-1
ebook ISBN: 978-1-64472-245-9
Library of Congress Control Number: 2020933378
Manufactured in Dongguan, Guangdong, China
Mfg. 12/2020

First edition
Visit our website at Highlights.com.
10 9 8 7 6 5 4 3 2

Design and Art Direction: Red Herring Design
Production: Margaret Mosomillo, Tina DePew, and Lauren Garofano
Editors: Marlo Scrimizzi, Laura Galen, and Christy Thomas
Cover Design: Red Herring Design
Cover Illustration: Tom Jay

Acknowledgements

Many people contributed to making this book. Without their creativity, dedication, and expertise, this gigantic book would not have been possible. We'd like to thank all the contributors!

WRITERS: Aubre Andrus, Teresa Bonaddio, Rachel Bozek, Janice Bridgers, Andrew Brisman, Sarah Chapman, Lisa Glover, Ted Heller, Jannie Ho, Laurie Kane, Joanne Mattern, Carmen Morais, Margaret Powers, Kimberly Stoney, Cy Tymony

ILLUSTRATORS: Tom Bingham, Hayelin Choi, Avram Dumitrescu, Jannie Ho, Tom Jay, Vicky Lommatzsch, Beegee Tolpa

TESTERS AND REVIEWERS: Ana Appel, Teresa Bonaddio, Andy Boyles, Mindy Burton, Sarah Chapman, Lisa Glover, Amanda Masters, Annie Rodriguez, Kimberly Stoney, Cy Tymony, Kehley Vellecamp, Sarah Weisman

OTHER CONTRIBUTORS: Jamie Bryant, Caitlin Conley, Patty Courtright, Christine Cully, Rachel Ginzberg, Psy.D, Lisa Glover, Magicorp Productions, Diane Power, Francesca Richer, Robin Weisman

We'd also like to thank those who previously created the activities for *Highlights* magazine that appear in the book.

CONTENTS

Things to Do Inside

Things to Do Outside

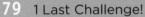

Things to Do in the Kitchen

Things to Draw

Things to Write

Things to Do with Your Brain

Things to Do with Color

Things to Do with Paper

Things to Build

Science Experiments to Do

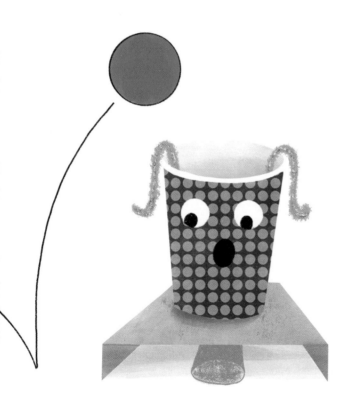

Do Great Things

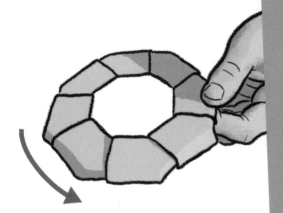

(More) Things to Do with Recycled Materials

INTRODUCTION

Dear Reader,

This book began with a simple idea: Create an activity book that captures everything you love about being a kid—and things that are important for you to know how to do. As we explored all the possible activities to include, we realized the idea wasn't so simple after all. Ultimately, it was the early days of Highlights that became our guide and inspiration. Before publishing the very first issue of *Highlights* magazine in 1946, the creators Caroline and Garry Myers thought about calling it *My Do Book*. This was fascinating to learn because choosing to *do* is more important than ever. *Do* is the driving force behind everything in this book.

The Highlights Book of Things to Do gives you the opportunity to create, make, play, invent, discover, explore, think, share, and laugh. Perhaps you were given this book to use whenever you are bored or have nothing to do. Or maybe because it's a good alternative to screen time. But we believe this book is so much more!

Our greatest hope is that you will think of this book as an adventure—something that you can pick up whenever you are curious. For instance, have you ever wished you could whistle really loudly with your fingers? Or that you could invent your own language? Maybe you've wanted to make a tool belt out of tape, or build a robot with an electric toothbrush. You'll be able to discover new ways of doing what you already know. You'll learn more about what you thought you knew. Most of all, you'll discover what you don't know yet. Because we believe that one of the best parts about doing is *discovering*. We hope you do, too.

The very last chapter of this book is called "Do Great Things." Maybe you've heard stories about kids who are changing the world in very big ways. However, doing great things doesn't have to be groundbreaking—it can simply mean being your best self. You can be your best self when you approach a problem or use your voice. You can hold the door open for someone or listen to yourself when you are stressed or angry. This chapter shows how all of us can do great things every single day, even if we're only making the world a better place for a few minutes. The word *do* is a powerful one, not only in what we create and invent but also in how we choose our actions.

Our last wish is a simple one: If you discover something in this book that you really enjoy or think is useful, we hope you will find out more about it. Maybe it will lead to a lifetime of doing great things for yourself and for others. Who knows what you'll love to do! We invite you to enjoy the adventure.

Your friends,
The Editors at Highlights

How to Use This Book

There are no rules on how to use this book. You can open it to any page you'd like—and come back to any other page that interests you. If you know you'd like to be outside, you can open up to the chapter called "Things to Do Outside." Or if you feel scientific, you can go to "Science Experiments to Do." If you need some inspiration on what to write, you can go to "Things to Write." And if you only have 10 minutes to spare, you might like to try our "6 Quick Challenges" at the beginning of every chapter. But you don't have to know what to do because we've given you more than 500 ideas to try.

STUCK? DON'T GIVE UP!

We've included a variety of activities that are simple, sort-of-simple, and not-so-simple. If you get stuck on a challenging activity, we encourage you to find a grown-up who can help you get unstuck. In fact, there are many activities in here that are perfect—and fun—to do with grown-ups.

And if you make a mistake, remember that you've already succeeded at being a doer. Doers aren't afraid of making mistakes because they reveal new discoveries—including how to do something different next time. For instance, when we first tried making the water microscope on page 272, we used plastic wrap as the "lens" and found that it did not successfully magnify objects. We learned that the lens needed to be smoother and more curved in order to work well. Then, lo and behold, an unexpected craft item stood out to us—the googly eye! We discovered that the clear cover of a googly eye was just the right shape and texture to hold water and magnify objects. If we hadn't been unsuccessful with the plastic wrap, we never would have been able to make an awesome water microscope.

USING RECYCLED AND ECO-FRIENDLY MATERIALS

You can make almost all of the projects in this book with materials that are already in your home. We encourage you to use recycled, scrap, or environmentally friendly products as much as possible in activities that ask for paper, cardboard, plastic bottles, plastic bags, plastic containers, food coloring, and similar items.

NOTE: We explored whether the activities that ask for plastic straws could be achieved with the same success using paper straws. When they can't, we recommend that you look into recycling plastic straws in your area before disposing of them. What's great about making and doing things yourself is that it challenges you to be resourceful, curious, and creative. These types of thinking are needed more than ever to address the environmental challenges of our time. We hope that this book will inspire you to consider what goes into the things you make and use, and how those things may impact the planet.

You can find more information about taking care of the planet on page 350. Learning about the environment, reflecting on your impact, and taking action all make a difference—whether it be working on recycling at your school (page 352), reducing your water use (page 352), or writing a letter to your federal, state, and local elected officials (page 135).

SAFETY FIRST!

Many activities ask you to work with things that are hot and/or sharp. It is important to learn how to safely use tools and equipment that can be dangerous to work with. We have noted when it is necessary to have a grown-up help you. We also tell you when a grown-up will need to use a tool or piece of equipment for you.

THINGS TO DO
INSIDE

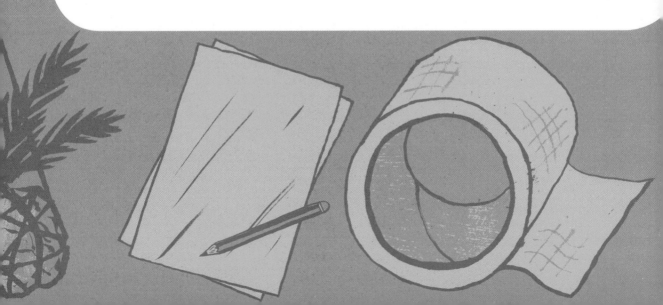

Quick Challenges

Go on a magnifying glass hunt in your home. See what you can find when you look at things really closely.

Wear something that makes you smile—fun socks, a colorful scarf, or just cheerful colors.

Invent a new holiday: Decide what it should be about and how to celebrate.

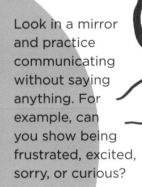

Look in a mirror and practice communicating without saying anything. For example, can you show being frustrated, excited, sorry, or curious?

Sort your books, clothes, or stuffed animals by color. Then organize them in the order the colors appear in the rainbow.

Take a poll of your friends and family on an issue you care about.

Can You Do These Tricks?

Give yourself some room to move, then try these tricky challenges.

Put a ball between your knees. Can you hop across the room without dropping it? Can you walk without dropping it?

Pick up a ball from the floor using just your elbows.

Sit up straight in a chair. Place a stuffed animal on your head. Stand up and walk around without letting it fall. Can you hop in place?

You need eight coins for this one. Sit on the floor with your legs straight. Can you place one coin in each space between your toes and hold the coins there? Can you let them go one at a time?

Balance on one foot. Can you touch your knee to your nose? Balance on the other foot and try it again.

Can you touch your left ear to your left shoulder? Can you do it on the right? Can you touch your nose to each shoulder?

Cup one hand and put it near your ear. Use your other hand to place a coin on your elbow so your elbow sticks out in front of you. Balance it there. Snap your arm down and try to grab the coin with your cupped hand before it falls. Try it with a stack of coins.

Sit down and take off your shoes. Then, without using your hands, see if you can take off your socks. If so, can you put them on again with no hands?

Inside Games

Stuck inside and tired of the usual games? Try these instead!

Toss It!

FOR 3 OR MORE PLAYERS

You Need

- Peanuts in the shell or plain popped popcorn
- Paper cups
- Paper bowls

1. Each player fills a cup with either peanuts or popcorn. Players hold their cups and stand about four feet apart in a circle. They each put an empty bowl in front of their feet.

2. One person says "Go," and players quickly toss peanuts or popcorn, one piece at a time, toward the bowl on their left. Whoever gets the most into a bowl wins.

Sock Stumper

FOR 2 OR MORE PLAYERS

You Need

- 5 tube socks
- 5 small objects

1. Gather five clean socks.

2. Look around your home for five small objects that are safe to touch. Place an object inside each sock.

3. Have your friends reach inside the socks without looking and try to guess what the objects are.

4. Take turns filling the socks with different items.

5. Bonus Round: Feel the objects from outside the sock instead of reaching inside.

Guess That Name!

FOR 4 OR MORE PLAYERS

You Need

- Slips of paper
- Bowl or hat
- Timer

This game is a twist on charades. The team who guesses the most nouns correctly after three rounds wins. To start, each player writes three nouns (people, places, or things) on three slips of paper, folds each slip to hide the word, and puts them in the bowl or hat. Players split into two teams and decide which team goes first. The other team sets the timer for one minute and says, "Start!"

Round 1: A person from the first team pulls a slip of paper from the bowl. They describe the noun on the slip to teammates without saying the actual word. When teammates guess the noun, the player puts it aside and pulls another slip of paper from the bowl, continuing to play the same way with each new noun. If teammates don't guess correctly, the player who's picking them can put the paper back in the bowl at any time, pick another, and continue playing until the minute is up.

After the minute, someone on the other team says, "Time," and the bowl is passed to a player on their team to do the same thing with the unused and unguessed nouns in the bowl. Continue taking turns until all the slips have been used. Then fold them and put them back in the bowl for the next round.

Round 2: Players can use only *one* word to describe each noun. Again, teams have one minute for each turn.

Round 3: Players must act out the nouns, with no talking allowed.

Bonus Round: If you want a super-challenging round, then repeat the play, but the actor can only use one sound as a hint.

Card Games

Want to play cards? Here are three quick-moving games to play with family or friends.

Hi, King!

FOR 2 OR MORE PLAYERS

1. Deal out an equal number of cards to each player and put aside any cards that are left over. Players sit so they are facing each other and place their cards facedown in a pile in front of themselves. Put one joker faceup in the middle of the table.

2. For every round, each player turns over a card at the same time and places it in a pile in front of themselves. If certain cards are turned over on anyone's pile, each player tries to be the first to do the correct action. If more than one action card is played, players must do the action of the highest card. The player who does the correct action last must pick up all the cards that have been played and add them to the bottom of their pile. The first player who has no cards left is the winner.

ACTIONS

If a KING is played, say, "Hi, King!"
If a QUEEN is played, clap your hands.
If a JACK is played, slap the joker in the middle of the table.
If a 10 is played, whistle or sing.

Tongues

FOR 4 OR MORE PLAYERS

Tongues is a card game that gets more fun the faster you play. The goal is to get four of a kind, such as four jacks or four aces.

1. Shuffle the deck and deal four cards to each player. Place the remaining cards in a pile facedown.

2. The dealer removes a card from their hand and slides it to the player on their left. Then the dealer takes a new card.

3. The player on the dealer's left removes a card from their hand and slides it to their left. Then they add the dealer's unwanted card to their hand.

Race to 24

FOR 2 OR MORE PLAYERS

1. Remove all jokers, kings, queens, jacks, and aces from an ordinary deck of playing cards.

2. Deal four cards faceup from the remaining pile so all players can see.

3. There are no turns. Each player plays every round.

4. Try to use all four cards to make 24 by using any math operation, such as addition, subtraction, multiplication, or division. Combine the operations any way you like to end up with the number 24.

5. The first player to say "24" and state a correct series of math steps that make 24 wins the hand. That player takes all the cards from that round, and four new cards are dealt. (If no player finds a combination that equals 24, the dealer puts one card back into the middle of the deck, then deals one new card from the top of the deck and everyone tries again.)

6. Keep playing until you use all of the cards. The player with the most cards at the end wins.

TRY IT HERE:

One winning combination would be:
2 x 6 = 12; 12 + 4 = 16; 16 + 8 = 24
Another way to get 24:
8 x 4 = 32; 32 − 6 = 26; 26 − 2 = 24

4. The game continues like this around the table, except when it gets to the last player before the dealer: They place their unwanted card in a discard pile in the center. The dealer continues to pick a new card after they have passed a card to the player on their left.

5. Players don't have to wait their turn, including the dealer, but they can't look at their new card until they've already slid an unwanted card to their left. It can get fast—everyone can slide their unwanted cards at the same time. The first person to get four of a kind quietly sticks out their tongue but continues to play.

6. As soon as you see someone with their tongue out, stick out your tongue right away! Keep playing. The last player to stick out their tongue loses.

Make Sound Effects

You can make many sounds with objects around your home. With permission, try these out and then make up your own.

THUNDER: Use two hands to hold one end of a piece of poster board or a flexible metal cookie sheet. Flap it back and forth. Or put some marbles into a plastic container, put the lid on, and gently shake it.

HORSE HOOVES: Bang two plastic cups upside down on a hard surface for clip-clop sounds.

RAIN: Pour uncooked rice into a paper bag.

CICADA: Drag a wooden craft stick along the teeth of a comb.

FOOTSTEPS: Fill a tray with gravel. Rock a block of wood back and forth in it. Or put your hands into a pair of shoes and tap them, heel to toe, on a hard surface.

FIRE: Crumple a paper bag. You could also crinkle plastic bags.

DOOR OPENING: For a creak, dip your finger in water, then run it across an inflated balloon.

DOOR SLAMMING: Make the door-opening sound above, then open a heavy book and slam it shut.

CHINA RATTLING: Rattle two metal spoons in a mug.

CLOCK STRIKING: Gently tap a spoon against a glass.

More Ideas

Can you come up with a play that uses at least three of these sound effects?

Tip

For cooler snow, put it in the refrigerator for 30 minutes before playing with it.

Make Your Own Snow

Don't wait for it to snow when you can make your own inside!

You Need

- ½ cup school glue
- 2 teaspoons contact lens solution
- Large bowl
- 1 ½ cups baking soda
- 1 ½ cups shaving cream
- Markers
- Sealable plastic bag

1. Mix the glue and contact lens solution in the bowl.

2. Stir the baking soda and shaving cream into the mixture.

3. Play and build with the snow. Use markers to add details. Store in a plastic bag.

Upside-Down Faces

FOR 2 OR MORE PEOPLE

You Need

- Turtleneck or scarf
- Washable markers
- Couch
- Pillows

1. Work on one person's face at a time. They should wear either a turtleneck or a very loose scarf to cover their neck. Check with a parent first.

2. Put two dots (for the nose) at the end of the person's chin. Draw two eyes on their neck directly under the chin.

3. The person then lies upside down on the couch, with the top of their head reaching down to the floor. Prop pillows under their neck, if needed.

4. Ask the upside-down face to talk. That's the best part! Try interviewing them, and take some photos or make a short movie.

More Ideas

If you have two couches across from each other or two beds near each other, you and your friend can both have upside-down faces and have an upside-down conversation.

Quick Skits with a Laundry Basket

With an empty laundry basket and some common household objects, you can put on a silly play.

FOR 2 OR MORE PLAYERS

1. Fill two laundry baskets—or any large containers—with about 10 different items from around the house, with permission. For example:

- hat
- scarf or necktie
- sunglasses
- costume jewelry
- hair clips
- trophy
- bathrobe
- flashlight
- photograph
- magnifying glass
- binoculars

2. Write some skit titles on index cards. Here are possibilities:

- *The Cage Escape*
- *The Lost Lunchroom*
- *Our Weird Class Trip*
- *The Best Birthday Ever*
- *Picture Day Fiasco*

3. Place the index cards facedown.

4. Divide players into two groups. Ask each group to select a title card. Then give each group one of the filled baskets or containers.

5. Set a timer for 10 minutes. In that time, each group must make up a play using its skit title and any or all of the items from its basket. After the timer goes off, each group performs its play for the other group. Create new title cards, mix up the groups, exchange baskets, and play again. Make up as many skits as you like!

More Ideas

You can also use laundry-basket theater for writing. Choose a title card and randomly select some items from a basket, then write a story that ties them together.

Make Bath Fizzies

Give your feet a soothing bath by dropping these balls into warm water. Or give them to someone who may also enjoy some pampering.

You Need

- Eyeglasses or goggles
- 1 large and some small bowls
- 1 cup baking soda
- ½ cup citric acid (found in the canning section of grocery stores)
- ½ cup Epsom salts
- ½ cup cornstarch
- 2 tablespoons olive oil
- 1 tablespoon water
- Food coloring
- Vanilla extract (optional)
- Ice-cream scoop
- Paper towels

1 **Put on eyeglasses or goggles to protect your eyes while mixing ingredients.** In a large mixing bowl, stir together baking soda, citric acid, Epsom salts, and cornstarch.

2 In a small mixing bowl, stir together olive oil and water.

3 Add the wet ingredients to the dry ingredients one teaspoon at a time, stirring quickly.

4 Divide the mixture into separate small bowls for making different colors. Add a few drops of food coloring to each bowl. If you'd like, mix in a few drops of vanilla extract for scent.

5 Spoon some of the mixture into an ice-cream scoop and press down hard to compact it.

6 Gently release the bath fizzy and place it on a paper towel. Repeat with more mixture. Let them dry for 24 hours.

Treat Your Toes

Fill a container big enough for both feet with warm water. Drop in a bath fizzy, then relax and let your feet enjoy the fizz!

Did You Know

When placed in water, baking soda and citric acid react with each other. This chemical reaction produces carbon dioxide (CO_2) gas, which bubbles up out of the water.

Set Up a Spooky Room

You can turn any room into a true fright with a little creativity. With permission, use eerie sounds, music, lights, and decorations, and then invite friends and family for a haunted tour!

CREEPY CRAWLIES: Start with any creepy decorations or toys you already have, such as fake cobwebs or little plastic spiders, and use them to set the mood.

EERIE SILHOUETTES: Draw a large rat on black paper, cut it out, and then tape or prop it up.

FLYING BATS: Cut out bats from black construction paper and fold their wings inward. Stick the bats to the wall so that their folded wings pop out.

SCARY SIGNS: Make warning signs for the walls or scary labels for bins. For example: *Don't Touch!* or *Stay Away!* Draw spiderwebs on the signs for extra creepiness.

SPOOKY SHADOWS: Bring in fallen branches or leaves and use them as decorations. If you have a flashlight, dim the room's lights after the sun has gone down. Then place the branches in front of the flashlight to cast spooky shadows around the room.

STRANGE SOUNDS: Play scary organ music or make your own recording of creepy sounds, like slow, heavy footsteps or the haunted meows of a ghost cat. (See page 12 for how to make sound effects.) Hide the device in a corner and play the recording.

A COSTUMED SURPRISE: Have a person in a costume jump out of a closet or from behind furniture to give your guests a fright.

Stretch!

Stretching and holding poses can help improve your concentration, strength, flexibility, and balance.

Before You Start

- Don't practice right after eating.

- Move into each pose slowly. Hold it as long as you can without discomfort. Don't overdo it.

- Focus on the parts of your body you're strengthening and stretching.

- Don't hold your breath. Let your breathing be comfortable and relaxed while you stretch, unless otherwise instructed.

- Come out of the pose by reversing the steps you took to get there.

Leg Stretch

Sit with one leg straight out in front of you, keeping your toes up. Bend your other leg, placing the sole of your foot against the inner thigh of your straight leg. Walk your hands down your straight leg. Stretch forward, keeping your spine straight. After a few breaths in the pose, can you lean out over your leg a little farther as you exhale? Hold the position, then walk your hands back up your leg until you are sitting up straight. Change legs.

This pose stretches your hips, back, and legs. It strengthens your legs and stomach muscles.

Balance Pose

Stand with your feet hip-width apart and your legs straight. Lean forward slightly from your hips, keeping your back straight. Reach both arms behind you, and fan out your fingers. Concentrate on one spot in front of you. Go up on your toes, focusing on staying balanced. Is it easier to keep your balance when your eyes are open or closed? If you tumble out of the pose, can you take a breath and find your balance again?

This pose strengthens your back, hips, legs, and ankles. It stretches your shoulders and arms.

Tortoise Pose

Sit with your knees bent and your feet flat on the floor, wider apart than your hips. Bend forward and reach an arm under each knee, from your inner leg outward. Then bring the soles of your feet together and let your knees open to the sides, resting on your arms. Spread your hands as you lean forward. Let your breath be comfortable and smooth as you curl inward, like a tortoise in its shell. Try to gently lower your head toward the floor each time you exhale. Does the feeling of this stretch change as you hold the pose?

This pose stretches your hips, hamstrings, back, and shoulders.

Squat Walk

Squat and try to put both feet flat on the floor. Place your palms together. Hold your hands with your thumbs against your forehead and your fingers interlaced. Widen your elbows. Once you feel strong in this position, try walking forward, lifting one hip at a time and keeping your back straight and strong.

This walk strengthens your shoulders, wrists, back, hips, and ankles.

More Ideas

Try practicing your favorite stretches often. Some may seem hard at first, but soon you'll be able to hold them longer.

Camel Pose

Kneel with your knees directly under your hips. Keep your spine straight and your knees hip-width apart. Place your hands against your bottom to press your hips and thighs forward with your elbows pointing behind you. Keeping your hips over your knees, move your chest up and back, with your head following, as if you're leaning back over a big barrel. Curve backward as far as you comfortably can. Keep the back of your neck long. You'll be looking forward and slightly up, rather than at the ceiling right above or behind you. **Do not throw your neck back.**

After several seconds, lean farther back and reach with both arms to hold onto your heels. Keep pressing your hips forward and breathe deeply through your nose. Place your hands against your bottom to come back up slowly and evenly. (Don't lean to either side as you come up.)

This pose stretches the front of your body and strengthens your back and core muscles.

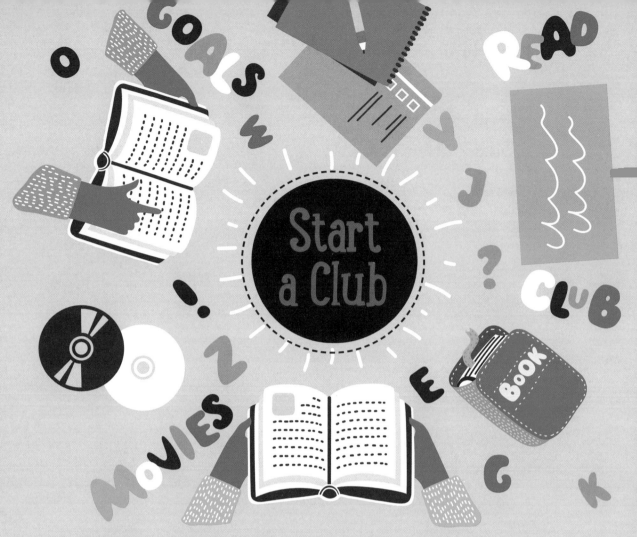

Start a Club

Have you ever thought about starting a club where you can do the things you enjoy with other people? You could try one of these ideas, or think up one of your own.

Share-and-Learn Club

Gather a group of friends or family members. You could start by asking everyone to write down things they can do, such as making a favorite meal, drawing superheroes, or writing stories. Then decide what skills you will all learn first.

You can organize it any way you want, either by pairing up members to teach each other or by having everyone learn a skill from one member. Keep going until you've all learned a lot of new skills.

Book Club

Find a few friends who also enjoy reading and talking about books. First decide how you want to choose books: by discussion and vote, by having each member get a month to choose a book, or some other way. After you've all read the "assigned" book, talk about it in your club. Here are some questions to get started: What words would you use to describe this book? Who was your favorite character? What do you think happens to the characters after the book ends? Would you like to change anything in the book? What might a different cover look like? You can also come up with awards, such as Phenomenal Page-turner, Awesome Adventure, or Coolest Character.

Movie Club

Gather together friends or family who enjoy watching movies. You can choose movies to watch together based on types of films, such as comedies or classics, or ones that feature the same actors, directors, settings, or anything else. Perhaps you could change where you watch the films each time. When the movie is over, look at the end credits and all the jobs and people involved. What was your favorite part of the movie? Did you like the costumes, the settings, the music? Give yourselves enough time to talk about all aspects of the film.

I Care Club

Is there a cause that is really important to you, or an issue you feel strongly about? Maybe you would like to make your school, town, or the world a better place. If so, then you could create an "I Care Club." To start, decide on an issue the club will tackle—perhaps you don't have clean playgrounds nearby, or there's something you would like to improve at school. Or maybe there's something in the news that's concerning or confusing to you. Talk to and invite people you know who also want to get involved with making positive changes around this issue.

You'll need at least one adult to help with your club. It could be a teacher, a community leader, a parent, or another adult you trust. They can help you navigate how to make an impact on the issue and help come up with ideas of what to do.

Together, the group can talk about the issue you've decided to focus on, and come up with what your goals are as a club. The goals can change later, but they will give you a place to get started!

Make a Tool Belt with Tape

Create sturdy duct-tape pockets to store tools, school supplies, or other small items.

1. Cut a piece of string that's long enough to wrap and tie around your waist. Then cut one piece of duct tape almost as long as the string. Put the duct tape sticky-side-up on a flat work surface. Place the string in the center of the duct tape.

2. Fold the duct tape in half, using the string as a guide. This is your belt.

4. On the back of each pocket, toward the top, cut two vertical slits that are as long as the belt is wide. The slits should be a few inches from each other and should not go through to the tops of the pockets.

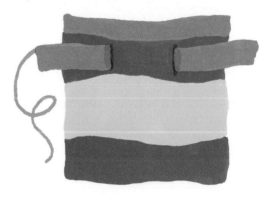

3. To create the pockets, cover the front and backs of each resealable plastic bag with duct-tape strips.

5. Weave the belt through the slits to complete your tool belt!

More Ideas

You can make a line of staples down the center of a duct-tape bag to create separate pockets. Staple around the left, right, and bottom edges of the pockets, about a half-inch from each edge.

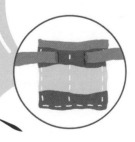

Tip
When practicing knot-tying, try using rope that is flexible. Avoid rope that is too stiff or stretchy. Braided nylon rope is a great choice.

Tie Four Useful Knots

Knots aren't just for tying shoelaces. Learn how, and when, to tie four useful knots.

Before You Start

The working end of the rope is the end that you move around to tie the knot; the standing part is the part of the rope, or other end, that is held in place as you form the knot. The standing part may also be the part that is attached to something, like a sled or an object being pulled.

working end

standing part

FIGURE EIGHT KNOT

Good for: Putting a stopper in a rope, like when you don't want a drawstring to slip through the opening in a hood or waistband.

1. Make a simple loop near the working end of the rope. Make sure the working end is the top part of the loop.

2. Pull the working end behind and under the standing part.

3. Pull the working end back through the loop. Keep the knot loose at this point.

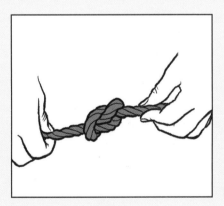

4. Pull the two sections of rope away from each other to tighten the knot.

More knots on next page

BOWLINE KNOT

Good for: Making a loop that can't change size, like what you need to attach a hammock to a tree, or tie a boat to a dock. Sailors have used this knot for centuries. It's also the knot used to secure a harness for rock climbing.

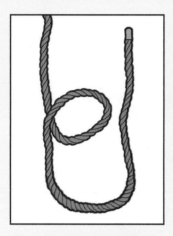

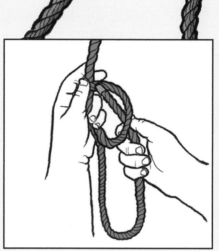

1. Lay the rope directly in front of you. The loop must have the working end on top of the standing part. Also, give some length (6–12 inches) between the end of the rope and the loop.

2. Grab the working end and put it through the loop from the bottom up.

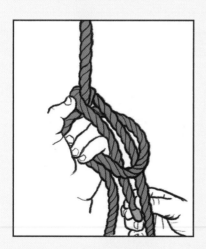

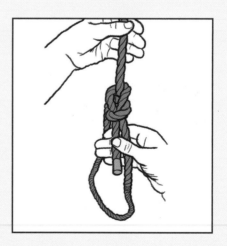

3. Bring the working end around the back of the standing part and then back down through the loop.

4. Grab each end of the rope and pull the knot tight.

TWO HALF HITCHES

Good for: Tying a rope to a tree or pole, like when you want to put up a tarp, a clothesline, or a hammock. A hitch knot is one that ties to an object.

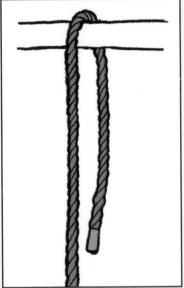

1. Put the rope around the tree or pole, with the working end on the right.

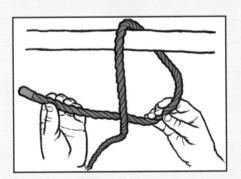

2. Cross the working end underneath the standing part.

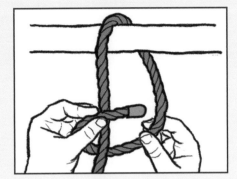

3. Wrap the working end around the standing part and bring it through the loop.

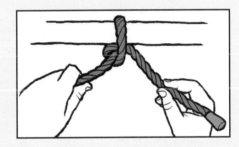

4. Tighten this first knot by pulling both ends of the rope.

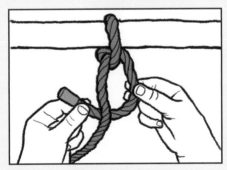

5. Cross the working end underneath the standing part again, just as you did in step 2.

Continued on next page

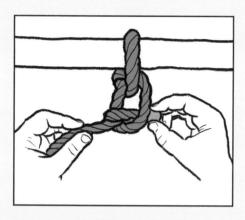 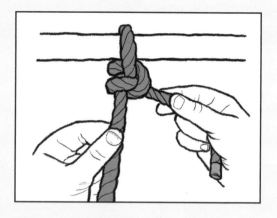

6. Wrap the working end around the standing part again and bring it in through the loop, like you did in step 3.

7. Pull both ends of the rope to tighten the knot.

SQUARE KNOT

Good for: Tying together the two ends of a single rope, or two ropes together. It should only be used for light needs, such as tying a package or tying up a bundle of objects. It should not be used for pulling or towing something.

1. Cross the two ends of rope, with the working end on top of the standing part.

2. Wrap the working end around the standing part.

3. Then pull the working end up in front.

4. Cross the two ropes together again so the working end is on top of the standing part.

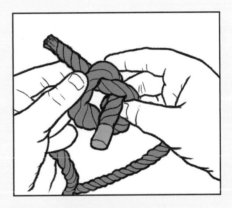

5. Wrap the working end around the standing part and pull the working end through the loop.

6. Once you've pulled the working end all the way through the loop, grab the four sections of rope and pull the knot tight.

Knit on Two Fingers

You don't need knitting needles to make something out of yarn. All you need are your hands.

You Need

- Skein of yarn (the thicker the yarn, the denser your knitting will be)
- Scissors

1. Hold your left hand in front of you, with your palm facing toward you. (If you are left-handed, hold your right hand in front of you.) Put the end of the yarn between your thumb and pointer finger. Leave a tail four-to-six inches long on your palm. You won't be knitting with the tail.

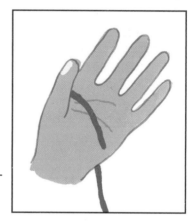

2. Grab the yarn that's behind your hand. Loop the yarn in front of your middle finger, starting from behind your pointer finger.

3. From the back of your middle finger, loop the yarn in front of your pointer.

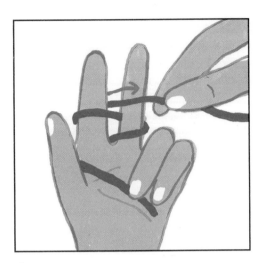

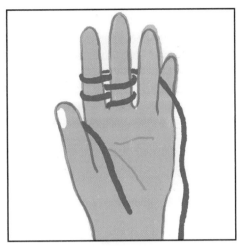

4. Repeat the loops: From the back of your pointer, loop the yarn in front of the middle finger and around the back.

5. Then loop the yarn around the front of the pointer. Each finger now has two loops of yarn. To keep the yarn in place, hold it in between your ring and pinkie fingers.

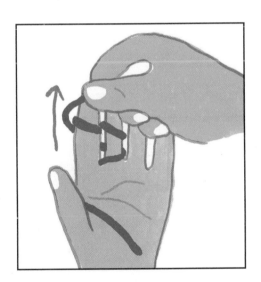

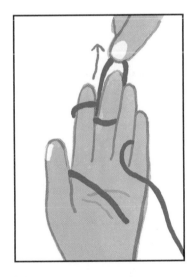

6. To make your first stitch, start with your pointer finger. Pull the bottom loop up and over the top loop and the fingertip.

7. Repeat with the middle finger: Pull the bottom loop up and over that fingertip. Pull gently on both ends of the yarn to tighten up the stitches.

Continued on next page

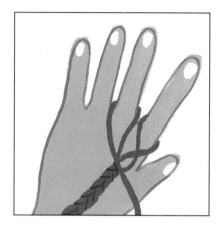

8. Remove the yarn from between your ring and pinkie fingers and then repeat steps 4–7 until your creation is the length you want.

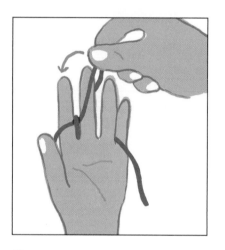

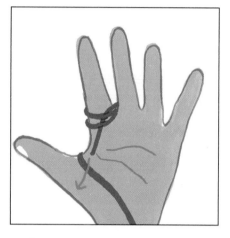

9. To end (or *cast off*), make sure you have only one loop left on each finger. Cut the yarn from the skein, leaving a tail six inches long. Move the loop from the middle finger over to the pointer.

10. Thread the tail through both loops, pull the loops off your finger, and pull tight to knot.

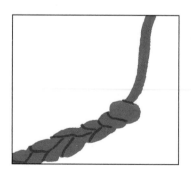

Tip

Try lacing knitted strands together to form bigger pieces: Cut a new piece of yarn and knot it to the end of a knitted strand. Weave the yarn back and forth between two strands. Pull firmly to join the strands.

Invent a New Language

Have you ever wanted to create a secret language? It can be easier than you might think.

You could start by following the rules of Pig Latin, which are to move and add sounds. In Pig Latin, if a word starts with a consonant sound, move it to the end and add the sound *ay.* For example: *dog = ogday* and *chicken = ickenchay.* And if a word starts with a vowel, then just add *ay* or *yay* at the end. For example: *orange = orangeay* and *are = areyay*.

To create your own language, you can move or add different sounds. For instance, you could add *goo* after the first syllable.

For example: *I'm hungry for a turkey sandwich* would be *I'mgoo hungoogry forgoo agoo turgookey sandgoowich.*

You can also create a language by substituting words. With this rule, you replace words with completely different, unrelated words. You'll need to write down a vocabulary list to keep the meanings straight.

To start, think of a common topic you talk about with your friend, such as video games. Create a list of gaming words, then substitute them with random words.

For example, say "garbage can" instead of "game controller," "eat" instead of "lose," and "umbrella" instead of "racing game." Your sentences could sound like this: *Hand me the garbage can. You have eaten enough umbrellas for one afternoon!*

That means: *Hand me the controller. You have lost enough racing games for one afternoon!*

Make an Indoor Hanging Garden

This garden art form has been around in Japan for hundreds of years. Here is how you can make a miniature plant for yourself—or to give as a gift.

You Need

- Plastic cover or old vinyl tablecloth, to protect your work area
- Garden gloves (optional)
- Small plant (Try ivy or a baby fern. Avoid succulents and cacti.)
- Soil (Use equal parts peat moss and bonsai soil. If you can't find bonsai soil, use potting soil with perlite. Add a handful of garden clay if you have it.)
- 2 buckets
- Water
- Moss (dry sphagnum)

1. Set up your work area. Spread out the plastic cover or tablecloth. Prepare the plant by gently shaking or brushing the soil away from its roots. Then gather the soil mixture in one bucket. Moisten it until it feels sticky and squishy enough that you can pack it between your hands. In the second bucket, soak the dry sphagnum moss in water for about five minutes.

Tip

This project can be very messy! If you want to protect hands and clothing, wear garden gloves and clothes that can get dirty.

2. Hold your plant in one hand and pack the soil around the roots into a ball. The size of the soil ball will vary, depending on the size of your plant. It should look and feel firm. If you need to, add water to keep the soil moist and workable.

3. Wring out the moss and then wrap it around the soil ball. Press it all around. It should also look and feel firm.

4. Tie twine around the moss, as shown below, to keep it in place. Wrap it around the ball in different directions for added decoration and support. Knot the end. Then tie a long piece of twine to the top of the ball for hanging in a sunny spot.

CARING FOR YOUR PLANT:
When the ball feels light, it's time to water it. Take it down, soak the ball in water, and then place it on a bowl or dish or let it hang outside until it's no longer dripping.

Games to Speed Up Clean Up

Here are some ways to add a little fun to cleaning up.

Beat the Timer

FOR 1 OR MORE CLEANERS

How long do you think it will take to clean your room? Five minutes? Ten minutes? Take a guess, and then set a timer for the amount of time you guessed. Start the timer, and see if you can finish before the timer beeps. It may take more than one try. Keep guessing until you beat the timer.

Pick a Stick

FOR 1 OR MORE CLEANERS

Look around your room. What needs to be straightened up? Books? Toys? Maybe your bed? Write each thing on its own craft stick. Put all the sticks in a cup. Then pick a stick to see what you'll clean first. When you're done with that stick, grab another. When all the sticks are gone, your mess should be gone, too.

Song Stop

FOR 2 OR MORE CLEANERS

One person (the DJ) starts the first song. As the music plays, the others clean as fast as they can (while still being thorough and careful). When the DJ pauses the music, freeze! When the DJ starts the music, start cleaning again. At the end of the song, someone else takes a turn as the DJ. Keep playing until the room is clean.

Create Your Own Time Capsule

1. Find an empty shoebox to use as the capsule.

2. Find things of importance to you today and place them in the box. Some suggestions are photos, movie tickets, lists of friends' names, a list of your predictions about the future, lists of popular TV shows, movies, clothing, stars, and songs, and your opinions about them. Don't put in anything that could decompose, such as food!

3. Close the box, and write your name and the date on it.

4. Put it in a cool, dry spot, such as the top shelf of your closet. Open your time capsule next year or several years from now. It will be interesting to see what changed and which predictions came true.

Tips

Do a big sort. Label empty boxes with group names such as *Papers*, *Artwork*, and *Sports Equipment*. Write *Give Away* on one box for things you don't want. Move everything from your floor to its proper box.

Toss out or recycle. If you have things that can't be used anymore, throw them away or see if you can recycle them.

Figure out where to put the things you'll keep. Tackle one box at a time. If the items already have a home, put them in it. If not, create a home for them. For example, stash hobby supplies in labeled plastic tubs.

Make cleaning a habit. The more often you clean, the less work it will be each time.

Car Games

When the trip seems to go on and on, try these games.

Zip

FOR 2 OR MORE PLAYERS

Before the game starts, a player chooses a number between one and nine, and tells everyone what it is. To play, take turns counting. The first player says "one," the next says "two," and so on. When you come to any number that contains the chosen number, you must say "zip" instead of the number.

For example, if the chosen number were three, you'd say "zip" instead of 3, 13, 23, and any of the 30s. If you get caught not saying "zip" when you should, you're out.

If you want a challenge, say "zip" if the number is a multiple of the chosen number (3, 6, 9, 12, etc.). Or say "zip" if the digits add up to the chosen number (12, 21, 30, 102, etc.).

City, State, Country

FOR 2 OR MORE PLAYERS

The first player chooses a city, state, or country and says it out loud. The next player must think of a city, state, or country that begins with the final letter of the first name. For example, if the first player says "Oregon," the next player could say "Nebraska." The next player could say "Alabama" or "Arkansas."

Players continue taking turns. If a player can't think of a place with the correct first letter, they are out. The last remaining player is the winner.

Stoplight Baseball

FOR 2 OR MORE PLAYERS

Take turns being "at bat." The person at bat scores a run whenever the car you're in passes under a green light. Stopped at a red light? That's an out. Stop signs count as outs, too. After three outs, it's the next player's turn. The player with the most runs after an equal number of turns wins.

3 Signs, 3 Minutes

FOR 2 OR MORE PLAYERS

Ask someone (but not the driver) to time you for three minutes. In that time, you and your opponent look for signs with numbers on them, such as speed limit, exit, and route signs. When you spot a sign, say the number out loud. If you are first to say it, you get to write it down. Add it to the next numbered sign that you claim, and then the next one. Whoever gets the highest total from three different signs in three minutes is the winner.

Virtual Hide-and-Seek

FOR 2 OR MORE PLAYERS

One person thinks of a place in the world to "hide" and doesn't tell anyone else. The rest of the passengers try to figure out where they are "hiding" by asking yes-or-no questions. You can decide the maximum number of questions that players can ask before the hider tells where they are.

Make Checkers to Go

Roll up this game and take it with you wherever you go.

FOR 2 PLAYERS

You Need

- Piece of felt, about 15 inches long and 10 inches wide
- Tacky glue
- 12 large craft sticks
- Scissors
- Pencil
- Ruler
- Felt in a different color
- Adhesive hook-and-loop dots
- 24 buttons, 12 of one color and 12 of another color

1. Use tacky glue to attach 12 large craft sticks, side by side, to the large piece of felt. Let them dry.

2. Trim off any extra felt.

3. Use a pencil and ruler to draw a checkerboard on the other side of the felt. Cut out squares of the different colored felt to fit in the squares, then glue these felt squares on every other space.

4. For playing pieces, attach the sticky side of adhesive hook-and-loop dots to the bottom of buttons—12 of each color.

Ways to Explore a Culture

On a map or globe, find a country that you'd like to learn more about. Then try out these ideas!

1 Learn a few words or a phrase in the language spoken there.

2 Find out what foods people eat for breakfast in that country. Try to find ingredients to prepare one of them.

3 Learn a game that kids play in that country and, if possible, play it.

4 Find out about a holiday that is important in that country.

1 Last Challenge!

Can you invent a new game that uses yarn, coins, and chopsticks?

THINGS TO DO
OUTSIDE

Time yourself to see how many cartwheels you can do in 30 seconds.

Quick Challenges

Start a nature collection.

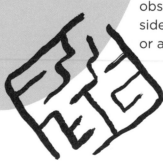

Go outside with a phone or tablet that has a microphone. Listen closely and record while you stay in one place. How many individual sounds did you capture?

Invent your own games by using whatever sports balls you have. You could play tennis-ball soccer or beach-ball baseball, for example.

Find a spot where you can lie on your back and watch the clouds go by.

Make a chalk maze or obstacle course on a sidewalk or driveway, or at a park.

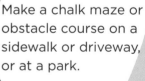

Make a Summer Hideout

Once there is no longer any frost in the spring, you can grow your own hideout or reading nook. It will be ready in the later part of summer, depending on where you live.

You Need

- Shovel
- Fertilizer
- 3 poles, about 1-inch in diameter, or 1-by-1-inch pieces of wood that are 10–12 feet long
- Scissors
- Twine cut to the following lengths:
  3 pieces that are 5 feet long
  6 pieces that are 9 feet long
  1 piece that is 2 feet long
- Package of pole-bean seeds
- Water

1. Choose a sunny spot outside for your hideout. Make sure an adult approves the spot you pick.

2. Prepare the soil by turning and loosening it with a shovel. Sprinkle fertilizer in the dirt.

3. Stand the three poles in a cone shape. Push the pole bottoms four-to-five inches into the soil.

Continued on next page

4. Use the two-foot piece of twine to tie the three poles together where they cross at the top.

5. Pat soil firmly around the bottom of each pole.

6. Tie each five-foot piece of twine from one pole to the next pole at the bottom of the cone.

7. Tie the nine-foot pieces of twine from the top of the cone to the bottom pieces of twine. You'll have two nine-foot strips between each pole.

8. Make a one-inch-deep hole in the soil at each nine-foot piece of twine and at each pole. Plant two beans in each hole.

9. Water the seeds once a day for the first week. Then water them twice a week, unless it rains.

10. As the plants grow, gently wrap the tendrils around the poles and twine so they can climb to the top. Enjoy your hideout!

Whistle Really Loudly

You can learn to whistle strongly and loudly. Follow the steps below and practice, practice, practice.

1. Wash your hands well.

2. Make an upside-down V with your index or pinkie fingers.

3. Put the two fingers that form the V in your mouth so that the point of the V is under the tip of your tongue.

4. Push your fingers back a bit so that your tongue curls backward.

5. Close your lips around your fingers. This allows air to pass only through the small triangular hole between your fingers.

6. Blow!

Tip

You can blow hard or soft. It doesn't really matter. Just move your fingers around and keep blowing until you find the right spot. Some people practice for several days before they get the hang of it. Don't give up!

Chalk Activities

TRIANGLE TOSS

FOR 2 OR MORE PLAYERS

On a flat sidewalk or other paved spot, use chalk to draw a big triangle. Divide it into five sections, as shown. Number the sections 1 through 5. Draw a line about two feet below the base of the triangle.

Players stand behind the line. Take turns tossing three pebbles onto the numbered sections. The highest total score for each round wins.

```
    5
   4
  3
 2
1
```

FOUR SQUARES

FOR 4 OR MORE PLAYERS

To play, you need four people, a big ball, some sidewalk chalk, and a flat, safe, paved spot. Draw a large chalk square (about eight-by-eight feet). Divide it into four equal squares.

Number the squares in order, moving clockwise from the upper left corner to the lower left corner: 1, 2, 3, 4. One person stands in each square.

The person standing in square 1 serves by bouncing the ball first in their square and then hitting it to another square. It should bounce once there, and then the person in that square hits it to another square.

If anyone hits the ball to the area outside of the squares, they are out. A person is also out by letting the ball bounce more than once in their square or by forgetting to let the ball bounce once before hitting it. The one who is out goes to square 4, and everyone else moves up a square to fill the empty spot. (If you have more than four players, the person who is out leaves the square and the new person moves to square 4.) Then play resumes with the person in square 1 serving.

Continue playing as long as you want. There are no winners or losers.

DRAW A 3-D FAKE HOLE

1. Using black chalk or charcoal, draw a shape with zigs and zags around the edge. A few steps away, draw an X on the ground.

2. Draw several dark lines inside the circle, starting from the edge farthest from the X and running straight toward it. Attach the lines to the corners of the zigs and zags—but draw them only inside the shape!

3. For shadows, add more darkness to the side closest to the X. Smudge the shadows with your fingers to make them fade from very dark to less dark.

4. With a thin piece of charcoal or chalk, draw a few zigzag lines that extend from the edges of the "hole." These are the cracks that make it look extra realistic!

5. Stand on the X and look at what you've drawn!

Weird Races

How many ways can you race with friends? Here are some silly races that you can try on a soft, grassy area. Make START and FINISH lines, then mark the boundaries of the course using rope, towels, or sticks.

STATION RACING
FOR 2 OR MORE PLAYERS

In a yard or a park, set up six "stations." At station one, players might do 10 jumping jacks. At station two, perhaps they hop along a hopscotch board forward and then backward. Station three might be hitting a target with a foam football, and so on.

Time each player as they race through the course. Who can get the best time?

ELBOWS ON KNEES
FOR 2 OR MORE PLAYERS

Place your elbows on your knees and keep them there as you race. (You can use your feet this time.)

NO FEET ALLOWED
FOR 2 OR MORE PLAYERS

Your feet may not touch the ground at any time. Use any other parts of your body to get from START to FINISH.

BELLY BUTTON UP
FOR 2 OR MORE PLAYERS

Your belly button must face up, toward the sky, all the way from START to FINISH. Imagine you are walking like a crab.

BEACHBALL BALANCE
FOR 4 OR MORE PLAYERS

In teams of two, players carry a beachball between their heads from START to FINISH. The fastest team wins.

HOLD YOUR TOES
FOR 2 OR MORE PLAYERS

Take off your shoes. Hold on to your big toes and don't let go of them until you reach FINISH.

Throw a Summer Fair

Set up a spot where friends, family, and neighbors can come together to have a fun day in the sun!

You Need

- An outdoor space you can use
- Outdoor tables, chairs, stools
- Beanbags, small buckets, rubber balls
- Craft materials, for a crafts table
- Games, such as cards, trivia games, etc.
- Toys and small items you don't want anymore

More Ideas

Set up a table where you can sell cookies and lemonade or sell cupcakes and set up a cupcake-icing station.

Before you begin, decide on what you want at the fair. It depends on how many people are helping. Each person can come up with an idea for a booth to run. There could be tossing games and craft-making tables. You could also have a yard-sale table with old toys and trinkets.

You might also have booths with games, such as Sprinkler Trivia, where a player must run through the sprinkler if they answer a trivia question incorrectly (or correctly, if it's a super hot day). Or you could make an obstacle course with cardboard boxes, outdoor furniture, and other found objects.

Play Tag Five Ways

Try these twists on the classic game of tag. You need at least three players. The more people you have, the more challenging the game.

DRAGON TAG

Line up. Each player holds the waist of the person in front of them. Then the dragon's head (the player in front) tries to "bite" (tag) the tail (the last player in line).

CHAIN TAG

The first player tagged joins hands with "It" and they run together, each using a free hand to tag others. Each person they tag becomes a new link in the chain.

SILLY-STEPS TAG

Before beginning the game, "It" chooses a silly step for the first round. All of the players, including "It," must do the silly step. No running, just the silly step. Once "It" tags another player, that player decides what the next round's silly step will be. Some silly-step ideas could be crab walking, tiptoeing, skipping, or hopping.

SHADOW TAG

Instead of tagging players, "It" steps on people's shadows. Try this in a gym, or in a well-lit backyard after dark. Your shadows will change as you run!

HIDE-AND-GO TAG

All players hide within shouting distance of one another. As the seeker finds each hider, they call out a number, starting with one, and make eye contact with that hider. Hiders stay where they are.

After everyone is found, the seeker shouts, "Go!" Players race to tag the person they think has the number just above theirs. (The person with the highest number chases the person who is number one.) If a player tags the wrong person, they both keep playing. The seeker doesn't chase anyone. Anyone who remains untagged wins.

Water Balloon Games

Cool off with these games that will help you beat the summer heat.

BALLOON BOWLING

FOR 2 OR MORE PLAYERS

Use empty cans or plastic bottles as pins and a water balloon as the ball. Set the pins on a flat surface outdoors and see how many you can knock down.

YARD TOSS

FOR 2 OR MORE PLAYERS

Place four rulers (or other markers) at varying distances. See who can toss a water balloon the farthest without bursting it.

EXPLODING TAG

FOR 3 OR MORE PLAYERS

Instead of tagging another player, "It" lightly tosses a water balloon at them (below the neck). If the balloon doesn't pop when it hits the player, they become "It"!

BALLOON TENNIS

FOR 2 OR MORE PLAYERS

Gently toss a water balloon back and forth with tennis rackets, taking a step back after each toss. See how far away from each other you can get without bursting the balloon.

Make Giant Bubbles

Use this recipe to make huge and long-lasting bubbles.

STIR UP THE BUBBLE SOLUTION

You Need

- 3 cups "soft" or distilled water
- Clean bucket
- 6 tablespoons of dish soap (Dawn works well)
- 3 tablespoons glycerin or corn syrup

1. Pour the water into a clean bucket.

2. Add the dish soap and glycerin or corn syrup. Corn syrup and glycerin make the soap film stronger.

3. Gently stir the ingredients. Try not to create suds.

4. Let the mixture sit for a few hours or overnight before using it, so the ingredients combine and any dirt settles on the bottom.

Tip

Blow bubbles on a cool, humid, calm day. When it's hot, dry, and windy, water evaporates faster from bubbles, making them pop.

CREATE A BIG-BUBBLE WAND

You Need

- Scissors
- Yarn or cotton string
- 2 straws (plastic, stainless steel, or any stiff material)

1. Cut a piece of yarn or cotton string so it's six times as long as a drinking straw.

2. Thread it through the two straws.

3. Tie the ends of the yarn or string together. Slide the knot inside one of the straws.

4. Using the straw pieces as handles, dunk the wand into the bubble solution to coat the straws and yarn or string. (Wet your hands, too.) Hold the straws together  as you lift them out. Pull them apart slowly to make a sheet of bubble film. Pull the wand through the air. Bring the straws together to close the bubble.

Jump Rope Games

Get out a jump rope—a long one if you are playing with more people—and play these fast-moving games.

A IS FOR APPLE

FOR 1 OR MORE PLAYERS

This game calls for fast thinking! Play alone or with a friend. As you jump rope, say this chant, filling in any word you choose for each letter. For example:

"*A* is for attic,

B is for baseball,

C is for camel . . ."

Continue like this for every letter of the alphabet. Each line should be said with only two turns of the rope. Start over if you miss a skip or if you cannot think of a word fast enough. Can you get to *Z*?

Another version: Let your partner call out any letter, and see if you can think of a correct word on the next jump.

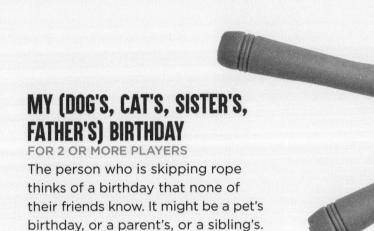

MY (DOG'S, CAT'S, SISTER'S, FATHER'S) BIRTHDAY
FOR 2 OR MORE PLAYERS

The person who is skipping rope thinks of a birthday that none of their friends know. It might be a pet's birthday, or a parent's, or a sibling's.

While jumping, the person says this chant, using two or four turns of the rope for each line:

"Do you know their birthday?

See if you can guess.

I can skip their birthday

And put you to the test."

That person then says, "Month first," using one turn of the rope for each word ("month" on the first turn of the rope and "first" on the second turn). Then they jump the birthday by using one rope turn per month (so they would jump three times for a March birthday).

Immediately after the last skip for the month, they say, "Now the day," on the next two turns of the rope ("now the" on the first turn and "day" on the second), and then jump until the day of the birthday is counted out.

See if anyone can guess the birthday.

HIGH WATER, LOW WATER
FOR 4 OR MORE PLAYERS

To play High Water, two people hold the ends of the jump rope. Start with the rope touching the ground, with the holders making "waves" by wiggling the rope. Other players take turns stepping over the "water" without touching the rope. After everyone has done this, the rope holders raise the rope a little higher and make waves again, and everyone crosses the water again. A player is out when they touch the rope. The last person in the game wins.

To play Low Water, two players hold the rope at shoulder level. Players try to pass, or "swim," under the rope without touching it. After each round, the rope is lowered. (To add a challenge, don't allow players' hands to touch the ground.) Any player who touches the rope is out, and the last person in the game wins.

Go Camping

Ready to explore the great outdoors? Here are some ideas to get you started on a camping adventure—whether in your yard or at a campground.

See how to tie knots on page 24.

MAKE YOUR OWN TENT

Create a simple temporary shelter for yourself. Be sure to pick a dry day to enjoy it.

1. Tie a rope between two trees.

2. Place an old towel on the ground below the rope.

3. Toss an old sheet over the rope, half on each side.

4. Pull the sheet to the edges of the towel, and place a few rocks along the edges on both sides to hold it in place.

NAVIGATE WITH THE SUN

You can find north, south, east, and west using the sun. The sun rises in the east and it sets in the west. Notice where the sun rises and sets. Then stand with "sunrise" on your right and "sunset" on your left. You'll be facing north. South will be directly behind you.

Safety Tip

Remember never to stare directly at the sun, and don't leave a telescope or binoculars where anyone, especially a young child, could use them to look at the sun. Looking directly at the sun can damage the eyes.

NAVIGATE WITH THE STARS

Know which way to go before starting
out on a starlit adventure.

North Star

1. Find the Big Dipper, as shown below. Then find the pointer stars on the side of the "pan." Draw an imaginary line between the pointer stars.

2. Extend the line up, away from the pan. The first bright star you come to is the North Star, or Polaris.

pointer stars

3. If you're facing the North Star, then north is in front of you, south is behind you, east is on your right, and west is on your left.

More camping on next page

BUILD A FIRE AT A CAMPGROUND

These instructions show you how to build a fire in a fire ring, fireplace, or grill, all of which are available in most campgrounds. Make sure fires are allowed in the campground and that you have an adult to help and supervise.

Definitions:

Tinder includes small twigs, dry leaves, and pine needles.

Kindling means small sticks.

Firewood refers to larger pieces of wood.

3. Place the smaller pieces of kindling in a cone shape around the tinder. Lean the tops of the kindling against each other to form the cone. Make sure to leave some small spaces in the kindling cone so air can get in and you can light the fire. Continue adding larger and larger pieces of kindling until you have two or three layers around the tinder.

1. You will need three kinds of wood to build your fire: tinder, kindling, and firewood. Only use local firewood to build your fire to help prevent the spread of harmful insects.

2. Place a small pile of tinder in the middle of the fire ring.

4. Place small pieces of firewood in a "log cabin," or square shape, around the cone.

5. Light the tinder in the bottom center of the fire. Be careful. It's fine to light the match and just drop it in.

6. Fire needs oxygen to build. Get on your hands and knees and blow at the bottom of the fire. Blow close to the ground, but not too close to the fire. Blow directly at the fire to avoid stirring up ashes and dirt. You can continue to blow on your fire as needed.

7. Once your fire is going strong, add bigger pieces of firewood. You can add them to the log cabin piece or around the cabin in cone form, with the tops of the firewood leaning against each other. Enjoy the warm fire. To keep it going, add more wood when the fire starts to die down.

8. When you're ready to put out the fire, give yourself some time—about 20 minutes. Pour lots of water on it. Use a long stick to spread out the ashes and embers and make sure they all get wet. You may need to pour more water over them. Check that the ashes are cool and there are no embers before you leave the site. There should be no steam or hissing noises coming from the fire.

More camping on next page

MAKE FOOD ON THE FIRE

Have an adult supervise while you make these tasty treats.

For how to make a sun cooker, see page 287.

CHEESY MELTS

Butter two slices of bread on one side. Place cheese between the unbuttered sides. Wrap the sandwich in three layers of foil and use metal tongs to place it on hot coals. Cook for three minutes, then flip it and cook for three minutes more. Let it cool before eating!

STUFFED S'MORES

Use a table knife to poke a slit in the top of a marshmallow. Put two chocolate chips into the slit. With the chocolate-chip side up, put the stuffed marshmallow on a stick and roast it over the fire. When it's browned, place it between two graham crackers.

Take Outdoor Photos

Try these tips for taking eye-catching photos when you're outside.

- Clean the lens with a soft microfiber cloth. Never use your fingers to wipe it (especially for a smartphone camera).
- Take photos in the early morning or late afternoon, when light is softer and warmer than at midday. The light at these times also makes interesting shadows and rich colors.
- If it's sunny, keep the sun behind you. Even if it's cloudy, keep the light source to your side or behind you.

- If you're photographing small children or animals, kneel down.
- Make sure that your subject's entire head is showing in the viewfinder.
- Hold the camera steady and level.
- Breathe out slowly as you click the shutter gently with a slow squeeze.
- Keep it simple. Pick out the most important thing you want to see and focus on it.

PHOTOGRAPH FALL CHANGES

Find a tree close to home or school with leaves that change color in the fall. Take a photo of the tree, from the same spot and angle, once or twice each week throughout the season.

You could print out the sequential shots at a small size, stack them in order, staple them together on the left side, and then watch the tree change from the first to last page. Or you could print them larger and mount them on a board.

Go on a Tree Search

Trees do a lot more than stand around all day. Among many things, they provide wood, fruits, and nuts for humans and other creatures, homes for wildlife, shade in hot weather—and the oxygen we need to breathe! Here's a look at five trees that you can find throughout the U.S. Can you find them all?

WEEPING WILLOW

These large trees are distinct and beautiful. They can be as wide as they are tall—from 45 to 70 feet. They have long, thin, bending leaves that are green on top and whitish underneath. The tree got its name because it seems to "cry" when raindrops fall to the ground from its hanging branches.

You may notice that there are no other trees that grow close to a weeping willow. That's because its long, underground roots soak up a lot of water from the soil, leaving little for other plants. For the same reason, the weeping willow often grows near bodies of water. These trees grow fast, up to eight feet per year!

Aspirin comes from experiments with the bark of weeping willows. Ancient Greeks and early Native Americans chewed the bark to relieve pain. But it also caused stomach trouble. A few hundred years ago, a scientist created a man-made version of the chemical in the bark and called it aspirin.

PINE

Many species of pine trees grow across the U.S. and Canada. Pines are part of a group of trees called *conifers*, which is a Latin word meaning "cone-bearers." Pines are also called evergreens because their leaves stay green all year long. Pines are strong, typically living from 100 to 200 years, but some live more than 1,000 years!

All conifers hold their seeds inside of cones instead of flowers. Each tree has both male and female cones. The male cone has pollen and the female cone has seeds. Wind or gravity carries the pollen from the male to the female cones. It's easy to tell pine trees from other conifers, though. While all conifers have long, thin, needle-shaped leaves, needles on a pine tree grow in bunches of two to five.

Wood from pine trees is used in buildings, furniture, and paper products. Some pines have large seeds that we can eat, called pine nuts. And of course pines play a big role at Christmas celebrations.

More trees on next page

WHY DO TREES HAVE RINGS?

A tree stump's rings give clues to the life of that tree. The rings are layers of its growth, and show things like how the weather conditions from year to year affected it. Rings are like the tree's fingerprints.

During spring, when a tree often gets plenty of water, it grows the most. It makes large cells to transport the water quickly. They form a wide, light-colored ring. In summer and fall, if water and nutrients aren't as plentiful, the tree grows less. It makes smaller, close-together cells that form a narrow, dark ring. One light ring and one dark ring make up one year of the tree's growth. Scientists study tree rings to learn about climate. A tree usually grows wide rings in warm, wet weather. If the weather is cold and dry, the rings are thinner. If there is a severe dry spell, the tree might not grow at all.

OAK

There are many different kinds of oak trees that grow all over the U.S. and Canada. Each oak starts as a tiny acorn with a cap on top. One tree can produce 2,000 acorns per year, but only one out of about 10,000 acorns becomes a tree. Acorns provide food for wildlife, such as squirrels, birds, and deer.

To identify an oak, first look for acorns. Then look at the leaves. Most oak leaves are lobed, which means they have knobs, or extensions. An oak's lobes grow out from a center line. Oaks can have rounded or pointed lobes.

The wood of an oak tree is strong and hard, which makes it great for building furniture, flooring, and drums. In the past, oak tree wood was used to build ships.

Oak trees are usually large with long branches, so they often provide great shade. They're also a symbol of strength and longevity.

ASPEN

When a strong wind blows, aspen trees do something special. They shiver! Most trees have round leaf stems. But the aspen's leaf stem is flat. This shape causes the leaves to blow from side to side, fluttering and shaking in even a light breeze.

Aspen leaves are roundish in shape and pointed at the tip. They are smooth, bright green or yellowish-green, and dull on the underside. In autumn, aspen leaves turn brilliant colors—gold, orange, red, and yellow.

The quaking aspen, which grows from New England to the Great Lakes, got its name because of the way it quakes, or shakes, in the wind. It's the most common type of aspen in the United States.

Cottonwood trees are related to aspens. They grow in the southern parts of the United States, and get their name because their seeds look like clumps of cotton.

MAPLE

Have you ever had real maple syrup? Maple syrup is made from the sap of the sugar maple tree, which grows in the eastern part of North America. Other common maples in the East are the silver maple and the colorful red maple. If you travel to the Rockies, you can see the bigtooth maple. Farther west, you can find the bigleaf maple on the Pacific Coast.

All of these maples have leaves with five lobes, or sections. The lobes and veins of maple leaves start from a single point, unlike those of oak leaves. Silver maple leaves have a soft, white coating on their undersides, and red maple leaves have rough, sharp edges. Maples are one of the most colorful trees in the fall. The leaves turn bright orange, yellow, red, or maroon.

Maple trees can live for more than 200 years. Their seeds are winged, and flutter down like helicopters as they fall from the tree. Baseball bats, certain musical instruments, and some types of paper are made from maple wood.

Listen and Look for Birds

Different types of birds not only have distinct coloring, they also have varied behaviors and abilities.

Wherever you live—city, suburb, or country—see if you can find these six North American birds.

CHICKADEE

Size: about five inches long
Shape: rounded body, narrow tail, large head, and short, dark beak
Colors: black cap, black throat, white cheeks, gray back and wings, pale underside

Six species of chickadee live in North America, and they look and behave alike. The black-capped chickadee, shown here, has the widest range.

The chickadee's name mimics its alarm call: *chick-a-dee*. More *dee* sounds added to the end send a more serious alarm. The male's song sounds like *see-bee*, *ss-see-bee*, or *see-bee-bee*. It starts with a high pitch on the first note, then drops to lower pitches. Many people find the song easy to imitate, sometimes prompting the bird to reply and even come closer, ready to face off with a rival.

Chickadees are curious and usually active, flitting from place to place, finding hidden food and sometimes hiding what they've found. They search out seeds and insect eggs among dry leaves. During the warm months, they take seeds one at a time from plants or from feeders. Then they fly off to eat the seed or to tuck it into a hiding place, such as a crevice in rough tree bark. In freezing weather, they survive mainly on eggs of insects and spiders. But they also eat seeds they stored earlier.

You can spot chickadees all year round, even in the wintertime.

Cool Fact: Chickadees can perch sideways or upside down.

AMERICAN CROW

Size: 17 inches long
Shape: trim body, heavy beak, medium-length tail
Color: black feathers, beak, and legs

American crows may not have flashy colors, but they are worth watching for their intelligence. These birds have learned to live just about anywhere except very dry regions. You may spot them in treetops or on the ground, feeding in fields or along roads.

Notice how resourceful and social crows are. In addition to the crow's hoarse *caaaw-caaaw* sound, they make a range of caws, croaks, gurgles, and other sounds. Their sounds have many meanings, such as "Here I am" and "I see an owl! Let's chase it away!" (Owls eat crow eggs and chicks.) Watch and listen. What might they be saying?

Crows' complex language is only one sign of their intelligence. Some crows also make tools. They trim a twig to size, then use it to pry insect larvae out of tight spaces.

Cool Fact: In experiments, crows have impressed scientists with their ability to solve problems.

BLUE JAY

Size: 11 inches long
Shape: trim with a pointed head crest and medium-long tail
Colors: blue wings with black-and-white markings, blue tail with black markings, blue crest, black across the back of the neck, white cheeks, black bill

Blue jays live throughout the Eastern and Central United States. Many live in forests. But you may see them in parks and yards. These crow cousins are large and loud, with a call that sounds like *jay! jay!* Like crows, they can make many sounds, such as those of other birds. No one knows why they often imitate hawks' calls, but perhaps it's to warn other birds that a hawk is nearby, or they might simply want a bird feeder all to themselves.

Some bird lovers chase blue jays away, because these strong birds can swoop down and take smaller birds' food and, sometimes, their eggs. But blue jays mostly eat seeds, berries, and their favorite, acorns. In fact, they help forests. They carry acorns and beechnuts far and wide, then stash them under leaf litter to eat later. One blue jay can carry up to five small acorns in its stretchy throat at once.

Cool Fact: Blue jays have strong family bonds and often mate for life.

More birds on next page

They sing their clear song early in the morning, just as the sun is coming up.

Robins look for food by hopping and running across the ground. You'll often see them standing with their heads turned, using one eye to look for worms in the ground. Once a robin spots a worm, it uses its beak to pull out the worm and eat it. Robins also eat insects and berries.

You may also spot a robin's nest or, after the eggs have hatched, eggshells on the ground. The color of robins' eggs is such a beautiful blue that many people have tried to copy it. The color is known as *robin's-egg blue*.

Cool Fact: No one knows why robins and many other songbirds sing so intensively around dawn. It might be to remind others that they are around and to claim the local territory as their own.

AMERICAN ROBIN

Size: 10 inches long
Shape: egg-shaped body, medium-short tail, short beak
Colors: rusty-red chest, grayish brown wings, black head, yellow beak

Robins are found all over North America. They are considered one of the first signs of spring.

HUMMINGBIRD

Size: most species are about three inches long
Shape: trim body, short tail, and long, thin beak
Colors: most species are green with white or green undersides, and a colorful (often red) or patterned chin patch

The telltale sign of a hummingbird, besides its tiny size, is the way it hovers as it uses its long beak and tongue to drink nectar from flowers. The wings beat up to 80 times per second—so fast that they look like a blur and make the sound that gives the bird its name. A few other birds may be able to hover, but only the hummingbird can also fly backward.

More than 12 hummingbird species live in North America. Most of them are so small that they look almost like an insect. In fact, if you think you see a hummingbird, look closer to see if it's an insect instead. Some species of moth—the "hummingbird moths"—look, fly, and feed similar to hummingbirds.

BLUEBIRD

Size: about seven inches long
Shape: egg-shaped body (not as round as chickadees), short tail, and short, black bill
Colors: all have blue heads and wings, but each species has distinct coloring over the rest of their bodies

Three species of bluebird live in North America. They are drawn to open fields and grasslands where they can spot insects from the air. Notice how they swoop down and land to grab their prey, then take off again.

Bluebirds nest inside trees, wooden fence posts, or nesting boxes people build just for them. Special setups have been designed to protect the eggs and chicks from raccoons and other predators.

If a bluebird pair nests near you, notice how they stay busy all summer. First, they work together to build a nest. Then the female lays four-to-seven eggs. While she sits on the eggs, the male stays busy hunting for insects and bringing them to his mate.

Once the eggs hatch, both parents stay busy flying in and out of the nesting cavity as they feed their chicks.

Cool Fact: Bluebirds can eat while flying, snatching insects out of the air.

Your family may be able to attract these birds with a special hummingbird feeder or by raising some of the many flower varieties that attract hummingbirds, such as day lilies or columbines. If you see hummingbirds feeding, watch how the birds interact. Often, one bird will claim a feeding site as its own, then chase away any other hummingbirds that try to use it.

Cool Fact: Hummingbirds must drink their body weight in nectar every day.

Watch for Insects

Choose a small area for your search: maybe a not-too-large branch of a bush or a 12-inch square patch of grass.

Tip
Carefully look through the leaves or blades of grass for insects and other small animals. A magnifying glass helps (but not with direct sun).

CRICKET

Follow the sound of a cricket after dark. Each time it chirps, take a few soft steps toward the sound. When it stops chirping, stand quietly until it begins again. After several stops and starts, you may be close enough to see it. Wait quietly. Even in the beam of a flashlight, it will lift its wings to chirp.

FIREFLY

Fireflies make their own light by producing a chemical reaction in their bodies. They use the light the way birds use songs—to show others where they are and to find a mate.

Watch for fireflies on warm nights in early summer. They tend to like moist areas like meadows and marshes. Take a nighttime walk and see how many you can find. You might also spot other living things that produce their own light. The young of some fireflies look like small glowing worms or caterpillars on the ground.

SPOT DIFFERENCES BETWEEN BUTTERFLIES AND MOTHS

Although there are exceptions, here are some typical differences:

MOTHS
- Fuzzy antennae
- Wings are usually down when at rest
- Nocturnal (active at night)
- Where to find them: around outdoor lights in the evening

FLOWER FLY

Flower flies are helpful garden insects that move pollen from one flower to another and eat aphids, tiny insects that can harm plants. You might mistake a flower fly for a bee or wasp since it has black and yellow stripes. But a flower fly can't sting, and its wings stick straight out when it stops flying instead of folding onto its back like a bee's. Still, the stripe disguise is enough to fool most insect eaters. They see the stripes and leave flower flies alone.

CICADA

Cicadas spend most of their lives in the soil, feeding on the juices of tree roots. Some kinds of cicadas come out of the soil after two years. You could hear them in any year. There are other kinds that live underground for as long as 17 years!

More Ideas

Try to figure out when you hear more insects buzzing: When it's hot or cool? When it's wet or dry? During the day or at night?

BUTTERFLIES

- Long, thin antennae with bulbs at the tips
- Wings upright and together when at rest
- Diurnal (active during the day)
- Where to find them: in a flower garden during the day

Look for Life in Ponds and Streams

Take a walk to a nearby pond or stream. Look in gravel areas, under small underwater rocks, or on the stalks of water plants. Put back any objects you move, so the animals you find can return to their habitats.

SNAIL

A snail makes its hard shell by secreting a substance that contains calcium, the same mineral that makes bones hard. The shell helps protect the snail from predators. Some snails live underwater, but many live in wet places on land. Land snails can survive during dry periods by closing themselves up in their shells and waiting for rain.

Look for different kinds of snails and snail shells in any moist place—including marshes, or even under dead leaves in the woods. Make sure to leave them where you found them.

WATER STRIDER

Water striders have their name because it's exactly what they do: they stride on the water. To see them, kneel down and look at the surface of a still pond. You can see the tiny imprints on the water that the striders make. They dart back and forth on their own endless highway.

MAYFLY

You might be able to find mayflies flying low over the water. Sometimes millions of them come out at once. As nymphs, mayflies eat all they need while living underwater. Once they become adults, mayflies fly above the water to mate and lay eggs. They soon die, in some cases after only a few hours or days.

EARTHWORM

Earthworms aren't everywhere in the U.S. and Canada, but they may be near you. You can dig a bit or look for earthworms under fallen leaves, rocks, or logs near ponds, streams, or other moist areas during the day or night. Walk quietly because worms can feel your steps. After a rainstorm, you can look for them on the ground or pavement. Sometimes you can find muddy trails left by worms. They tunnel into soil, which allows water and air to reach the roots of plants and trees.

Worms stay away from the bright sun, which dries them out. They get oxygen through their wet skin. Without moisture, they die. They're fragile creatures, so be careful with them!

See how to build a wormarium on page 304.

More Ideas

Sit quietly next to a pond or stream and simply observe. What living things do you see? Do they travel alone or in groups? What noises do they make?

Make Spontaneous Art

You can easily turn nature into your own work of art. Keep your eyes open when you're outside and look for fallen pieces of nature that you can transform.

Before You Start

Keep in mind that plants are living things. Try to only collect items that have fallen on the ground and won't be disturbed in their natural habitat.

1. Start by collecting objects. You could gather just one type of object in similar shapes and sizes, like acorn caps, stones, or leaves, or you could find a variety of items in different sizes, shapes, and colors.

2. Find a plain, open space and put your objects into patterns: Can they make a spiral, fan, or flower image? Can they spell out a word? The possibilities are endless.

3. Leave your work of art for others to discover. It might brighten their day!

Start a Bucket Garden

You don't need a garden plot or a lot of space to grow vegetables outside. You can have success with just some buckets or containers.

You Need

- Plastic pail or metal bucket
- Hammer
- Nails
- Stones or gravel
- Soil
- Sand
- Peat moss
- Seeds for any of the following: leaf lettuce, carrots, radishes, beets, basil, dill
- Water

1. Begin your bucket garden when the weather is warm and there are no longer any frosts at night.

2. Ask an adult to help you punch a dozen holes in the sides of your bucket about two inches up from the bottom, using a hammer and a large nail. This will let water drain out. Pour in small stones or gravel up to the level of the holes. Then fill the rest of the pail with soil, sand, and peat moss mixed together, leaving several inches at the top empty.

3. Plant your seeds a few inches apart. Cover them with no more than one-fourth inch of the soil mixture. Pat the earth over the seeds and sprinkle lightly with water. Within a week, most of the seeds will sprout. When they have grown four or six leaves, snip off enough so that the plants that are left will have room to spread a little.

4. Set your container in a spot outside that gets a lot of sun. Water the soil deeply when it feels dry to your finger.

5. Enjoy your harvest of tasty vegetables!

Make a Plaster Cast of Animal Tracks

Even the tiniest plants and animals can leave an impression on the earth. You can make a plaster cast to remember their details.

You Need

- Milk carton or cardboard box, for a frame
- Scissors
- Small tub of plaster of paris
- Water
- Resealable plastic bag

3. Using two parts plaster of paris and one part water (start with two cups of plaster and one cup of water), mix your plaster and water in a sealed plastic bag. Make sure to squish out all the clumps. Then open the bag and pour it over the animal track into the cardboard frame.

1. Explore muddy grounds to discover an animal track. Clear the area around it.

2. Place a cardboard frame around the area you want to cast. Press it into the ground a little. If you are using a milk carton, first mark a two-inch area in the center of the carton. Cut off the rest of the top and the rest of the bottom, and you'll have a two-inch high frame.

4. Leave the plaster to harden for 15 minutes to an hour. Timing may vary, depending on the weather. Remove the cardboard when the plaster is hard and dry, and clean off any dirt. You can use some water and a brush, if needed.

More Ideas

If you don't like the look of dirt in your cast, you can paint it any color you'd like.

Create a Butterfly Resort

Use some simple objects to attract butterflies to your yard.

- Lay out several rocks in the sun for butterflies to bask on.
- Pour water into a saucer and place it next to the rocks.
- Make butterfly food by mixing four parts hot water to one part granulated sugar until it dissolves. Let it cool. Place a few cotton balls in a shallow dish and pour the sugar water over them. Place the dish beside the rocks and water saucer.

1 Last Challenge!

Find three or four sticks. Lay them on the ground and see how many shapes you can create (you can break them into smaller pieces).

THINGS TO DO IN THE
KITCHEN

Quick Challenges

Make a snack using only foods that grow on trees or underground.

With an adult, use a blender to mix a dollop of honey with equal parts yogurt and frozen fruit. Pour the mixture into an ice-cube tray, add a craft stick to each cube, and freeze them. Use a fork to loosen them, and enjoy!

Upgrade your lemonade by mixing in crushed and washed mint leaves, mashed seedless watermelon, or mashed strawberries.

Use a toothpick to draw a cheerful picture on a banana's peel for the next person to find. (The lines of the drawing will turn brown.)

Plan and help make a meal at home.

Be adventurous! Try two new foods that you've never tasted before. You could also try mixing that food with something you really like.

Plant What You Eat

Before you toss those seeds or pit, think about growing a plant of your own. Here are some simple ways to make those seeds grow.

White Grapefruit

1. Take plump seeds from one or two white grapefruits and soak them overnight in warm water.

2. Fill a small container with about two inches of garden soil. Add the grapefruit seeds, pressing down firmly. Sprinkle more soil over the seeds until they are covered.

3. Keep the soil moist. The seeds will sprout in about two or three weeks.

Avocado

1. Wash the pit and remove any bits of avocado. Then poke three toothpicks into the sides of the pit, and place it on the top of a glass filled with water. The round end of the pit should be down, and the pointed end should be faceup. Keep it out of direct sunlight, but in a warm place.

2. Be sure there is always some water covering the bottom of the pit. It will take two-to-six weeks to sprout. As the roots and stem begin to grow, the pit will split. When the stem is about six inches long, cut it in half, to about three inches tall.

3. When the roots are thick and new leaves have formed on the stem, plant it in a large pot (about 10 inches across) filled with rich soil. The pit should be a bit exposed above the soil. Keep it watered so the soil is moist, and put it in a place that gets plenty of sunlight.

More planting on next page

Pineapple

1. Cut off the top two inches of a fresh pineapple before you cut into the rest. Keep the leaves attached. Scoop away the soft fruit around the hard core and then let your pineapple top dry for a day or two.

2. Cut off some of the lowest leaves. When the inside of the pineapple is dry, plant it in a pot filled with sandy soil. Cover the pineapple with soil so that only the leaves show. Keep it wet until the new leaves grow. Pineapples grow best in a sunny spot.

Herbs and Spices

Many herbs and spices are seeds. You might find cardamom, celery, anise, mustard, sesame, or poppy seeds on your family's spice shelf.

Try planting some of them to see if they will grow. You can fill an egg carton with potting soil and plant a different kind of seed in each cup. Use half an ice-cream stick to label each section so you'll know which plant is which when the seeds grow.

Water the seeds carefully whenever they are dry and keep them in a sunny spot. When a plant is about as tall as a matchstick, it should be transplanted to a larger container.

Fruit or Vegetable?

That depends on whether you're talking about cooking or botany (plant biology). A chef might say that a fruit is the sweet or tart part of a plant that contains a lot of sugar, while a vegetable is an edible plant part with lower sugar content.

Scientists name plant parts by how the plant uses them, not by how we use them. Botanists talk about leaves, stems, flowers, roots, and so on. The word *vegetable* doesn't have a scientific meaning. In botany, the fruit of a plant is usually the seed-bearing part that can grow into a new plant. So botanists call the tomato a fruit, but many chefs call it a vegetable. Whatever you call them, they're good to eat.

Birthday Treats for Pets

Celebrate with these special birthday snacks for your best friend.

Safety Tips
- Check with your vet before feeding new foods to your pet.
- Ask an adult for help with anything sharp.

Cat Snack

1. Mix together two tablespoons of tuna fish, one tablespoon of shredded cheese, and one teaspoon of oatmeal.

2. Press the mixture into a muffin-tin cup to shape it. Carefully tap the treat out and place it on a cat dish.

3. Top with small cat treats.

Pup Cake

1. Mix together two tablespoons of dry dog food, one tablespoon of peanut butter, and one tablespoon of mashed banana.

2. Press the mixture into a muffin-tin cup to shape it. Carefully tap the treat out and place it on a dog dish.

3. Add banana slices. Top with a dog treat.

Very Bunny

1. For rabbits, slice their favorite fruits and vegetables.

2. Stack the pieces in layers.

3. Top with their favorite treat.

Play Food Pranks

You don't have to wait until April Fools' Day to play these tricky pranks.

Brown *E*'s

Cut a few *E*'s out of brown construction paper. Place them in a brownie pan and cover the pan with foil. Tell your family to help themselves to some "brown *E*'s."

May-Oh No

Save an empty mayonnaise jar and fill it with vanilla pudding. Wait until there are people around, then scoop some of the pudding from the jar into a bowl and dig in. Pretend not to notice the horrified looks from your audience.

Leek in Sink

Place a leek in your sink and tell your family, "Oh, no! There's a leek in the sink!" This also works with a clog-type shoe. ("There's a clog in the sink!")

Pear in Shoebox

Place a pear in a shoebox. Hand the box to a friend and say, "I saw some shoes that I thought you would like, so I bought you a pear."

Not Your Average Nachos

Make nachos for dessert! Add yellow food coloring to vanilla yogurt to make "cheese sauce" and add green food coloring to coconut flakes to make "lettuce." Top cinnamon pita chips with the "cheese sauce," "lettuce," diced strawberries as tomatoes, and raisins as black beans. Add a dollop of vanilla yogurt as the sour cream on top.

Fold a Napkin Into Creative Shapes

Tip

Press down on the crease of every fold you make so the napkins hold their new shapes.

Spruce up your dinner table with these impressive creations. To make them, use a large, square napkin or a square sheet of paper towel.

Silverware Pocket

1. Fold the napkin in half by folding the right side over to meet the left.

2. Fold it in half again, this time from the bottom up.

3. Fold just the top layer from the top left corner to the bottom right corner.

4. Turn the napkin over. Fold the right side in toward the center.

5. Fold the left side in and tuck the bottom corner into the diagonal pocket.

6. Turn the napkin over. There's your pocket for silverware!

More napkins on next page

Table Boat

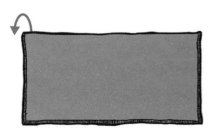

1. Fold the napkin in half by folding the top down to meet the bottom.

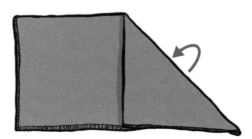

2. Take the top right corner and fold it down to the center of the napkin.

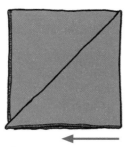

3. Pick up the bottom right corner and fold it over to meet the bottom left corner.

4. Pick up the top left corner and fold it down to meet the bottom right corner.

5. Now slip your fingers into the bottom of the napkin. Find the center, between all the layers, and flip the bottom edge up all the way around, like you're making a cuff.

6. Make the cuff big enough so the boat will stand up. Then set your sailboat afloat—just not in your soup!

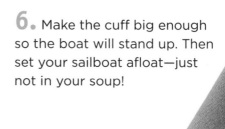

Dress Shirt

1. Fold the four corners of the napkin into the center.

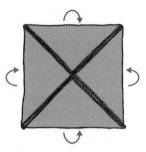

2. Fold both sides into the center.

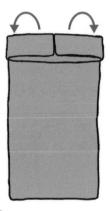

3. Turn the napkin over and fold down a one-inch strip from the top.

4. Turn the napkin over. To make the shirt collar, fold the top corners toward the center on a diagonal.

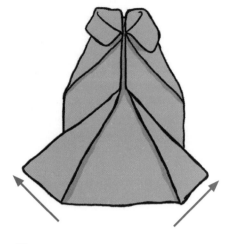

5. To create the sleeves, fold the bottom flaps outward to form wide, diagonal strips.

6. Fold the bottom of the napkin upward, and tuck the edge underneath the shirt collar. Your napkin is now properly dressed for dinner.

More napkins on next page

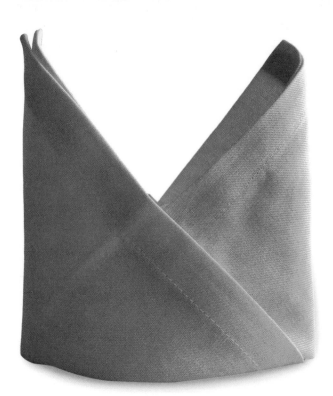

Crown

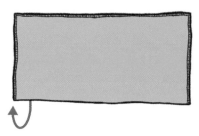

1. Fold the napkin in half by folding the bottom up to meet the top.

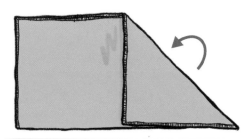

2. Take the top right corner and fold it down to the bottom center of the napkin.

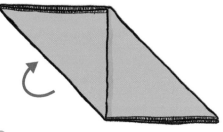

3. Now take the bottom left corner and fold it upward to the top center.

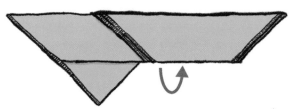

4. Flip the napkin over and rotate it so the longer sides are horizontal. Take the whole bottom right side and fold it up to meet the top of the napkin. Make sure there's a triangle shape pointing down on the left.

5. Put your hand underneath the napkin on the right side and pull down the point to reveal another triangle shape.

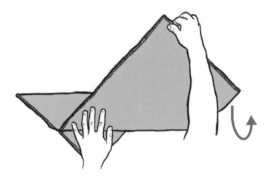

6. Now take that point and unfold it upwards.

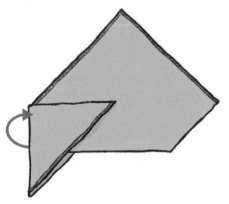

7. Fold the triangle shape on the left in half vertically by taking the far left corner of the napkin and folding it toward the center.

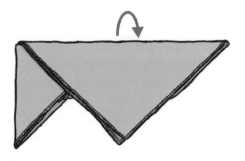

8. Take the top point and fold it down.

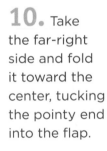

9. Turn the napkin over and flip it upside down so the straight edge is on the bottom.

10. Take the far-right side and fold it toward the center, tucking the pointy end into the flap.

11. Your crown is finished, so pick it up and pop it open. Crown each plate to make your dinner guests the kings and queens of the table.

Make Salsa

Try these three tasty recipes for salsa. Have an adult help with anything sharp.

You Need

- ½ cup diced sweet bell pepper
- ½ cup diced tomato
- ¼ cup diced red onion
- 1 tablespoon lime juice
- 1 tablespoon chopped cilantro or parsley
- ½ teaspoon sea salt
- 1 teaspoon olive oil

Sweet Salsa

Put the ingredients listed above into a bowl.

Stir in:
- ¼ cup crushed pineapple, drained
- 1 teaspoon white balsamic vinegar
- ½ cup diced mango

Corny Salsa

Put the ingredients listed above into a bowl.

Gently mix in:
- ½ cup corn kernels
- ½ cup canned black beans, drained and rinsed
- 1 finely diced garlic clove
- ½ cup diced avocado
- 1 teaspoon diced jalapeño pepper*

Spicy Salsa

Puree the ingredients listed above with:
- ½ cup roasted tomato puree
- 1 finely diced garlic clove
- 2 teaspoons diced jalapeño pepper*

Stir in
- ½ cup peeled and diced cucumber
- A few drops of hot sauce (optional)

*Have an adult help handle jalapeño peppers. The oils may irritate your eyes and skin.

Cook Easy Lasagna

Are you in the mood for some cheesy, delicious Italian food? Try this shortcut lasagna, which takes less than an hour to make.

You Need

- Square baking dish
- 24-ounce jar pasta sauce
- 10-ounce package ravioli, thawed
- 1 cup shredded mozzarella cheese
- Vegetables, such as spinach, sliced black olives, diced red bell pepper, or sliced mushrooms (optional)
- Dried parsley flakes
- Aluminum foil

1. With an adult, preheat the oven to 350°F. Spoon a thin layer of pasta sauce on the bottom of a baking dish.

2. Place a layer of ravioli on top of the sauce. Sprinkle a quarter cup of the cheese over the ravioli. Add a layer of vegetables, if desired.

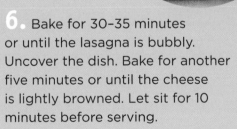

3. Continue layering the sauce, ravioli, cheese, and vegetables until all ingredients are used.

4. Add a final layer of cheese, then sprinkle with parsley flakes.

5. Cover the dish with foil.

6. Bake for 30–35 minutes or until the lasagna is bubbly. Uncover the dish. Bake for another five minutes or until the cheese is lightly browned. Let sit for 10 minutes before serving.

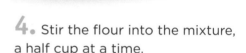

Knead Challah Bread

Challah is a soft, chewy bread with a hint of sweetness.

You Need

- 1 large and 1 small bowl
- 1 cup plus 1 tablespoon warm water
- 1 packet dry yeast
- 1/4 cup vegetable oil
- 1/4 cup honey
- 1 1/2 teaspoons salt
- 3 eggs
- 4 cups flour, plus more for kneading
- Clean, damp cloth
- Cookie sheet
- Butter or cooking spray
- 1 egg yolk

1. Pour the cup of warm water and the yeast into a large bowl. Stir until the yeast dissolves.

2. Stir the vegetable oil, honey, and salt into the large bowl.

3. Beat the eggs in a small bowl. Pour them into the large bowl and stir.

4. Stir the flour into the mixture, a half cup at a time.

5. Knead the dough on a clean, flour-covered surface for five minutes. Add small amounts of flour until the dough is no longer sticky.

6. Place the dough back into the bowl and cover it with a damp cloth. Let it sit for two hours to rise.

7. With an adult, preheat the oven to 350°F.

8. Push down the dough in the bowl. If you want, mix in one of the flavors at right (optional).

9. Divide the dough into thirds. Roll each third on a flour-covered surface to form a long rope. Braid the ropes together.

10. Grease the cookie sheet with butter or cooking spray. Place the braided dough on the sheet. Tuck the ends underneath.

11. Beat the egg yolk and one tablespoon of water in a small bowl. Brush the mixture over the braided dough.

12. Put the braided dough into the oven, bake it for 25–35 minutes, and remove it when the top is golden brown.

Extra Flavors

For sweet or savory breads, mix the ingredients in a small bowl and add them to the dough in step 8.

Cinnamon Apple
2 tablespoons cinnamon
¼ cup diced apples
¼ cup honey

Chocolate Marshmallow
½ cup chocolate-hazelnut
  spread
½ cup marshmallow creme

Sweet Fruit
¼ cup brown sugar
¾ cup pomegranate seeds

Bruschetta Braids
1 cup chopped sun-dried
  tomatoes
2 tablespoons chopped garlic

Blend a Slime Smoothie

Mix a quick, tasty—and green—smoothie!

You Need

- 1 cup milk
- 1 cup fresh spinach
- 1 cup pineapple chunks
- 1 cup mango pieces
- Blender

Put all the ingredients into a blender. With an adult, blend the mixture until it's smooth.

Bake Leftover Pies

Turn leftovers into these miniature pies after Thanksgiving or another big meal.

You Need

- 12-cup muffin tin
- Butter or cooking spray
- Puff pastry sheets, enough for 12 four-inch squares
- Filling: choose one from the right
- 1 beaten egg white

1. With an adult, preheat the oven to 400°F.

2. Grease a 12-cup muffin tin with butter or cooking spray.

3. Defrost puff pastry sheets, then flatten and cut into twelve four-inch squares.

4. Press each square into a muffin cup.

5. Make the filling: Mix the ingredients for one of the pies at right. Each filling makes three mini pies.

6. Add several tablespoons of filling into each pastry square. Then fold the points of the square over the leftovers so they meet in the middle.

7. Brush the tops of the mini pies with the beaten egg white.

8. Put the mini pies into the oven, bake them for 15–20 minutes, and remove when the tops are golden brown.

MASHED POTATOES
1/3 cup mashed potatoes
2 tablespoons gravy

SPICED SWEET POTATOES
2/3 cup cooked sweet potatoes
2 tablespoons maple syrup
1/2 teaspoon cinnamon

TURKEY
1/3 cup turkey
1/4 cup stuffing
2 tablespoons gravy

Chocolate Banana Treats

Make a sweet dessert with bananas, chocolate, and your favorite toppings.

You Need

- 4 bananas
- Butter knife
- Cookie sheet
- Wax paper
- 8 craft sticks
- 1 cup semi-sweet chocolate chips
- Toppings, such as granola, candy, nuts, or sprinkles

1. Peel the bananas and cut them in half. Place them on a cookie sheet lined with wax paper.

2. Put a clean wooden craft stick into the cut end of each banana. Place the tray of bananas in the freezer for about an hour.

3. When the hour is almost up, melt the chocolate chips on the stove or in the microwave with an adult's help.

4. Remove the bananas from the freezer. Carefully dip them into the melted chocolate. Sprinkle or roll them with whatever toppings you'd like.

5. Put the bananas back on the lined cookie sheet and freeze for three-to-five hours. Then eat and enjoy this tasty treat!

Easy Ice Pops

They're cool, fruity, and don't take long to make!

You Need

- Ice-pop forms or 3-ounce paper cups
- Ingredients for one of the flavors at the right
- Aluminum foil and craft sticks, if using paper cups

1 Wash your hands and any fresh fruit before you begin. Have an adult help with anything sharp or hot.

2 Choose an ice-pop flavor from the right and follow the instructions for that flavor. You can make them in store-bought, ice-pop forms or in three-ounce paper cups. Use aluminum foil to cover the tops of the paper cups and poke a clean craft stick into each pop through the foil before freezing.

3 Once the pops are frozen solid, remove them from the forms (or tear away the paper cups) and enjoy!

Berry Nice

You Need

- 1 cup fresh or frozen strawberries, green tops removed
- ½ cup milk
- 2 tablespoons honey
- Blender

1. Put strawberries, milk, and honey into a blender. With an adult, blend until creamy.

2. Pour the strawberry mixture into each form or paper cup, almost to the top. Put the sticks in them and place in the freezer.

Tropical Treat

You Need

- Mango sorbet
- Chopped pineapple
- Orange juice

1. Put a spoonful of mango sorbet into each form or cup. Add chopped pineapple until each cup or form is two-thirds full.

2. Add orange juice almost to the top. Put the sticks in them and place in the freezer.

Lemonade Freeze

You Need

- Sweetened pink lemonade mix
- Water
- Fresh or frozen raspberries

1. Mix up sweetened pink lemonade using three-fourths as much water as the instructions call for.

2. Fill each form halfway with fresh or frozen raspberries. Pour the lemonade mixture into the forms or cups almost to the top. Put the sticks in them and place in the freezer.

Cocoa Cooler

You Need

- Hot cocoa mix
- Hot water
- Mini marshmallows or marshmallow creme

1. Prepare hot cocoa. Add mini marshmallows or marshmallow creme. Set it aside until the cocoa cools to room temperature.

2. Pour the cocoa mixture into each form or paper cup almost to the top. Put the sticks in them and place in the freezer.

Great Icy Grapes

You Need

- Sliced grapes
- Grape juice

1. Fill each form or cup halfway with sliced grapes.

2. Add grape juice almost to the top. Put the sticks in them and place in the freezer.

Make Rock Candy

Cook up some sugar and crystallize a sparkly treat.

You Need

- 2 cups sugar plus a few tablespoons
- Plate
- 3 wooden skewers, trimmed to about 6 inches
- Water
- Wire rack
- 3 heatproof jars or glasses
- Medium saucepan
- Wooden spoon
- Food coloring (optional)
- Flavor extract, such as vanilla or peppermint (optional)
- Spring-loaded clothespins
- Masking tape

1. Pour a few tablespoons of sugar onto a plate. Dip the end of each skewer into water. Roll the end of the wet skewer in sugar. Coat only the bottom inch or two. Set the skewers aside to dry on a wire rack.

2. Fill the jars with hot water and set aside.

3. Working with an adult, boil one cup of water in a saucepan. Add one cup of sugar. Stir slowly and carefully. (Splashes can burn!) Once the sugar dissolves, add the second cup of sugar and stir again. Bring to a boil, and simmer for a minute or two. Remove the pan from the heat, and let it cool for 20–30 minutes. The liquid should still be warm.

5. Attach a clothespin to the top of each skewer. Balance the clothespins on the tops of the jars. The skewers should hang straight down with the end of each skewer about a half inch above the bottom of the jar. Tape the clothespins and skewers in place if they are wiggly.

4. Empty the water out of the jars. Add a few drops of food coloring and flavoring to each jar if you want. Have an adult pour the warm sugar solution into each jar. If you need to, stir to combine.

6. Place the jars in a safe spot that doesn't get hot or sunny. Wait 5-to-14 days, until rock candy forms on the end of the skewer. Break the crust at the top of the jar, pour out the extra liquid, and remove the candy. You may need to set the jar in hot water to warm it up before you can pull the candy out.

Why It Works:
There are many, many tiny bits of sugar dissolved in the warm water. There are so many that the bits keep bumping into each other. Some of the bits stick together to make crystals.

Puzzling Snacks

Set up each of these food puzzles with the snacks on these pages, or use others with the same shapes if you prefer. The answers are on the bottom of the page.

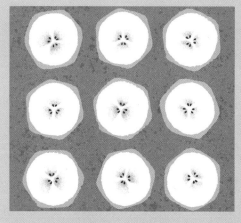

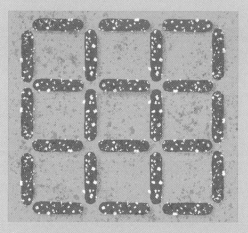

1. Slice a banana into nine pieces and lay them in three rows of three slices. Can you rearrange them to make three rows of four slices?

2. Set up nine pretzel-stick squares as they are in the picture. Now eat eight pretzels to leave two squares.

3. Set up six cups—three empty and three containing juice—as in the picture. Can you arrange them so that every other cup is empty? You can move only one cup.

Answers: 1. Arrange the slices in a triangle with four pieces making up each side. **2.** Leave the big square around the outside and the small square in the middle. Eat all the other pretzels. **3.** Pour the juice from the fourth cup into the first cup. **4.** Take three grapes from the bag and put them in the first cup. Take three more and put them in the second cup. Now drop the bag holding the last three grapes into the third cup. **5.** Place the cracker on top of the cracker in the middle. **6.** Have the pretzels spell the word *TEN* in block letters.

102   THINGS TO DO IN THE KITCHEN

4. Place three empty cups on a table and nine grapes in a plastic bag. Can you place three grapes in each cup and still have three in the bag?

5. Place five crackers as they are in the picture. Now add one more so that each diagonal row has four.

6. Set up nine pretzel sticks in a row. Rearrange them to make ten without breaking any pretzels.

1 Last Challenge!

You can do this alone or with friends. First, wash hands. Each player gets the same ingredients on a plate. They could be carrot sticks, hummus, sliced cucumbers, purple grapes, and string cheese, for example. Players have three minutes to turn the foods into a picture. It can be a scene, a face, something abstract, or anything you want.

THINGS TO DRAW

Quick Challenges

Draw a picture using a single line—don't take your pencil, pen, or marker off the paper.

Write one letter of the alphabet, then try to turn it into a picture of a familiar thing.

Find an object you'd like to draw. Without looking at your pencil or paper, draw the object by slowly following its edges with your eyes, moving your pencil along the paper as your eyes move.

Draw a picture of yourself by looking at a photo or sitting in front of a mirror.

Think about what you had for breakfast this morning. Draw the shapes you saw.

Draw your current mood. Use colors.

Ways to Start Drawing

It might seem hard to draw something from memory or your imagination, but anyone can draw with a bit of practice. Warm up with these activities.

You Need

- Scrap paper or a notebook
- Pencil
- Eraser
- Markers or colored pencils (optional)

Lines

Think of a line as a dot going for a walk. Draw a dot on your paper. See where it goes!

Could a straight line be uncooked spaghetti or an airport runway?

Could a wavy line be hills, waves, or rooftops in a faraway city?

How dark can you make a line without breaking your pencil?

How light can you make a line and still see it?

Draw a zigzag line with sharp corners or a line with lots of loops. Drawing these—or other lines— might help you feel better when you're sad or mad.

More practice on next page

Shapes

Use lines to create shapes, then mix and match them to make anything you like. Shapes are everywhere. Look at objects around you and see what shapes you can find within them.

Trees come in all shapes and sizes. Try drawing this one, or create one of your own.

You can use shapes to draw different animals. Give these a try!

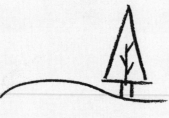

Can you come up with some other simple shape drawings?

Patterns

Patterns can be found in nature, on clothes, and on all sorts of things everywhere you look. If you draw one line or shape over and over, you'll make a pattern.

Here are some patterns to try. What others can you create?

More practice on next page

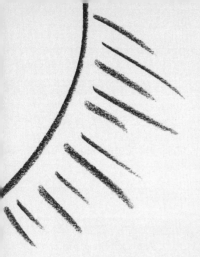

Shading

Shading makes objects appear to have depth on flat paper. Using patterns is just one way to create shading.

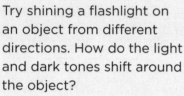

The greater the distance between pencil marks, the lighter in tone an object appears to be. Smaller distances between marks make darker, shaded tones.

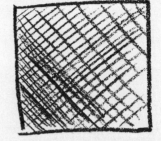

Try shining a flashlight on an object from different directions. How do the light and dark tones shift around the object?

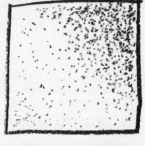

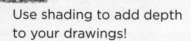

Use shading to add depth to your drawings!

Textures

Patterns and shading can also help create texture—how something feels. A rough texture has lots of light and dark pencil marks next to each other. A smooth texture has gradual changes between the light and the dark marks, and can be made by blending pencil strokes together.

Draw a lot of tiny dots to show a bumpy texture, such as an orange peel.

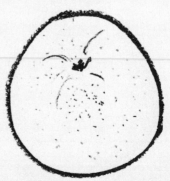

Upside Down

This method may seem strange, but when you draw something upside down, you can more easily see the shapes and lines and not get confused by how you think the subject should look.

Find a simple picture or photograph you'd like to draw and turn it upside down. As you draw, focus on the lines, shapes, and spaces you see instead of the bigger picture.

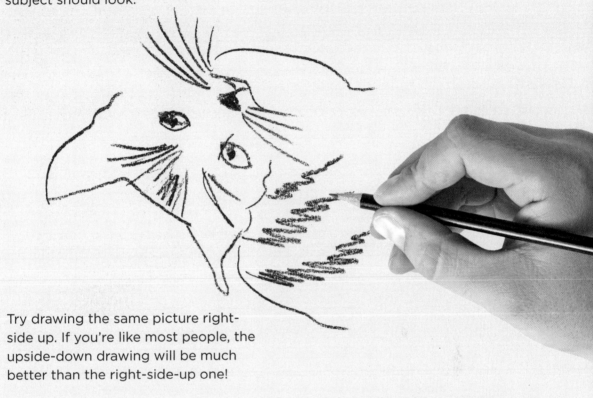

Try drawing the same picture right-side up. If you're like most people, the upside-down drawing will be much better than the right-side-up one!

Make lots of small, fine lines to give the look of grass or short hair.

What other textures do you see around you? Try drawing them!

Create Three Illusions

Optical illusions are drawings that trick your eyes when you look at them. Try drawing the illusions below.

Seeing Double

A Rubin's vase is an illusion in which a person can see a vase, two faces, or both. Can you draw your own Rubin's vase, so the vase's sides are also the profile of two faces, as in the example above?

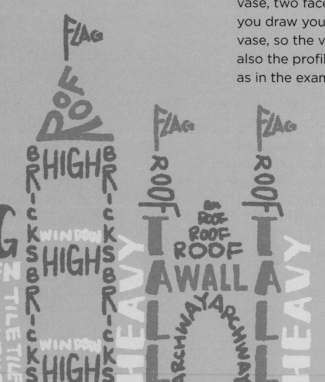

Word Art

You've probably written a story before, but have you ever written a drawing? Using only words, see what images you can create.

Colorful Squiggles

1. Draw a squiggly line on a piece of paper.

2. Draw eight dots along the line.

3. Fill the page with lines that jump from dot to dot.

4. Color the design any way you want. You can also use shading to create depth (see page 110).

How to Draw Comics

BY JANNIE H

IT'S EASY AND FUN TO DRAW COMICS! LET'S START WITH DRAWING FACIAL EXPRESSIONS. A LOT OF EMOTION CAN BE SHOWN IN THE EYES, EYEBROWS, AND MOUTH.

DRAW DIFFERENT EXPRESSIONS

HAPPY

SAD

SURPRISED

WORRIED

OVERWHELMED

ANGRY

EMBARRASSED

SCARED

TIRED

BORED

IN LOVE

SILLY

SOME COMMON SYMBOLS

SLEEPING

IDEA

CONFUSED

KNOCKED OUT

TRY IT!

TIP:

HOLD UP A MIRROR AND USE YOUR OWN FACE AS A REFERENCE!

DESIGN YOUR OWN CHARACTER

WHO'S IN YOUR STORY? SOME-
ONE YOU KNOW? A PET?
GET TO KNOW YOUR
CHARACTER WITH THIS
PERSONALITY SHEET.

- NAME:
- AGE:

- FAVORITE FOOD:
- FAVORITE SUBJECT IN SCHOOL:
- WHAT DOES HE/SHE DO FOR FUN?

ALL CHARACTERS CAN BE BROKEN
DOWN INTO SIMPLE SHAPES. LOOK
AT DIFFERENT SHAPES AND TRY
TO IMAGINE WHAT THEY CAN BECOME.

HOW TO DRAW SUPER CHICKEN

1
2
3
4

5
6
7
8

HOW TO DRAW SHELLY THE EGG

1
2
3
4
5

WHAT IS YOUR STORY ABOUT?

STORY IDEAS CAN COME FROM ANYWHERE! TO QUICKLY GET STARTED, THINK OF 3 THINGS:

① CHARACTERS   **②** SETTING   **③** PROBLEM

LET'S PUT THEM IN A SIMPLE 3-PANEL COMIC.

FOR EXAMPLE:

Panel 1: SUPER CHICKEN, WHERE IS YOUR CAPE?

Panel 2: OH NO, NOW I CAN'T SAVE THE WORLD!

Panel 3: ACTUALLY, I CAN. AFTER MY LAUNDRY IS DONE.

INTRODUCTION → THE SET UP. FIRST CHARACTER TALKS.

BUILD-UP → THE SECOND CHARACTER RESPONDS.

PUNCHLINE END WITH SOMETHING SURPRISING OR UNEXPECTED.

TELL YOUR STORY WITH ART AND TEXT

COMICS IS THE ART OF STORYTELLING WITH ART AND TEXT TOGETHER IN PANELS.

THOUGHT BUBBLE

SPEECH BUBBLE

MAKE SURE THE TAIL IS DIRECTED AT THE CHARACTER'S MOUTH.

SOUND EFFECTS

BANG!   POOF!   ZING!

WHAT OTHER SOUND EFFECT WORDS (ONOMATOPOEIA) CAN YOU COME UP WITH?

SUPER CHICKEN SAVES THE DAY

THE END

Draw a Map

Make a map of an imaginary place and see how far your mind will travel.

You Need

- Blank paper (graph paper works well)
- Pencil
- Colored pencils or markers

Here are some words to know:

Cartouche (car-TOOSH): the title of the map in a themed frame.

Icons and Symbols: images that describe important things on a map. For example, $\bigwedge\!\!\bigwedge\!\!\bigwedge$ = *water*.

Key (or Legend): a box that lists the meanings of icons and symbols on the map.

Compass: the key to directions (N=north; S=south; E=east; W=west).
Note: When looking straight at the map, north should always be at the top of the page.

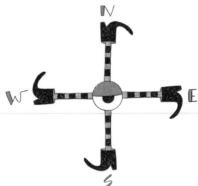

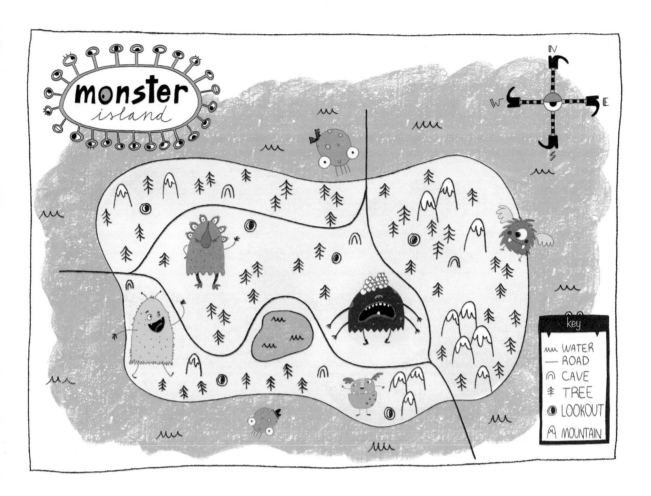

1. Think about a theme and purpose for your map. Are you leading someone to buried treasure? Showing someone where dragons live? Or how to navigate a haunted forest or some other imaginary place? Give your map a title, then draw a cartouche at the top.

2. Draw the borders of your map and fill in the space with various icons, like those for roads, mountains, and bodies of water, to represent important landmarks.

3. Include a key (or legend) to tell the reader what your icons mean.

4. Add a compass to show the directions on your map.

5. Once you're done drawing your map, color it in and share it with a friend.

6. Use your new skills to make a map of your home or neighborhood.

Hand Lettering

Lettering can express a lot—a style, a sense of seriousness or playfulness, or a mood. Try your hand at the lettering activities below.

You Need

- Scrap paper
- Pencil
- Eraser
- Colored pencils or markers

1. Pick one letter to start with and draw it in pencil with simple lines to make its structure.

2. Draw a new outline around the basic letter you made in step 1. Leave some space between your new outlines and the original structure.

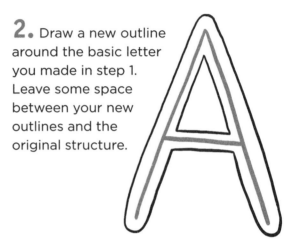

3. Erase the inner line, or color over it, to complete your letter.

4. Try using different types of outlines around letters and words to express emotions or moods.

Here are some examples:

More Ideas

Try to hand-letter the whole alphabet or your name, with each letter expressing a different feeling.

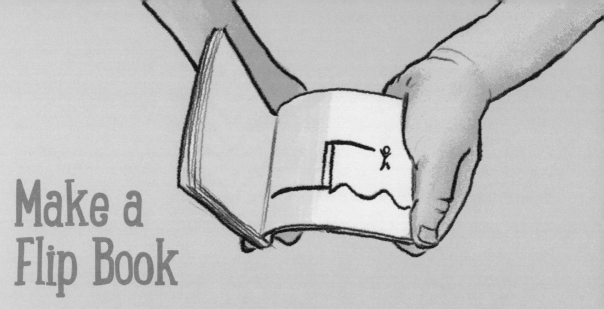

Make a Flip Book

A flip book is a picture story that moves when you flip through it. The secret to making a flip book is knowing how to space the pictures on the pages.

You Need

- 3-by-5-inch index cards
- Black permanent marker
- Other markers, for a cover (optional)
- 2 large craft sticks
- 2 rubber bands
- Tacky or school glue (school glue isn't as strong)

1. Come up with a sentence or story idea. Make it short and simple. For example, "A swimmer jumps off a diving board into a pool." Think of how you'd like to begin and end the story.

2. Illustrate your story. It's best to start with a simple drawing, because you'll need to make 16–20 pages.

3. Start with one index card. Place it in front of you horizontally, with the long side facing you. Use the marker to draw the first image on the unlined side. Make sure to have the focus of your drawing be in the middle or toward the right side of the card.

4. Put the second card on top of the first. You'll be able to see through the top card because the marker is very dark. Trace the parts of the image that you want to have on the second card (the base of the diving board, the water, and the side of the pool).

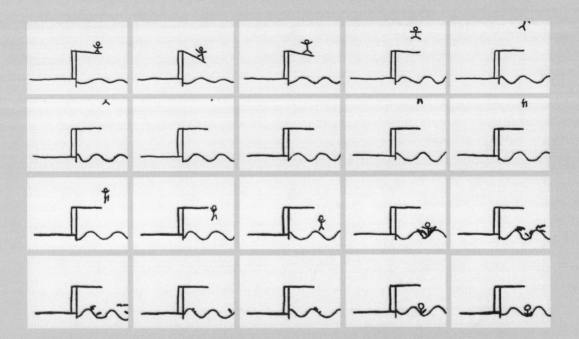

5. To show motion as you flip pages, each picture of the swimmer has to be a bit different from the one before it. Continue making small changes as you go from page to page.

6. You can also make a cover for your book. Come up with a title and draw a picture for it.

7. Stack the index cards in order and line up the left edges. Put the cover on top if you have one. Use large craft sticks and rubber bands to make a clamp for gluing. Slide the clamp onto the stack.

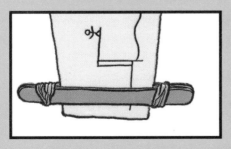

8. Apply glue along the spine and allow the glue to seep between the cards. After the glue dries, repeat the gluing process on the top and bottom corners of the spine. When all of the glue has dried, take off the clamp.

9. Hold the spine of the book with your left hand and flip through it with your right thumb.

Be a Cover Artist

Create a new cover for a book and design it your own way.

You Need

- A favorite book
- Pencil
- Blank paper
- Markers or colored pencils

1. Skim through your book and gather inspiration for cover ideas. Write down a list of words that the story brings to mind.

1. YELLOW + GREEN
2. SILVER SHOES
3. HOME
4. ADVENTURE
5. EMERALD CITY

2. Flip the piece of paper over and draw frames. Using your list for inspiration, sketch cover ideas into the frames. Play with the size and placement of images, the book title, and the author's name in your design.

3. Lay the book on a new piece of paper. Trace around the book's outer edges with a pencil. Now you have the frame in which to draw and color the cover idea you chose!

More Ideas

Come up with your own idea for a book and create a cover for it!

Drawing Games

Grab some friends and family members and get drawing with these games!

Back-to-Back Artists
FOR 2 PLAYERS

Sit back-to-back with a friend or family member. Each of you gets paper and something to draw with. Draw something on your paper and tell your partner what you have drawn. Your partner then draws the same thing on their paper. Keep adding more to your drawing, describing each detail to the other player so they can draw the same thing. After completing a picture, compare your drawings to see how well you described what you were doing and how well your friend followed your directions.

Double Doodle
FOR 2 PLAYERS

You and a friend each doodle something quickly, then switch papers and add to each other's doodle. Keep switching and adding until you've turned the doodles into something or you've filled up the pages.

More games on next page

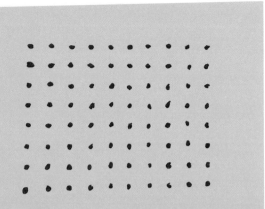

Dots and Boxes
FOR 2 OR MORE PLAYERS

Cover a piece of paper with rows of evenly spaced dots. Taking turns, each player connects two dots with a line, either side to side or up and down. If the line completes a box, the player puts their initials in it and takes another turn. When all spaces are boxed in, the player whose initials are in the most boxes is the winner.

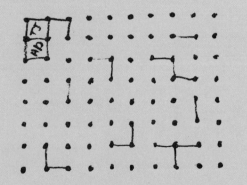

Building Character
FOR 2 OR MORE PLAYERS

1. Fold a blank piece of paper into four sections, back and forth.

2. The first player draws the head of a creature on the top section, and then folds it under so other players can't see the drawing.

3. The next player draws on the second section, and then folds that section back before handing it to the next player.

4. Continue until all sections are used. Then unfold the paper and see what monstrous creature you've created!

The Top Story

FOR 3 OR MORE PLAYERS

1. All players get paper and a pencil. Each person thinks up an imaginary newspaper headline and writes it at the top of their paper.

2. Players pass the papers to the person on their right so that everyone gets someone else's headline. Below the headline, players draw a picture to illustrate it. They then fold back the headline so that just the picture shows. Again, they pass the papers to the right.

3. Players now write a new headline for the picture they receive. They fold back the picture so that just the new headline shows. They pass the papers again.

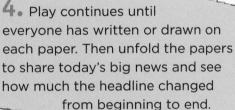

4. Play continues until everyone has written or drawn on each paper. Then unfold the papers to share today's big news and see how much the headline changed from beginning to end.

1 Last Challenge!

Draw a crazy, silly line on a big piece of paper. It can be squiggly, jagged, or any style you want. Can you turn it into an animal or monster? Find a squiggle that looks like a horn, a tail, or a nose, and get started!

THINGS TO
WRITE

P.S. Write back!

Quick Challenges

Write a letter to yourself. You can talk about how you're feeling today or what's on your mind. Date it, and put it in a place you know you will remember. Then take the letter out a year from now and read it. If you want, add the letter to a time capsule (see page 37).

Come up with a fictional character and write a description of them. What does your character like to do?

With a friend, write down predictions of what kids' lives will be like 50 years from now. When you're done, compare your thoughts.

Try writing a tongue twister. It's helpful to use a dictionary to find words that begin with the same letter. See page 152 for examples.

Come up with some title ideas for a book, movie, or TV show.

Pick an object and describe it in as many different ways as you can. You might say that a sweater feels like a cozy hug and is the color of pink peonies. A tree could seem powerful and protective.

Write in Secret Code

If you and a friend want to pass secret messages, then write to each other in code. Choose one of the ideas below or come up with your own.

Before or After

Replace each letter in your message with the letter that comes before or after it in the alphabet. If you use the letter before, *A* would become *Z*. Here's an example of using the letter that comes before:

RDD XNT KZSDQ = SEE YOU LATER

Leapfrog Letters

Read every second letter and ignore the others.

ATPAELRK BAYT WLXUENPCNH = TALK AT LUNCH

Number Code

Substitute numbers for letters. You could use the letter's position in the alphabet, so 1=A, 2=B, 3=C, etc. Or reverse the alphabet to make it trickier, so 26=A, 25=B, 24=C, etc. Here's an example of reversing the alphabet:

7-19-22   11-26-8-8-4-12-9-23

18-8   1-22-25-9-26

= THE PASSWORD IS ZEBRA

The Shopping List Code

1 mop
3 breadsticks
2 peaches
6 peanut-butter cookies
7 fruit bars
6 fish sticks
2 dozen eggs
2 onions
3 ice-cream bars

The number before each word tells which letter to use. The first letter in mop is *m*, so that is the only letter to save. Do the same with all the other items on the list. Now the grocery list has new meaning.

1 Mop
3 brEadsticks
2 pEaches
6 peanuT-butter cookies
7 fruit bArs
6 fish sTicks
2 dOzen eggs
2 oNions
3 icE-cream bars

Your message: **MEET AT ONE**

Notes and Letters

Writing a personal note to someone shows that you are thinking about them. You can also write letters to businesses, organizations, or government officials about something important to you.

Sometimes you might know just what to say when you write a letter or card. Other times, it's hard to find the right words. Here are some ideas to help you get started.

Before You Start

Try jotting down your thoughts before you write a letter. It also doesn't hurt to write a draft of your letter to see what works and what doesn't.

Thank-You Note

A thank-you note can be more than just thanking someone for the gift you received. You can also wish the person well and share news about yourself.

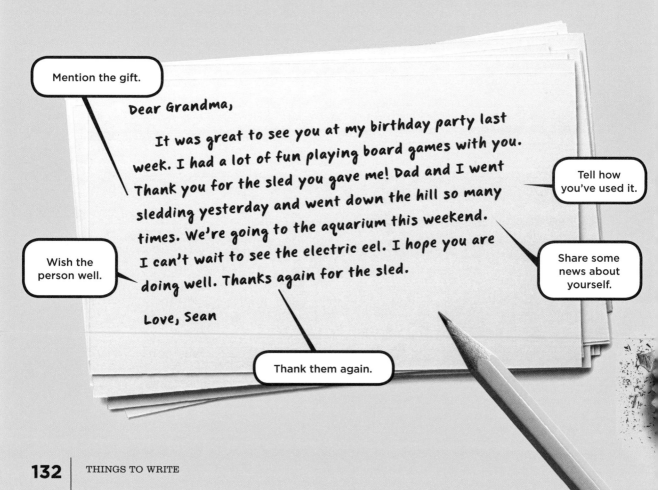

Mention the gift.

Dear Grandma,

It was great to see you at my birthday party last week. I had a lot of fun playing board games with you. Thank you for the sled you gave me! Dad and I went sledding yesterday and went down the hill so many times. We're going to the aquarium this weekend. I can't wait to see the electric eel. I hope you are doing well. Thanks again for the sled.

Love, Sean

Tell how you've used it.

Share some news about yourself.

Wish the person well.

Thank them again.

A Letter to a Friend

A handwritten letter is the perfect way to tell a friend a funny story or just say hello.

> Put your address at the top right so your friend can write you back.

75 Willow Street
Flisk, MT 55562
July 1, 2023

> Add the date you wrote the letter.

> Ask what is new with your friend.

Dear Alex,

How are you? My summer is great but I'm super bored today. I could have texted you, but a letter seemed more special. Plus, it takes more time to write!

> Explain first why you are writing.

I miss talking and joking around with you. Remember the skateboards we made for Horatio Hamster? I hope we can see each other soon.

> End your letter with a wish for the future.

Your friend,
Ava

> Close a letter to a friend with a short expression like *Your friend* or *Take care*.

P.S. Write me back!

> If there's something you forgot to say, add it at the bottom with *P.S.*

A Letter to Your Favorite Author

When you finish a really good book, you can write a letter to the author to tell them how much you liked it. They'd love to hear from you!

> Address the letter to *Author* and the author's name.

> Put your address at the top right.

15 Suffolk Road
Atlanta, GA 11135

> Send the letter in care of (*c/o*) the publishing company of the author's latest book.

> Type or neatly handwrite the letter.

Author Anabelle Gomez
c/o Trapper Books, Inc.
5482 Main Street
New York, NY 10099

> Add the date.

October 3, 2021

> Tell the author why you are a fan.

Dear Ms. Gomez,

> Use *Mr.* or *Ms.* and the author's last name.

I love your books so much. My favorite is *Don't Look Under the Sofa*. Carly is so messy! I laughed when she found her turtle under the sofa. Where do you get your funny ideas? I like to write stories, too.
　　When does your next book come out? I can't wait to read it. Thank you for reading my letter.

> Thank the author for reading your letter.

Your fan,

> End with *Yours truly* or *Your fan*.

Lizzie Perez

Lizzie Perez

> Write your first and last name.

> Tip
> To increase your chances of getting a reply, include a stamped envelope with your name and address written on the front.

A Letter to Your Senator or Representative

Maybe you've heard or seen something in the news that concerns you. Or maybe you would like to change something in your city, town, or state. One way to take action is to write a letter to someone in the government. You can write to federal, state, or local elected officials.

Tips

• For advice on what to write, talk with a parent, teacher, or trusted adult.

• To find out more about your elected officials, visit **usa.gov/agencies**.

Put the date first.

Type the letter and be sure to proofread it.

April 27, 2022

When writing an address, always use the phrase *The Honorable* before a senator or representative's name.

The Honorable John Smith
United States Senate
Washington, DC 20510

Find out the name and address of your senator or representative at the website above.

Dear Senator Smith,

Explain who you are.

Use *Senator* or *Representative*.

My name is Jacob Phan, and I am a student at Lincoln Middle School in Claymont. My science class recently studied the Great Lakes. It is one of the world's most important ecosystems, but invasive species are harming it. I learned that the U.S. Senate will be voting on whether to give money to solve this problem. I hope you will vote yes on this bill. Millions of people and animals depend on the Great Lakes for drinking water, and we need to protect this ecosystem for our future. Thank you.

Sincerely,

Jacob Phan

Jacob Phan
354 Park Street
Claymont, MI 77730

Include a thank you.

Explain the issue you are writing about. Be as specific as possible, and include the name of the bill or law, if you know it. Say how you want your representative to vote, and why.

End with *Sincerely*.

Type your name and address to get a reply.

A Sympathy Note to a Friend

When someone you know loses a loved one or experiences another loss, writing a sympathy note is a nice way for you to let them know that you care about them.

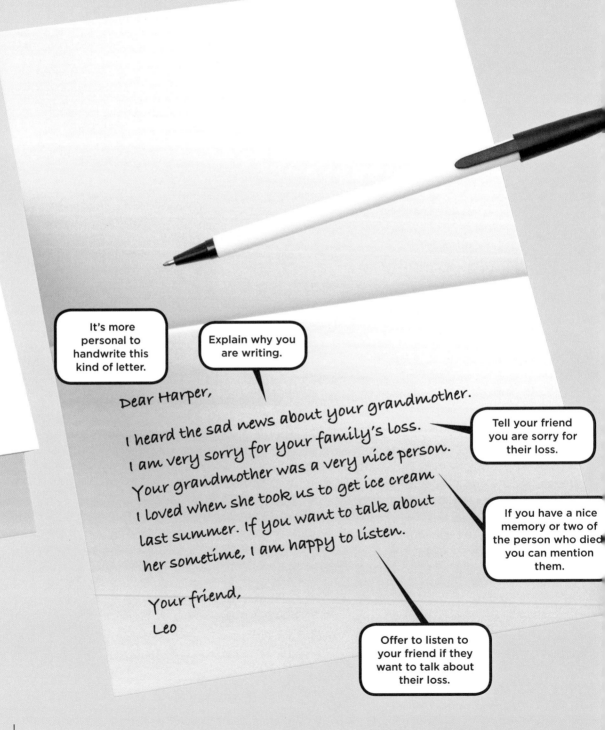

It's more personal to handwrite this kind of letter.

Explain why you are writing.

Tell your friend you are sorry for their loss.

If you have a nice memory or two of the person who died, you can mention them.

Offer to listen to your friend if they want to talk about their loss.

Dear Harper,

I heard the sad news about your grandmother. I am very sorry for your family's loss. Your grandmother was a very nice person. I loved when she took us to get ice cream last summer. If you want to talk about her sometime, I am happy to listen.

Your friend,
Leo

How to Start a Journal

A journal can be a great way of organizing your thoughts to learn more about yourself and the world around you. Find a blank book and get started!

You Need

- Blank book or digital app
- Pencil or pen

1. Decide on the purpose of your journal. Think about what you are curious about, what you'd like to pay more attention to, and what you would like to express. For example, you might want to keep a dream journal, a nature journal, or a general daily journal.

2. Pick out a notebook or a secure, private digital app (adult-approved) to house your thoughts. Books and digital apps come in many varieties, so pick the one you like best.

3. Choose where you want to write in your journal. Private time alone with your thoughts is important. If you are not able to find a space alone, journal anywhere that you feel comfortable. Some good places might be: your room, the library, or a train, bus, or car.

4. Make time to journal regularly. You can set a schedule of once a day or once a week, but the key is to create a special time to share your thoughts with yourself. Over time, you will have records of the past that will help you reflect and remember!

Record Your Dreams

Dreams can inspire your imagination or help you look at problems in a new way. To help you remember your dreams and understand what they might mean, keep track of them in a dream journal.

1. Choose a small notebook for your dream journal, and keep it by your bedside. Decorate it if you want. No one else has to read it unless you want them to.

2. Most dreams slip away when you get out of bed, so grab your journal as soon as you wake up and write down whatever you can recall. You might remember only a small part of it or what you felt like in the dream.

3. You don't have to use only words. You can draw pictures to show what you remember or how you felt.

4. Write the date of your dream and give it a title, such as "I Can Fly" or "The Chase." You can also label the type of dream it was: Funny, Crazy, Adventurous, Scary, etc.

5. As you fill the notebook, go back and flip through your old dreams. You might find similar plots or themes. Enjoy all the creative ideas your brain came up with.

Rewrite!

Can you write new lyrics for a song from an unusual point of view?

First, choose a simple melody to write lyrics for. Then use your imagination to come up with another perspective. Maybe ants on a picnic? Birds watching humans on their cell phones? Aliens approaching Earth in a rocket ship?

The example here is a hungry dog's version of "Itsy Bitsy Spider." See if you can write a different song based on this tune.

I'm a hungry little puppy
Just sitting on the floor.
You're at the dinner table,
Eating more and more.

It smells so delicious.
Would you share with me?
I promise to tell no one.
Please say you will agree.

My tongue is hanging out and
I'm begging, family, please.
I'd really like some steak, but
will settle for some peas.

My paws are in the air, see?
I'm begging—proud I'm not.
I'll show you all my tricks and
Everything you've taught.

Your dinner, it is done, now.
The kids are washing dishes.
Perhaps, instead of me, you
Should have gotten fishes!

I shuffle to my bowl, and
What is this I see?
Steak and potatoes
Are waiting here for me!

Poems

People have written poetry to express their thoughts and emotions for thousands of years. The poet Robert Frost said, "Poetry is when an emotion has found its thought and the thought has found words."

Poems can be about anything and take any form. See if you can write your own poem about something you're feeling, thinking about, or imagining. Below are a few different styles to try out.

Rhyming Poem

One of the easiest poems to write is a four-line rhyming poem. To keep it simple, make only the second and fourth lines rhyme. Keep every line about the same length, and say the poem aloud to make sure you like how it sounds. Write rhyming poems to celebrate birthdays, share with your family, or make your friends laugh.

In the middle of the night
I hear an acrobat.
It's not a trapeze artist,
It's just my crazy cat.

Let me tell you about my dog.
His name is Mister Fred.
I love him, though he slobbers
And takes up my whole bed.

Tip

You may want to read some poems for inspiration. Think about what the poet is saying and let that inspire you to write what you want to say.

Let It Out!
by Eileen Spinelli

There is a poem
  inside of me.
It buzzes like a
  bumblebee.
It tickles like a
  fuzzy chick
And bounces like a
  pogo stick.
It gurgles like a
  waterspout.
It whispers softly,
  "Let me out."
If you feel just a
  wee bit funny
And thumpy like a
  frisky bunny
And jumpy like a
  kangaroo—
Could be there is a
  poem in you!

Happy birthday to my grandma,
Today's a happy time.
I love you and I miss you,
And that is my whole rhyme.

When it's very hot outside,
My favorite way to cool
Isn't lemonade or ceiling fans—
It's jumping in a pool.

After you've written some short, rhyming poems, try a poem that has two stanzas:

In the middle of the night
I was awoken by a ghost.
"I need sliced bread," he said.
"I want to make some toast."

"How can you eat?" I asked.
"You do not have a tummy."
"It's not for me," he said.
"It's for my friend, the mummy."

Haiku

A *haiku* is a poem that has only three lines and doesn't rhyme. The first line has five syllables, the second line has seven syllables, and the last line has five. This style of poetry originated in Japan.

Haikus are often used to make observations. Try writing haikus about things that you notice. You can even hang them around the house to deliver messages to your family!

Our kitchen is glum.
The freezer cries out for more
Vanilla ice cream.

My room is spotless.
A rare wonder of the world.
How long will it last?

Dirty bathtub ring
Reveals what I did today:
Football in the mud.

Thanks, Mom, for dinner—
Pasta with homemade meatballs.
My favorite meal.

The dishes are clean.
In the dishwasher they sit.
Still too hot to touch.

More poems on next page

Limerick

A limerick is a five-line poem with a surprise ending. The first, second, and fifth lines rhyme. The third and fourth lines are shorter, and they rhyme with each other. Think up a surprise ending and write your own!

Tip
Think of words that can be rhymed easily, such as run, hat, jump, and glad, and use them at the end of lines.

There once was a hamster named Pete
Who was looking for something to eat.
He was not in the mood
For hamster pet food,
So he decided to try Cream of Wheat.

There once was a dog on a farm
Who worked as a farmer alarm.
But the chickens complained
That the dog wasn't trained:
He was seen with a wolf arm in arm!

There was a boy in my class
Who enjoyed cutting the grass.
He wanted the height
To be exactly right,
So he used rulers and a magnifying glass.

Sound-Effects Poem

Some poems imitate sounds. For example, the poem below imitates the sound of bees. To create your own, first choose what you would like to write about. Then write down all the sound words you can think of related to that subject. Use those words to help you create a poem.

Sting!
Humdrum honey
  rumble fuzz
Daisy crazy
  bumble buzz
Drowsy browsy
  strummer wing
Harum-scarum
  grumble sting!

More Things to Write

When you have a few minutes to spare, try out one of these short writing ideas. See what you can come up with!

Perfect Professions

When writers come up with names for their characters, there are often specific reasons for them. Maybe the name sets a mood, says something about the character, or is just funny. Here are some character names that fit their professions. Can you come up with more?

Here are some examples:

Contractor: I. M. Builder

Diner Chef: Patty Cook

Swimmer: Will Float

Author: Page Turner

Chauffeur: Mercedes D. Driver

Valet: Parker Carr

Track and Field Coach: Miles Long

Banker: Rich N. Cash

Bodyguard: Justin Case

Words of Wisdom

Proverbs, or words of wisdom, are short sayings that express a bit of helpful advice. You may have heard this one: "A penny saved is a penny earned." What proverbs have you heard in your family? Can you come up with your own words of wisdom?

Oops!

We all make mistakes. Luckily, most mistakes aren't serious, and sometimes they're funny when they're in the past. Write about one of your funny mistakes.

The Whole Alphabet

Can you write a sentence using every letter of the alphabet? It's not easy! The best-known example is "The quick brown fox jumps over the lazy dog."

Sue Justice
Lawyer

Hunter N. Skye
Astronomer

Barry D. Treasure
Pirate

Writing Games

Gather some friends to play these word games.

A Line at a Time
FOR 2 OR MORE PLAYERS

One player writes a sentence and passes the paper to another player, who continues the story with a line that rhymes with the first. For example, the first player might write, "I could go for something to eat," and the second player might write, "Do you want a meal or something sweet?" Continue taking turns until you have completed the story— or run out of rhymes.

Character Play
FOR 2 PLAYERS

With a partner, decide on two characters from books, movies, your imagination, or the real world that could have a conversation. Maybe Harry Potter and Peter Pan, Goldilocks and Baby Bear, or a lion and a hippo who both want to drink from the same watering hole.

One of you starts the conversation on paper, writing a sentence as one of the characters. The other player writes a response as the second character. Keep going back and forth until you have written for about 10 minutes. Then read your script out loud, with each player reading their character's part.

Spin a Silly Story
FOR 3 OR MORE PLAYERS

1. Cut out at least 20 pictures from old magazines, catalogs, or newspapers.

2. To play, turn the pictures over, so no one knows which one is which. Deal an equal number of pictures to each player. Players keep the pictures facedown in a pile.

3. The first player flips over their top picture and begins a story by saying something related to it. For example, if the image is a parachute, they might say, "Last summer, I went parachuting for the first time ever. All was going well, but suddenly . . ."

4. The second player then flips the top picture in their pile to continue the story. For example, if the picture shows a brown bear, they might say, "The wind picked up, and I was carried away. Luckily, a local bear was out for a drive in his convertible, and I landed in the passenger seat."

5. The next player flips a picture and uses it to continue the story.

6. When you're finished with one story, mix up the pictures and play again.

1 Last Challenge!

Write a poem or a story about an inanimate object. For example, imagine what a fork would say about being put in the dishwasher or what a sock would say after being reunited with its mate.

THINGS TO DO WITH YOUR
BRAIN

Quick Challenges

Challenge yourself to a game of checkers or chess, moving the pieces for both sides.

Can you say the alphabet backward in less than 30 seconds? Test yourself.

Learn the lyrics to a song you like.

Write down your first and last name, then mix up the letters to see how many new words you can make from them, using as many letters as you'd like.

Can you name 10 words that start with the letter *Q*?

Try to make a few sentences in which the words begin with the letters of your name. For example, T-E-D could be *Try eating doughnuts*. Make up sentences for everyone you know.

Play Games for One

These games are good for rainy days or whenever you have some time alone.

Ditto

Write down any three-digit number (such as 345), put a comma after it, and write the same number again (345,345). Next, divide that new big number number by 7. Divide the answer by 11. Then divide the new answer by 13. Your final answer should be the same number that you wrote down at the beginning!

Alphabet Game

List the letters of the alphabet down the left side of a piece of paper. Look around for things beginning with each letter. Write the names of the objects next to the letters on your list. Try to find something for every letter.

Name a Number

See if you can name . . .

10 animals

9 things you did today

8 people you'd like to know better (or at all!)

7 things you know about your city or town

6 kinds of fruit

5 planets in our solar system

4 first names that are the same when spelled backward or forward

3 things you want to do more of

2 people you admire

1 letter of the alphabet that's not in any of the 50 state names

You can also make your own number list of things to name.

Brain Teasers

Can you solve these mind-bending puzzles?
Answers are on page 169.

Pencil Puzzler

Try to draw this design on a piece of paper without lifting your pencil from the paper or crossing over any lines.

Sea Shapes

How many triangles can you find in this fish?

Interlocking Rings

If you cut just one of these interlocking rings, they will all come apart. Which ring?

Logically Thinking

Use the clues to figure out the batting order of these five friends.

1. Abby is right before or right after Grace.

2. David is right before or right after Kira.

3. Jason is not right before or right after Abby or David.

4. Kira will bat first.

5. Abby will not bat last.

Coin Conundrums

Gather nine pennies and see if you can solve these puzzles.

1. Arrange six pennies in a triangle, as shown. Can you turn the triangle upside down by moving only two pennies?

2. Place four pennies on the table. Can you arrange them so each penny is touching the other three pennies?

Head Scratchers

1. What gets wetter and wetter the more it dries?

2. Before Mount Everest was discovered, what was the highest mountain in the world?

3. What is as big as an elephant but weighs nothing?

4. What belongs to you, but other people use it more than you do?

5. I am an odd number. If you take away one of my letters, I become even. What number am I?

6. Which is heavier, a pound of feathers or a pound of bricks?

7. What yes-or-no question can never be answered with a yes?

8. What do the words *flour, then,* and *thirsty* have to do with numbers?

The "You Night Did" States

Can you figure out what state names are listed below in a tricky code? HINT: Sound them out!

1. Collar raw dough
2. Why owe mean
3. Eel annoy
4. Chore jaw
5. How why he
6. Mare real end
7. Messy chew sits
8. Miss us hip pea
9. Awe rig in
10. Row dial end

State Those States Quiz

1. Which four state names have double *N*'s?
2. Which four state names start with *New?*
3. Which three state names have just four letters?
4. Which three state names begin and end with *A?*
5. Which state's name is hidden inside another?

Try These 22 Tongue Twisters

Big dogs dig bones.

Swiss wristwatch

Greek grapes

Frogs favor fables.

Reese's recess rocked.

Chai tea and tai chi

The sun shines on the shop signs.

Kate creates cakes.

Thelma sings the theme song.

A big black bug bit a big black dog.

Crisscrossed crispy piecrust

Some swans swim sideways.

Bella blows blue bubbles.

See Shawn's shoe shelf.

The green glass gleamed.

Nick picks bricks.

Mike might like to bike to Spike's.

"Swim, Stan, swim," sang Sam.

Brook's brown book is bigger than Blake's black book.

Story time: A timeless story telling time.

Penelope plays piano perfectly

Two tired toads tied twine.

The Tricky Circle

Can you draw a circle with a dot in the middle of it without lifting your pencil from the paper? It's possible—try it!

See if you can do it without reading the solution below.

How to do it:

1 The trick is to fold a corner of the paper into the center. Then make the dot on the paper just above that corner.

2 From the dot, draw a line halfway to the fold.

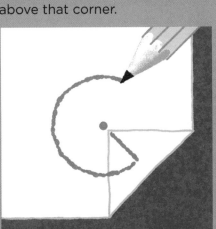

3 From there, begin drawing the circle; you'll start on the folded section, then move off it. Continue until you get to the opposite edge of the folded piece.

4 Keeping your pencil on the paper, unfold the corner and finish drawing the circle.

True or False Trivia

Decide if the statements below are TRUE or FALSE. Answers are on page 169.

1. Florida has a longer coastline than California.

2. Maine is the only state whose name has just one syllable.

3. The Everglades, one of North America's largest swamp areas, is really a 60-mile-wide, slow-moving river.

4. When bald eagles get older, they often wear toupees.

5. A parrot once sang the U.S. national anthem at the Super Bowl.

6. Dinosaurs existed on earth longer than humans have (so far).

7. A person can survive about 20 days without eating but only 2 days without drinking.

8. More than half the bones in the human body are in the hands and feet.

9. The United States has more tornadoes than any other country.

10. Snowflakes are actually colorless. They look white because they reflect light.

11. The pinkie has the strongest muscle in the human body.

12. In warmer weather, crickets chirp faster.

13. Only female mosquitoes bite.

14. A typical person's blood vessels, laid out end-to-end, would be about 100,000 miles long.

15. All ladybugs are female.

16. Baby giraffes are about six feet tall when they're born.

17. Koalas are not bears.

18. It takes one year for a centipede to cross all of its legs.

19. One name for a group of kangaroos is *mob*.

20. Spiders have eight legs, which means they're not insects.

21. Long tails helped dinosaurs keep their balance while doing ballet.

22. Emperor penguins ruled Antarctica until democracy was established in 1847.

23. Eighty percent of Earth's oceans are unexplored.

24. Underwater volcanoes spew ice cubes, not lava.

25. Whales have belly buttons.

Picture THIS

Each circle below shows a common phrase. Think about how the words are arranged and see if you can figure out the phrase. For example, in the first one, the word *EGGS* is over the letters *EZ*. So the answer is *eggs over easy*. Can you get them all? Answers are on page 169.

1.
EGGS
EZ

2.
choice
choice choice
choice **choice**
choice

3.
BANANA

4.
PANTS PANTS

5.
P
I
Z

6.
STAND
I

7.

TAKE TAKE

8.

OVER
OVER
OVER
OVER

9.

222222DAY

10.

SETTLE

11.

CA just SE

12.

hurr I cane

13.

GET
IT

More Ideas

Can you come up with a *Picture THIS* puzzle? Think of simple, common phrases that you hear.

It's Knot Impossible

Here's a challenge for you and a friend.

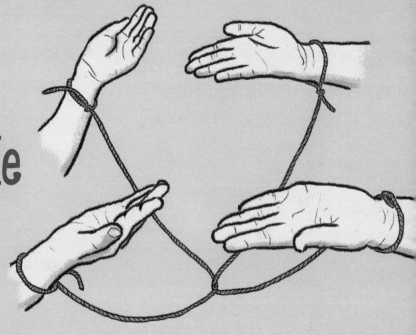

See if you can do it without reading the solution.

1. Get two pieces of string, each about four feet long. (The diagram shows strings in two different colors so it is easier to understand.)

2. Tie each end of one string loosely around your friend's wrists, but not so loosely that they can slip a wrist out of the string.

3. Have your friend tie one end of your string loosely to your left wrist. Then link the strings as shown above, and have your friend tie the other end loosely to your right wrist.

4. Now you're ready to start. Can you unlink yourselves without cutting or untying the strings? It's *knot* impossible!

How to do it:

1 Take the center of your string and tuck it under the string circle around your friend's wrist, pulling it out toward their fingertips.

2 Loop the center of your string up and over their hand.

3 Tuck your string loop under the circle around their wrist, and you're free!

Stump Your Friends

See if your friends can solve this coin-and-cup trick.
It'll be harder than they think!

1. Place three cups and ten coins on a table. Ask a friend or family member, "Can you put all ten coins into these three cups so there's an odd number of coins in each cup?" Let your volunteer try as many times as they want. They won't be able to do it.

2. Now offer to show them how it's done. Say, "It's easy. First, you drop four coins into the first cup." If your friend points out that four is an even number, say, "Yes, but I'm not done yet."

3. Say, "Then drop three coins in the next cup."

4. Say, "Now drop the three remaining coins into the last cup."

5. Pick up the middle cup and place it in the first cup. Point to the first cup and explain, "Now there's a total of seven coins in this cup. And that's an odd number."

Magic Tricks

Your friends and family will be amazed when you pull off each of these magic tricks.

Insider Tips

- Pick one trick and perfect it. Start with a simple trick that doesn't require elaborate props.

- When you think you have mastered the trick, try it out on friends or family members. Ask them for feedback to help you improve.

- Turn your trick into a performance: Before doing the trick, tell a joke or story or just talk directly to the audience. You want to seem casual and relaxed.

- Try to misdirect your audience by getting them to look away from what you are doing.

- Practice, practice, practice!

The Jumping Rubber Band

Put a rubber band around the first and second fingers of your left hand and close your hand into a fist. When you open your hand, the rubber band has jumped to your third and fourth fingers.

How to do it:

1. Use your right index finger to put the rubber band around the first and second fingers of your left hand, near the base of the fingers.

2. Now here's what you don't want your audience to see: After pulling the rubber band onto your left fingers, keep pulling on the band with your right index finger, long enough to close the third and fourth fingers of your left hand into your palm and inside the rubber band. Move your right hand away.

3. When you close your first and second fingers into your fist, put the tips of them inside the rubber band, too, as shown.

4. To the audience it will look as if you just closed your left hand into a fist with the rubber band around the first two fingers. But really, the tips of all four fingers are inside the band. When you straighten your fingers, the band will jump to the new fingers.

Now You See It, Now You Don't

Fool your audience with this disappearing coin trick.

The first four steps show how the trick looks to you.

1. Hold a quarter in front of you with your right fingertips. Say, "Observe that I have a quarter in my hand."

4. Pretend that you are grabbing the quarter with your left hand as you say, " . . . and these magic powers . . ."

The last two steps show how the trick looks to the audience.

2. Put your other hand in front of both the quarter and your fingertips so the audience can't see them. Say, "Before your eyes, I will make it disappear!"

5. Hold your left fist out to the side while pointing toward it with your right hand. Say, " . . . the quarter will disappear."

3. Open the fingers of your right hand slightly, and let the quarter drop into your palm as you look at your audience and say, "With these magic words . . ."

6. Keep pointing with your right hand as you wiggle your left hand and say whatever magic words you want to use. Then say, "One, two, THREE!" Open your left hand wide to reveal that the quarter is gone!

More tricks on next page

Predict the Future

When you guess the right number, your friends will be shocked!

You Need

- 6–10 sugar packets
- Pen
- Small caddy or container for the sugar packets
- Scrap paper
- Clean, dry mug

1. Do this step ahead of time, when no one is watching: Take a sugar packet and write the number *2* on the front. Flip the packet over so the number isn't showing. Place it into the caddy with the other sugar packets, but make sure it's the second packet in the stack.

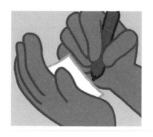

2. Perform the trick for your audience: Pick up the paper and pen, and say, "I'm going to predict something I think is about to happen." Write the number *2* on the paper without letting anyone see what you're writing, fold the paper, and set it aside.

3. Point to the caddy of sugar packets and explain, "I have a bunch of sugar packets here. I'm going to take out a few of them." Then carefully remove a stack of six-to-ten sugar packets from the caddy. Make sure the packet with the number *2* is the second one in your pile and that the number is not showing.

4. Now say, "I'm going to write a number on each packet and drop it into this empty mug." Ask someone to check the mug to confirm it's empty. Then write the number *1* on the front of the first packet, show it to your audience, and drop it into the mug.

5. Write the number *2* on the second packet and show it to the audience. Make sure they don't see the back. Then drop the packet into the mug. Write the number *3* on the next packet, and so forth, until all the packets are numbered and in the mug.

6. Ask a person from the audience to put their hand over the mug, shake it well, and then pour out the packets onto the table. Spread them out and say, "Now I'll remove all the packets that don't have a number showing." Set those packets aside.

7. Put the remaining packets back in the mug, and explain, "Let's do this again, until there's just one sugar packet left." Ask your friend to shake the mug again and pour it out. Then remove the packets that don't have a number showing. Keep repeating this step until there is only one sugar packet left with a number showing.

8. The last remaining sugar packet will have a number 2 on it. Pick it up carefully and show it to your audience without letting them see that there is also a number 2 on the back. Tell them, "Well, that's interesting. Number two is left."

9. Put that sugar packet aside and say, "I made a prediction of which number would be left. And guess what it was?" Unfold your piece of paper and reveal that you had written a 2. Your audience will be amazed!

Mind-Reading

Just when your friends think you're done with your bag of tricks, you can surprise them by reading their minds in these games.

Brain Waves

1. Send your partner out of the room, and ask someone in the group to pick a number from one to ten. Tell the group that you intend to use brain waves to tell your partner the number chosen.

2. When your partner comes back into the room, have them place their fingertips on your temples, with one hand on each side. Your partner will already know that by placing their hands there, they will be able to feel the muscles behind and above your eyes move slightly when you grit your teeth.

3. You should grit your teeth the same number of times as the number chosen by the group. At the same time, your partner should talk to the audience to distract them. With a serious expression, your partner should then announce the number. You can guess other numbers, like birthdays, with this trick, too.

Pick a Number

1. Ask a friend to pick any number without telling you what it is, for example, **23**.

2. Tell them to double the number **(23 x 2 = 46)**.

3. Have them add 10 **(46 + 10 = 56)**.

4. Tell them to divide the new number in half. **(56 ÷ 2 = 28)**.

5. Have your friend tell you this new number **(28)**.

6. Tell them to concentrate really hard on the original number **(23)**.

7. Pretend you are reading their mind. In your head, subtract 5 from the number your friend gave you in step 5. This will give you your friend's original number **(28 − 5 = 23)**!

A Three-Letter Word

1. Ask your friend to think of a three-letter word. Now ask them to think about the middle letter of that word.

2. Tell your friend to think of a fruit that starts with that middle letter. (If they can't think of one, then start over at step 1 with a new three-letter word.)

3. Ask your friend to think of the last letter of the fruit. Then say, "Think of something really big that starts with that letter."

4. When they're ready, say, "I'm reading your mind now . . . yes, is your word *elephant*?"

Most people think of the same words and fruits when they play this game, so their answer will most likely be, "How did you know?"

Card Tricks

Get comfortable handling playing cards before doing these tricks. Look on page 160 for some tips on performing tricks. Once you have some practice, you'll be ready to impress your friends and family.

I've Got Your Number

Find your friend's secret card with this spelling trick.

1. Ask your friend to shuffle a deck of cards. Then say, "Take any nine cards from the deck and place them on the table facedown." Set the rest of the deck aside.

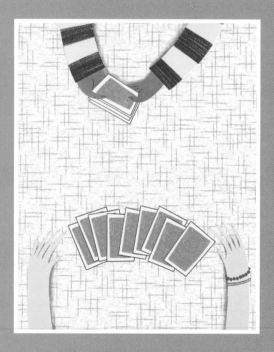

2. Ask your friend to count their cards to make sure they have nine. Then have them fan out the cards so only they can see them. Say, "I don't want you to think that I can see your top or bottom card, so look at the third card from your left in your hand. Remember that card's number and suit." You should turn away when they look at their cards, so they don't think you are peeking.

3. Ask them to hold their cards in a stack facedown. Then explain the rules: "Now you're going to deal out your cards facedown into a pile. First, think of the number of the card you picked. Then, spell out that number silently, putting down one card for each letter. For example, if the card was a two, you would put down three cards for *t*, *w*, *o*. I'll look away, so tell me when you're done." When your friend is finished, tell them to place the rest of their cards on top of the pile.

4. Ask your friend to pick up the pile and hold it facedown. Say, "A card is always known by its number and suit, such as the four of diamonds or jack of clubs. You've already spelled out the number, so now deal two cards facedown to spell out the word *of.*" Then place the rest of the cards on top.

5. Ask your friend to pick up the cards again. Say, "Now deal the cards facedown to spell out the suit silently, one card for each letter. For example, if the suit was hearts, you'd put down six cards for *h*, *e*, *a*, *r*, *t*, *s*. Then drop the rest of the cards on top." Make sure to look away until they're done.

6. Ask your friend to pick up the cards facedown one last time. "Now I want you to deal all the cards, one by one. This time, place them faceup so we can see them." Pay attention as they deal, and remember the fifth card they put down.

7. When all the cards are on the table, tell them to think hard about the card they picked. Say that you can hear their brain and you know which card they're thinking of. Then announce what the fifth card was.

More tricks on next page

Mix-Up Mystery Trick

Your audience will think they're mixing up the cards, but you have a surprise in store.

1. Put the cards in order, from ace to king, within each suit (hearts, diamonds, clubs, and spades). Stack the suits.

2. Now fan out the prepared deck to show your friend. Point out that the cards are grouped by suit.

3. Close the fan and put the cards facedown in a pile on the table.

4. Tell your friend to cut the deck. (This means to lift up part of the deck without shuffling, put it facedown on the table, and then put the rest of the deck on top of it.) Then have them cut it again. People usually think this has mixed the cards.

5. Deal the cards facedown one by one into 13 piles. You will end up with 4 cards in each pile.

6. Wave your hands over the cards and say some magic-sounding words.

7. Turn over each of the 13 piles. Your friend will see that the cards have "magically" separated from their suits and regrouped themselves into each pile by number!

Why It Works: Cutting the deck without shuffling doesn't mix up the order of the cards; it just changes the starting point of the deck. Since the cards remain in order, when you deal out 13 piles (the number of cards in each suit), you'll automatically regroup the cards by number.

1 Last Challenge!

Try this riddle: A man is looking at a photograph of someone, and his friend asks who it is. The man says, "Brothers and sisters, I have none. But that man's father is my father's son." Who is in the photograph? Answer below.

ANSWERS

**PAGES 150–151:
BRAIN TEASERS**
PENCIL PUZZLER

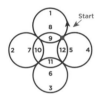

SEA SHAPES
19 triangles

INTERLOCKING
RINGS
The green one

LOGICALLY
THINKING
Answer: Kira is first, then David, then Abby, then Grace, and Jason is last.

COIN
CONUNDRUMS

HEAD
SCRATCHERS
1. A towel
2. Mount Everest
3. An elephant's shadow
4. Your name
5. Seven
6. They both weigh the same—one pound.
7. Are you asleep?
8. If you remove one letter from each word, you get a number. *Flour* contains *four*, *then* contains *ten*, and *thirsty* contains *thirty*.

STATE THOSE
STATES QUIZ
1. Connecticut, Minnesota, Pennsylvania, Tennessee
2. New Hampshire, New Jersey, New Mexico, New York
3. Iowa, Ohio, Utah
4. Alabama, Alaska, Arizona
5. *Kansas* is hidden in *Arkansas*.

THE "YOU NIGHT
DID" STATES
1. Colorado
2. Wyoming
3. Illinois
4. Georgia
5. Hawaii
6. Maryland
7. Massachusetts
8. Mississippi
9. Oregon
10. Rhode Island

**PAGES 154–155:
TRUE
OR FALSE TRIVIA**
All of the answers are true except for 4, 5, 11, 15, 18, 21, 22, and 24.

**PAGES 156–157:
PICTURE THIS**
1. Eggs over easy
2. Multiple choice
3. Banana split
4. A pair of pants
5. Zip up
6. I understand
7. Double take
8. Leftovers
9. Tuesday
10. Settle down
11. Just in case
12. Eye of the hurricane
13. Get over it

**PAGE 169: ONE
LAST CHALLENGE:**
Change "is" to "equals" to make it clearer. So: My father's son = That man's father. Since the person talking is an only child, he has to be "my father's son." So "that man's father" is the person talking, and "that man" in the photo is his son.

THINGS TO DO WITH
COLOR

Quick Challenges

While listening to music, use different colors to draw what you hear. Use paint, crayons, colored pencils, or markers.

Try painting with cotton swabs, plastic utensils, small sponges, or other materials you can find around your house. You could also try painting on a material other than paper.

Look at a painting or color photograph in your home. How many colors can you find in it?

In the fall, find different colored leaves. Make a collage using one leaf of each color you can find.

Put together an outfit that uses at least five different colors.

If you have a box of crayons, try organizing them from darkest to lightest.

The Color Wheel

A color wheel is a diagram that shows how colors are related. Notice how all the colors on the right side of the wheel are *cool* while those on the left side are *warm*.

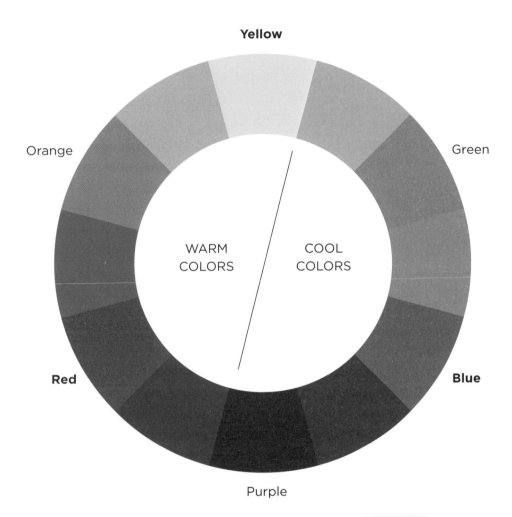

Did You Know

You can use the wheel to mix colors. You can make any color from the primary colors, which are red, yellow, and blue. You'll make secondary colors, such as green or orange, by mixing two primary colors. Tertiary colors are a mix of a primary color and a secondary color.

Play with Paint

You don't need an easel to start painting. Check out these projects to help you learn how to mix colors and make art that pops!

Mix and Make Colors

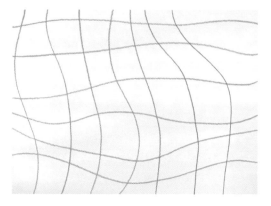

1. Spread newspaper on your work area. Draw a grid on your paper in pencil by making at least five horizontal lines and five vertical lines. Use a ruler to draw straight lines, or you can make the lines wavy.

2. Set up your palette—the place where you will mix paints. Use red, yellow, blue, white, and black paint. Put a quarter-sized blob of each color along one edge of your palette.

3. Mix new colors (see MIX IT UP). Try to paint a different color in each space on the grid. Can you paint only warm colors on one side and cool on the other? (Look back at page 173 to see which colors are warm and cool.)

4. Once the colors dry, use black paint to outline the shapes on the grid.

Mix It Up

Follow these tips for mixing paints.

- Do your mixing on the palette, not on your paper.

- Use the brush to scoop up a little paint. Place it on the palette. Then scoop up a bit of another color. Mix the colors together, adding more of either color until you like your new color.

- Clean the brush in water between colors. "Paint" the water on a paper towel to dry the brush. If the brush still has color on it, put it in the water and try again.

- If you are using watercolors, dip the brush in clean water before mixing. The paint should be watery and brush on easily.

More painting on next page

Create Different Values

The *value* of a color refers to how light or how dark it is. You can change the value of a paint color by adding black or white. Add white to make a color lighter. This lighter color is called a *tint*. Add black to make a color darker. The darker color is called a *shade*.

1. Mix blue and yellow on your palette to make green. Paint a stripe of the green down the middle of a page. Mix very little black into the green on your palette. Paint a stripe of the new color to the right of the first stripe. Then add a bit more black to the green and paint a stripe of this color again to the right. Keep going until you've filled the right side. These are shades of green.

2. Start with the green again. Add a little white and paint a stripe to the left of your first green stripe. Then add a bit more white to the green and paint a stripe of this color again to the left. Keep going until you've filled the left side. These are the tints of green.

3. You can make tints and shades for other colors, too. For light colors, such as yellow, paint the first stripe to the left of the middle. Yellow is already light, so you will be able to make more shades than tints. For dark colors, such as purple, paint your first stripe a little to the right of the middle. Purple is already dark, so you will be able to make more tints than shades.

Make Complementary Colors

Complementary colors look bright and noticeable when they're together. They're opposite each other on the color wheel, and like the saying goes, opposites attract. They attract the eye!

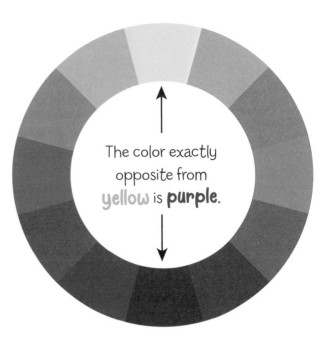

The color exactly opposite from *yellow* is **purple**.

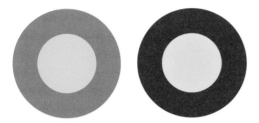

1. Paint two circles of yellow. Paint orange around one of the circles and purple around the other. Which yellow looks brighter?

2. Paint two circles of red. Paint orange around one of the circles and green around the other. Which red looks brighter?

3. Paint two circles of blue. Can you figure out what the complementary color of blue is? (Hint: Look at the color wheel and see which color is exactly opposite blue.) Paint the complementary color around one blue circle, and choose a color close to blue to paint around the other circle. Which blue looks brighter?

4. If you want someone to really notice a color, put it next to its complement. Paint a picture using complementary colors. Choose any color on the wheel and use it to paint whatever you like. Then surround that object with its complementary color. Somebody may *compliment* you on your color selection!

Make a Rainbow with Light

You don't need to wait for a rainy day to see a rainbow. You can make your own rainbow inside with a few items.

Tips

• This works best when it's dark out.
• Set up in the kitchen or bathroom where you can work near a sink.

You Need

- Hand mirror
- Pan or shallow bowl
- Water
- Dark room
- Small flashlight or cell phone with light
- Masking tape (optional)

2. Pour water into the bowl until it is a little more than halfway up the mirror.

1. Put the mirror into the pan or bowl, mirror-side up. Make sure the mirror is leaning at a slight angle.

3. Place the bowl in a dark room. Shine the flashlight on the part of the mirror that is underwater. Move the flashlight around until you see a rainbow on the wall or ceiling.

4. If you see only white light on the wall, adjust the angle of the mirror. Make sure the angle is more flat than steep. Tape the mirror in place if you need to. You can also add or take away water or try different mirrors and flashlights.

Did You Know

• White light is a mix of seven colors: red, orange, yellow, green, blue, indigo, and violet. When light passes from air into water, the light bends. But each color in light bends a little differently from the others, so the colors separate.

• The phrase ROY G. BIV can help you remember the order of the colors in the rainbow (R for Red, O for Orange, Y for Yellow, etc.).

air   water

More Ideas

• Put a glass of water on a sheet of white paper. Shine a flashlight through the glass to make a rainbow on the paper.

• Spray water from a garden hose on a sunny day using the mist setting. Look for a rainbow in the mist.

Wandering Colors

Watch colors magically move and change through water.

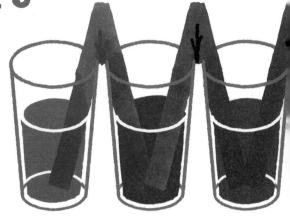

You Need

- 7 clear cups
- Water
- Red, blue, and yellow food coloring
- Paper towels
- Scissors

1. Set the cups close together in a row. Starting with a cup on one end, pour water into every other cup until they're each about three-quarters full. You should have water in four cups.

2. Add several drops of red food coloring to the water in the first cup. Add blue food coloring to the third cup, yellow to the fifth cup, and red to the seventh cup. **Note:** You can use fewer cups and fewer colors if you'd like.

3. Cut paper towels into six equal strips. They should be about two inches wide. Then fold them in half. Fold each strip into a V shape. If needed, trim the ends so they can sit in the cups.

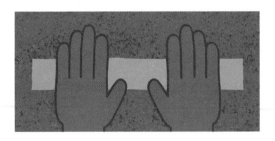

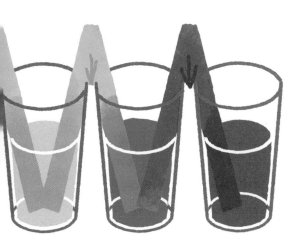

Tip

If you want to shorten the amount of time for this to work, dampen the paper-towel strips before folding them into V shapes.

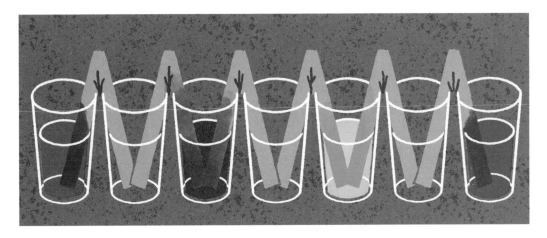

4. Place a V in every cup, as shown. The ends of the paper towels should touch one another in the cups. The colors should start traveling immediately, but it will take up to three hours to see the full results.

Did You Know

Water spreads up a paper towel because it's attracted to the tiny holes and spaces in the fabric. Water also likes to stick to water, so the water in the towel pulls even more water up from the glass.

Milk and Color

Create a surprising burst of color in a plate of milk!

You Need

- Whole milk
- Plate
- Food coloring
- Liquid dish soap
- Cotton swabs

1. Pour milk slowly onto the plate until it covers the bottom.

2. Squeeze a drop or two of food coloring into the center of the milk. Repeat with the other colors. Try not to let the colors overlap.

3. Dab some dish soap onto the end of a cotton swab. Touch the soapy tip of the swab to the center of the milk. Watch what happens!

Did You Know?

Milk contains a mixture of water and fat, and soap likes to stick to both of those things. When you put soap into the milk, it spreads out, sticking to the water and fat. The food coloring moves along with it.

Make Pavement Paint

Want to create artwork on a sidewalk or driveway? Instead of using chalk, you can make your own pavement paint and mix as many colors as you'd like.

Safety Tip

To avoid clogging pipes, don't wash pavement paint down a sink drain. Rain will clean off the pavement, or you can use a hose.

You Need

- Water
- Small, recyclable plastic containers
- Cornstarch
- Food coloring
- Old paintbrush or foam brush

1. Make sure it's okay to paint on the sidewalks, rocks, or driveways of your choosing. Wear clothes that you don't mind getting food coloring on.

2. Pour a third cup of water into the container.

3. Slowly stir in a quarter cup plus two teaspoons of cornstarch until it's dissolved.

4. Add a few drops of food coloring and stir until it's blended well. You'll need to stir the paint often to keep it smooth.

5. Repeat the steps above to make different colors. Try mixing multiple colors of food coloring together.

6. Begin painting! Pavement paint appears watery when you first brush it on, but the color darkens and looks more chalklike as it dries.

7. When you're done, clean the containers and brushes outdoors with water.

Create Tie-Dye Patterns

Express your true colors by creating patterns on a white pillowcase or T-shirt. Begin by prepping the materials and then try one or all of the tie-dyeing techniques on the next page.

You Need

- White, 100% cotton pillowcase or T-shirt*
- Plastic cover or old vinyl tablecloth, to protect your work area
- Plastic or rubber gloves
- Washing soda or soda ash (both can be purchased where laundry detergents are sold)
- Hot water
- Aluminum foil roasting pan
- Ice cubes
- Shoelace
- Rubber bands
- Raised wire rack
- Tie-dye kit
- Plastic wrap

We used a pillowcase for this project, but any white, 100% cotton item will work.

Preparation and Dyeing

1. Wash your pillowcase or T-shirt to remove fabric sizing, which prevents dye from working. (Sizing is a substance added to some fabrics to make them "crisp.") Make sure you don't use fabric softener and don't dry your items yet. They should be wet when you start dyeing.

2. Wear clothes that you don't mind getting dye on. Set up your work area. Spread out the plastic cover or tablecloth. Have an adult handy when you begin working with the dyes.

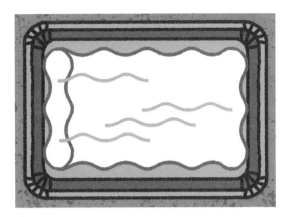

3. Put on the gloves. First, you'll presoak the pillowcase. Read the washing soda container to see how much you'll need. Add that amount into the foil pan and add hot water to fill the pan halfway. Stir gently until the washing soda is completely dissolved. Soak the pillowcase in the mixture for 20 minutes. (This will help the dye absorb into the fabric and make the colors pop.)

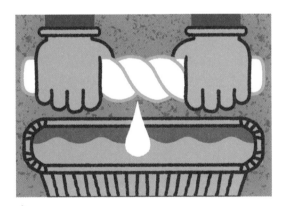

4. After 20 minutes, remove the pillowcase from the water and wring it dry. Do not rinse. Dump out the leftover mixture.

5. Choose one of the dye techniques on the next page. Follow the instructions for scrunching, gathering, or banding the pillowcase. Then place it on a raised wire rack over the foil pan to keep your design sharp and prevent muddied colors.

6. Prepare your dyes by following the tie-dye kit instructions. Apply the dye. Hint: For more colorful designs, be sure to apply the dye inside the folds. You could also flip your fabric and apply dye to the other side.

7. To keep the fabric damp and help the dye set, wrap or cover the fabric in plastic wrap. Let it sit for at least the amount of time that your dye kit recommends. Letting it sit for 12–24 hours will give you more vibrant colors.

8. Remove all bands or ties and rinse the pillowcase in cold water until the water runs clear. Wash and dry separately from other garments the first few times.

Continued on next page

Ice Technique

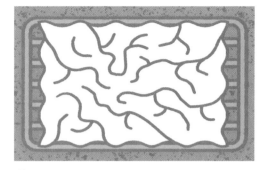

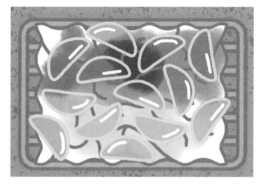

1. Lay your pillowcase on a flat surface, then loosely scrunch it and move it onto the raised wire rack over a foil pan.

3. Follow step 6 on page 185 and apply dye over the ice. Then follow steps 7 (wrapping ice and pillowcase in plastic) and 8.

2. Place bunches of ice cubes on top of the fabric.

Swirl Technique

1. Lay your pillowcase on a flat surface. Starting at the center, twist the fabric in a clockwise direction.

Shibori Technique

3. Pull the ends of the lace toward you as you push the fabric to scrunch it tight. Tie the lace together tightly. Put it on the wire rack over the pan and then follow steps 6, 7, and 8 on page 185.

1. Lay your pillowcase on a flat surface. Put a shoelace across the bottom short edge. Roll the edge over the lace. Continue rolling it all the way to the top.

2. Shape the rolled pillowcase into an upside-down U.

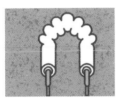

2. Continue twisting the fabric until it's gathered into a tightly swirled circle.

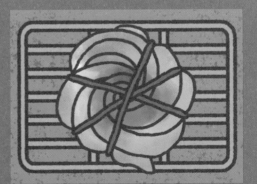

3. Secure the shape with rubber bands in all directions. Put it on the wire rack over the pan and then follow steps 6, 7, and 8 on page 185.

Weird Ways to Paint

There are lots of ways besides paintbrushes to get paint on paper. Try out these creative ideas to add an extra "pop" to your artwork.

Paint Popper

1. Cover an area outside with newspaper. This can get messy!

2. Cut the cardboard tube in half.

3. Tie a knot near the opening of the balloon. Cut off the other end.

4. Slide the balloon over the tube. Secure it with tape.

5. Squeeze some paint into the tube. While holding the tube, aim at a sheet of paper and pull back on the knotted end of the balloon. Release. Repeat with different colors.

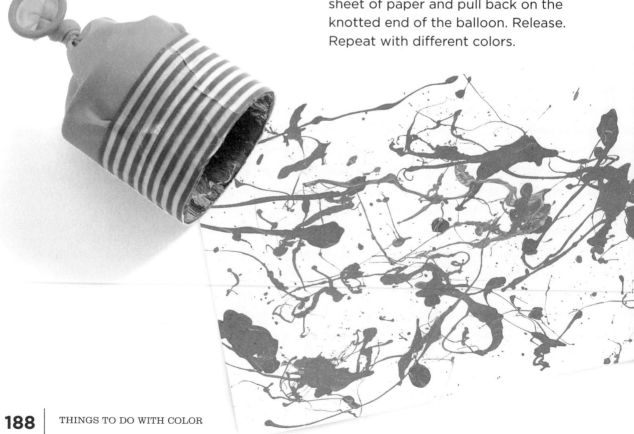

Spin Art

You Need

- Shoebox (lid not needed)
- Duct tape or masking tape
- Thumbtack
- ½-square-inch piece of cardboard
- Pencil
- Paper (watercolor or mixed media paper is best), cut to fit in the box
- Acrylic or tempera paint
- Water

1. Add a piece of duct tape to each corner of the shoebox to seal the seams.

2. Put the thumbtack into the middle of the cardboard square and set aside.

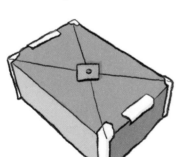

3. Place the box upside down and draw a diagonal line from one corner to its opposite. Repeat with the other two corners. Then insert the thumbtack and cardboard where the two lines intersect.

4. Turn the box over and put the paper inside. If the thumbtack points through the bottom, be careful to avoid it.

5. Add water to each color of paint so it's a bit runny, but still creamy. Put a few drops of paint on the paper and then put the box on a flat surface and give it a spin.

6. Add more paint and spin in the other direction.

More Ideas

- Try changing the speed of your spins, moving the thumbtack, or adding paint to a different part of the paper.

- Add eyes or other details to make monsters or other creatures.

More weird ways on next page

Shaving-Cream Art

You Need

- Plastic cover or old vinyl tablecloth, to protect your work area
- Plastic or aluminum foil pan (the size of your paper or bigger)
- Blank cardstock
- White, unscented shaving foam
- Scrap cardboard
- Food coloring
- Wooden craft stick or paintbrush

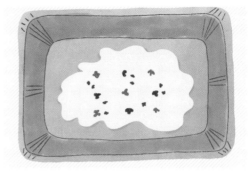

2. Drip food coloring onto the surface of the foam.

3. Use the tip of a wooden craft stick or the end of a paintbrush to blend and swirl the colors together.

1. Spread out the plastic cover or tablecloth and place your pan on it. Spray a small amount of shaving foam into the bottom of the pan. Then spread the foam in the pan with your hand (or with a piece of cardboard) to make a smooth surface a little larger than the size of your cardstock.

4. Press your cardstock onto the foam and gently massage the back of it to help the color transfer.

5. Slowly pull the cardstock off of the foam. Then scrape the extra foam off with some cardboard. Make sure to remove all of the foam before letting the cardstock dry. You can throw away the extra foam or rinse it down the sink.

6. To continue making prints, add more foam to the pan as needed (on top of the used foam), smooth out the surface, and repeat steps 2–5.

Tips

• A thin layer of foam works best.

• Try combining different colors to see how they blend together.

• Be careful not to leave the cardstock on the foam for too long, or it will soften and the colors will be blurry.

More weird ways on next page

Bubble Painting

1. Do this project outdoors on a calm day. Cover the work surface with a layer of newspaper. It's best to wear old clothes and shoes that you don't mind getting messy.

2. Place a piece of paper on the work surface. Anchor it with small stones if necessary.

3. Pour a quarter cup of dish soap into a plastic container.

* If you don't have a bubble wand, use craft glue to attach a craft stick to a shape cut from a plastic lid with holes punched in it, a section of a berry basket, or a spice-jar insert.

4. Start by adding a half teaspoon of food coloring to the soap. Stir with your bubble wand to mix the color well. Add more food coloring to get a stronger color.

5. Repeat steps 3 and 4 with different colors and containers, rinsing the wand between each color you make.

6. Dip the bubble wand into one of the colors, and blow bubbles toward the blank paper from one-to-two feet away.

7. Continue blowing bubbles onto the paper until you're happy with the color. Then rinse the wand and blow bubbles with the other colors you've made.

8. When you are happy with what you have, set the paper aside to dry. The painting can be a piece of art, or you can use it to make gift wrap, book covers, or notepaper.

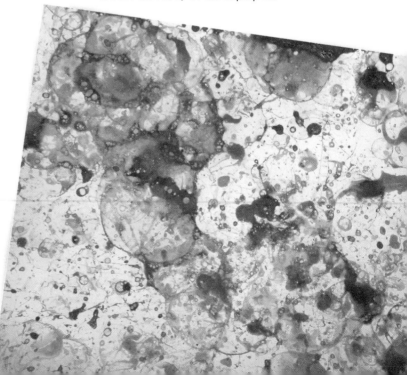

Paint a Mural

Find a friend and get painting!

FOR 2 PAINTERS

You Need

- Old newspapers or a tarp, to protect your work area
- Blank paper
- Tape
- Painter's tape
- Paint
- Paintbrushes
- Jars or old cups, ⅔ full with water, for rinsing

1. Cover a large area of a garage floor, driveway, or other surface with lots of newspaper or a tarp. Tape together enough paper to create a large mural, and use painter's tape to attach it to the newspapers or tarp.

2. You and your painting partner can first think about what you'd like to paint. You can each decide on something different, but tell each other your ideas and help come up with more. Maybe you want to paint your neighborhood or your dream bedroom. It can be anything.

3. Next, kneel at opposite ends of the paper and begin to paint. After a few minutes, step back and look at what's been painted. Decide how the two things might go together. Paint the section between them to connect them into a scene.

Tips
• When you're drawing on the hot rock, be sure not to touch it with your hands.
• To make the crayons melt more, draw slowly, or hold the crayon in one spot.

Crayon Rocks

Use these rocks for paperweights or decoration, or keep them to add to your art collection.

You Need

- Small, smooth rocks
- Cookie sheet
- Hand towel
- Aluminum foil
- Wax crayons
- Tongs
- Oven mitt

1. Have an adult help you with anything hot. Preheat the oven to 350°F. Wash the rocks to get rid of any dirt. Dry the rocks and put them on the cookie sheet. Bake them for 10–15 minutes. Meanwhile, lay a hand towel out in front of you and put a sheet of foil on top of the towel. Peel back the paper on your crayons.

2. With tongs or an oven mitt, take one rock out at a time, and put them on the foil. Take a crayon and press the pointy end against a rock. The crayon will start to melt. Draw on the rock with one or a bunch of colors.

3. Using the tongs, carry your rocks to a safe place where they can cool down and dry.

Design T-Shirts with Chalk

Try out a new way to use chalk by making your own colorful T-shirt.

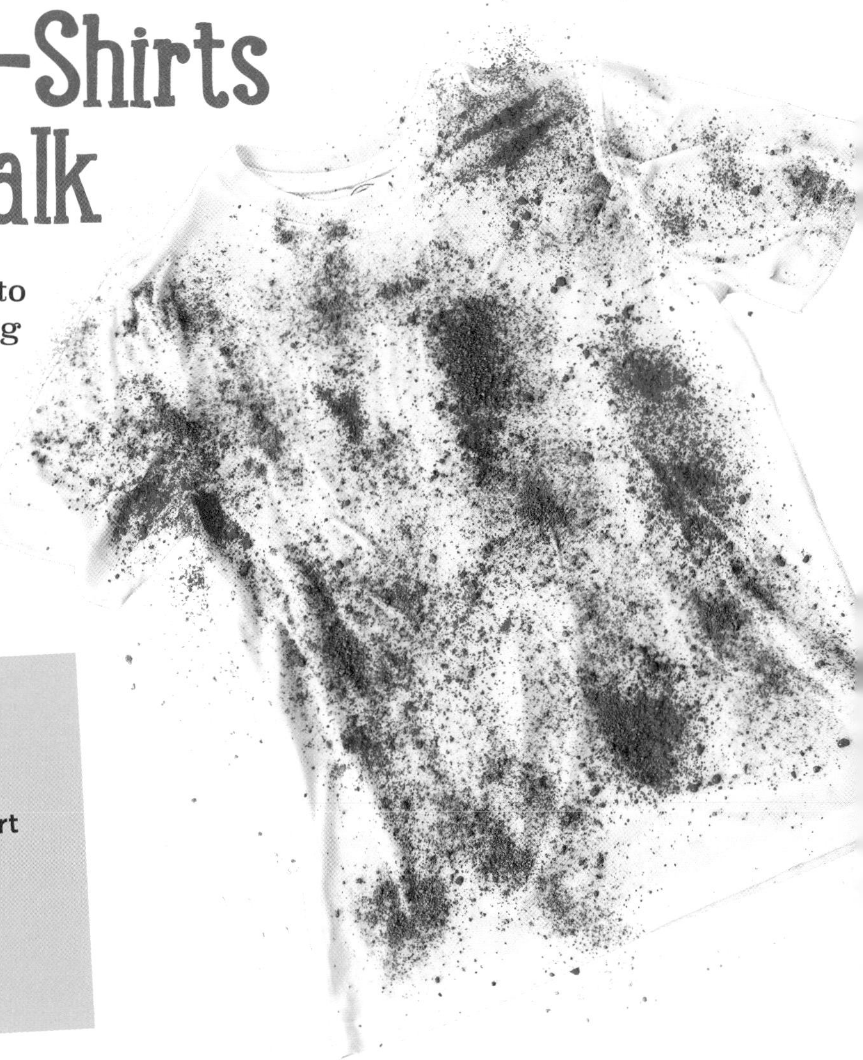

You Need

- Sidewalk chalk
- Freezer bags
- Hammer
- White cotton T-shirt
- Vinegar
- Trash bag
- 2 old towels
- Iron

1. Sort the chalk by color into separate freezer bags. With help from an adult, hammer the chalk into powder.

2. Soak the shirt in plain vinegar for 10 minutes.

3. Lay the trash bag flat on the ground outside. Place the vinegar-soaked shirt flat on top of the trash bag.

4. Throw handfuls of the chalk powder at the shirt. Let it sit for at least three hours.

5. Turn the shirt inside out and place it between two old towels. Ask an adult to iron the shirt between the two towels and then wash the shirt by itself in cold water.

NOTE: Colors may fade slightly when washed.

Sculpt Clay

Learn how to sculpt beautiful clay food with these techniques.

You Need

- Any type of clay, but polymer clay is best
- Dental floss
- Chalk
- Paintbrushes
- Old toothbrush
- Toothpick or plastic knife

Make a Spiral

This is how to make bumps and twists.

1. Roll out two thin snakes of yellow and white clay.

2. Hold them side by side, then twist together.

3. Use dental floss to cut the length you need for your corn on the cob.

Make Dust

This will add color or shading to objects.

1. Rub chalk on paper to create chalk dust.

2. Use a paintbrush to paint the colorful dust onto the clay, like adding purple dust to make a radish.

Add Texture

You can make rough or smooth surfaces.

1. To make a rough or crumb-like texture, like that of an orange, press the bristles of an old toothbrush against the clay.

2. To create smooth textures, like a potato or tomato skin, spread the clay with the toothbrush handle.

Flatten and Carve

Roll the clay, then cut out a shape.

1. Roll balls of green clay in your hands.

2. Using the handle of a paintbrush like a rolling pin, flatten each ball.

3. Use a toothpick or plastic knife to cut out shapes.

4. Carve details with the toothpick.

5. Overlap the shapes to make things like lettuce leaves and asparagus tips. Mold the edges with your fingers.

1 Last Challenge!

Create a self-portrait with a variety of colorful materials, like tissue paper, bottle caps, yarn, or whatever you can find in your craft supplies.

THINGS TO DO WITH
PAPER

Quick Challenges

Draw a character on cardstock and cut it out. Then design clothes for them.

Can you fold a piece of paper in half more than seven times? It's really hard!

How many pieces of paper do you use in a typical day?

Place a penny under a piece of paper and rub the paper with the side of a crayon. Can you do it well enough to see Abraham Lincoln's profile? Draw a hat and a body for him.

Place leaves or other objects on dark-colored construction paper in a sunny place. After a few hours, remove the objects to reveal a "sun print."

Start a paper collection of old newspapers, envelopes, wrapping paper, or other recycled paper products to use in future projects.

Make an Aerobatic Airplane

You may not have seen this type of paper airplane before, but it really soars!

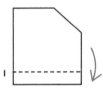

You Need

- 8½-by-11-inch piece of paper

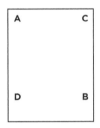

1. Put the paper down on a surface, as shown. Fold corner *A* down to meet *B* so the edges line up.

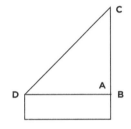

2. Fold *C* down to *D* so the paper looks like this.

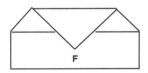

3. Fold *E* down toward *F*.

4. Turn the paper clockwise. Fold *H* up to *G* so the edges line up.

5. To make wings, fold down the top layer along the dotted line *I*. Turn the paper over and fold down in the same way.

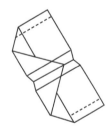

6. To make the wing tips, fold the wings up about a quarter of an inch, as shown by the dotted lines.

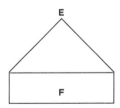

7. Fold the tail in at an angle, as shown by the arrow and dotted lines.

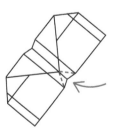

8. Give it a test flight. Grip the bottom of the plane and throw it hard. The plane will glide in large circles.

Build a Paper Helicopter

Create this helicopter that spins when you throw it.

You Need

- Construction paper
- Ruler
- Scissors
- Pencil or pen
- Paper clip

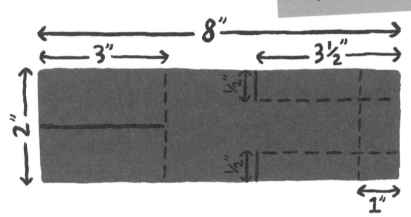

1. Cut out a two-by-eight-inch rectangle from the paper. With the ruler, copy the lines shown above onto it.

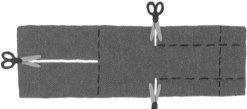

2. Cut along the solid lines. (There should be three cuts.) Fold, crease, and unfold along all the dotted lines.

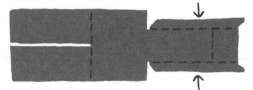

3. Fold the top and bottom sections along the dotted lines, as shown, toward each other.

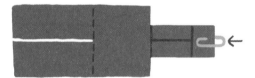

4. Fold the end inward and secure with a paper clip.

5. Fold the propeller sections down in opposite directions.

6. Throw the helicopter as you would a paper airplane. Watch it spin as it falls!

Create a Twirling Flyer

Make this flyer and watch it twirl!

You Need

- Cardstock
- Ruler
- Pencil or pen
- Scissors
- Low-heat glue gun or tacky glue
- Paper straw

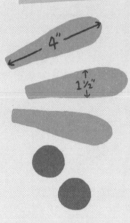

1. Cut out three petal shapes from cardstock. They should all be the same size.

2. Cut out two one-inch circles.

3. Glue the petal shapes to one of the circles. Have an adult help with anything hot. Let it dry. If you're using tacky glue, it will take longer.

4. Glue the second circle shape on. Let it dry.

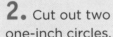

5. Snip three equal slits into the paper straw, as shown, and carefully bend back each tab.

6. Glue the three tabs to one of the circles. Let it dry.

7. Spin the straw quickly between the palms of your hands, let it go, and the flyer will take off.

Make Your Own Paper

Recycle paper scraps and tissue paper into unique pieces of paper. First, make your mold, deckle, and paper pulp. Then use them all together to make paper.

The Mold and Deckle

The mold is a screen attached to a frame. It strains water from the paper pulp. The deckle makes the shape of the paper.

You Need

- Old wooden picture frame that fits inside the large tub used for the pulp
- Piece of fiberglass screen or an old window screen
- Scissors
- Staple gun or stapler
- Duct tape
- Cardboard (thicker is better)
- Pencil
- Ruler

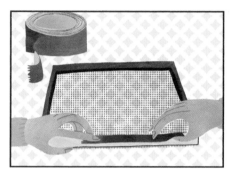

2. Use duct tape to completely cover the wood part of the frame. You've made the mold!

3. Trace the outside of the mold onto cardboard. Put the mold aside.

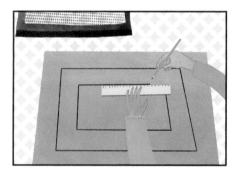

4. Using a pencil and ruler, draw a smaller rectangle inside the larger one. It must be smaller than the screen inside the mold. This will be the size of your paper.

1. With an adult, cut the screen so it's a bit larger than the opening in the picture frame. Staple or duct tape the screen to the frame. Make sure the screen is stretched tightly.

5. Cut out the frame shape. Wrap the cardboard completely with duct tape. You've made the deckle!

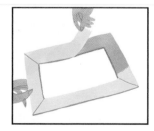

The Paper Pulp

Paper pulp contains fibers of paper mixed in water.

You Need

- Scrap paper, such as watercolor paper, newspaper, or tissue paper
- Paper towels
- Bucket or bowl
- Water
- Old blender (no longer used for food) or a large glass jar with a lid*
- Cornstarch
- Large tub

Old blenders can be found at yard sales and secondhand stores.

Tips

- If you use an old blender to mix, use newspaper and watercolor paper.
- If you use a jar to mix, use mostly tissue paper (about two-thirds of the mixture) and the rest paper towels and newspaper.

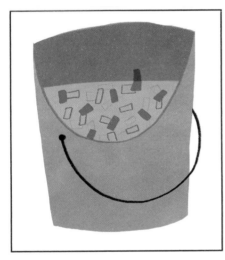

1. Tear the paper into small pieces. Put one cup of paper pieces into a bucket and cover with water. Let it stand for a few hours or overnight. Then strain the leftover water into the tub.

2. Fill the blender or jar halfway with water. Add only a handful of soaked paper pieces. Put the lid on and blend or shake until the mixture is mushy. Mix in one tablespoon of cornstarch. Pour the paper pulp into the large tub and continue blending or shaking until all the paper pieces are used.

Continued on next page

The Finished Paper

Use your mold, deckle, and paper pulp to create cool-looking paper!

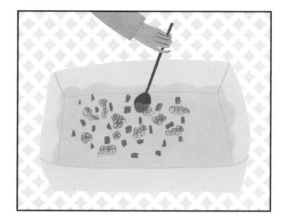

1. Work in a place that can get wet. Layer old towels on a hard, flat surface. Stir the pulp in your big tub. Do the bits of paper move around freely in the water? If not, add more water and stir again. If you want, stir in some add-ins.

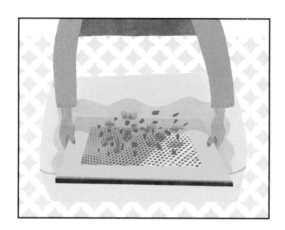

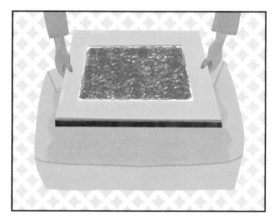

2. Hold the mold screen-side up. Place your deckle on top of the mold and hold them firmly together. Leading with one edge, dip the mold and deckle into the paper pulp.

3. Once the mold and deckle are underwater, hold them flat and bring them slowly out of the water. You will see a mush of wet paper pulp on your screen.

4. Lift the deckle straight up off the mold and set aside. Rest one edge of the mold on the towels. Gently lower the mold pulp-side down onto the towels.

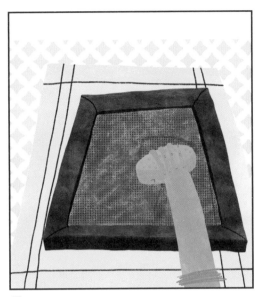

5. Use a sponge to press on the screen. Press all around the mold to squeeze out as much water as you can.

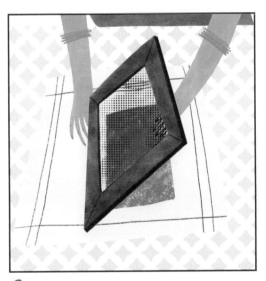

6. Make sure that the paper is sticking to the towel. You might need to use a finger to hold down the edge. Carefully lift the mold, leaving the paper on the towel.

7. Choose a way to dry your paper. You can leave it on the towel, peel it off and press it on a window, or lay it flat on a waterproof surface.

Paper Beads

Find some used colorful paper to make these beads. This is a good project to do with friends.

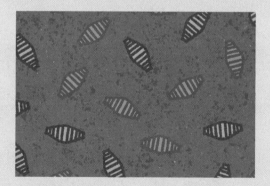

You Need

- Scrap poster board or thick paper
- Ruler
- Pencil
- Scissors
- Colorful paper, such as wrapping paper, pages from old magazines, or calendars
- Straw
- Glue
- Ribbon or string

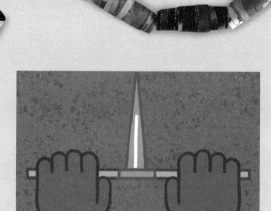

3. Place a triangle with the picture-side down. Lay the straw across the one-inch edge. Roll the triangle around the straw twice, as shown. Add glue to the rest of the triangle and continue rolling. Gently slip the straw out, and let the bead dry.

1. Draw a 1-by-10-inch triangle on the poster board or thick paper. Cut it out.

2. Trace the triangle many times onto your colorful paper. Cut out the triangles.

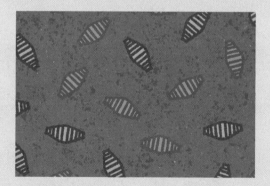

4. String the beads onto ribbon or string to make a necklace or garland. If you want different-sized beads, try using bigger or smaller triangles.

Layer 3-D Designs

You can make a 3-D effect with 2-D paper.

1. Think of any outdoor scene. It should have three distances: close to the viewer, farther back, and in the distance.

2. On black paper, draw the outline of each part of your scene. Cut them out.

3. Lay the cutouts of the farthest part of the scene (the clouds) on a piece of tracing paper. Layer another piece of tracing paper on top and then put the next closest part of the scene (the house) on top. Repeat the same process with the closest part of the scene (the trees).

4. Glue each cutout to the tracing paper beneath it.

5. Put all three layers of tracing paper and cutouts on a piece of white paper. Glue them in place along the top edge only.

Make a Papier-Mâché Fruit Bowl

Create both useful objects and awesome art with papier-mâché.

You Need

- Newspaper
- Balloon
- Plastic lid (about 4½ inches across)
- Masking tape
- 1 cup flour
- 1 cup water
- 1 tablespoon salt
- Pin
- Acrylic paint
- Non-toxic sealant, such as Mod Podge

1. Rip the newspaper into three-by-eight-inch strips. You'll need a lot of paper strips.

2. Blow up the balloon. Tape a plastic lid to the end of the balloon opposite the knot to form the base of the bowl.

3. To make the papier-mâché paste, mix the flour, water, and salt until it's a creamy paste with no lumps.

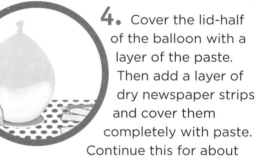

4. Cover the lid-half of the balloon with a layer of the paste. Then add a layer of dry newspaper strips and cover them completely with paste. Continue this for about five more layers of strips. Let it dry for a day or two.

5. When it's completely dry, pop the balloon, carefully remove the lid and tape, and trim the edges of the bowl.

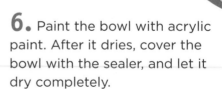

6. Paint the bowl with acrylic paint. After it dries, cover the bowl with the sealer, and let it dry completely.

7. Use the bowl for storing fruit that you peel, such as oranges and bananas, or other objects.

Paper Snowflakes

Try this 3-D twist on the classic snowflake.

1. Tape two pieces of paper together to form a long sheet.

2. Starting at a short side of the paper, fold accordion pleats, like you would to make a fan.

3. Staple the folded paper in the middle.

4. Snip the two ends at angles. Then cut out small triangles along the top and bottom edges of the folded paper.

5. Spread the folds open until the ends meet and form a circle. Tape the ends together.

6. Tape string to the snowflake and hang it up.

Make Your Own Books

After you make these books, fill them with your own art or stories.

Mini Notebook

1. Cut two 3-by-11-inch strips of paper. Overlap the strips and tape them together to make one long strip.

2. Accordion-fold the taped strip into two-inch sections. Trim off any extra paper.

3. If you want book covers, cut two two-by-three-inch pieces of the gift cards or other heavier paper and decorate. Tape one end of the strip to the back of each cover.

Twig Book

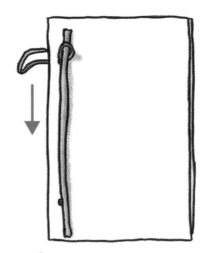

3. Push the rubber band from the back through the front of the top hole. Put the twig into the loop of the rubber band in the front of the book.

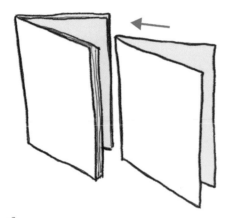

1. Take five pieces of paper and fold them in half vertically. Insert them into one another.

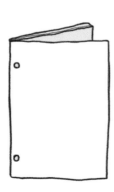

2. Punch two holes on the left, folded side: one about an inch or more from the top and one an inch or more from the bottom.

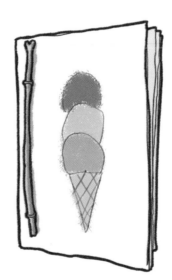

4. Do the same thing with the bottom hole and the other end of the rubber band. Start writing and drawing!

More books on next page

Tiny Little Book

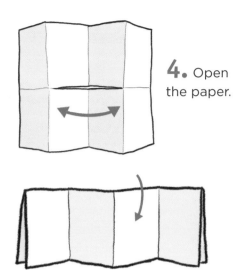

4. Open the paper.

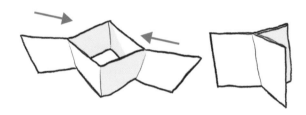

5. Fold the paper down, so the long sides meet.

1. Fold the piece of paper in half, as shown above. Then unfold it.

2. Fold the paper the other way, so the short sides meet, then fold the right edges back to meet the left side, as shown.

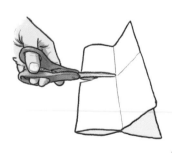

3. Unfold the paper and then fold it in half, so the short sides meet again. Cut along the center until it meets the next fold.

6. Hold both sides of your paper and gently push them toward each other. Crease the folds well.

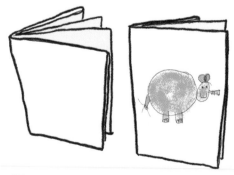

7. Fold along the spine of your new little book. Decorate the cover, if you'd like.

Ribbon-Bound Journal

You Need

- Thin cardboard or brown paper bag
- Paper or cardstock
- Ruler
- Pencil
- Scissors
- Quarter
- Hole punch
- Paint or markers
- 3-foot-long piece of raffia or ribbon

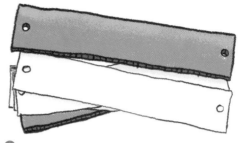

3. Place the paper strips between the cardboard strips.

1. Cut out two 2-by-11-inch strips of cardboard and four strips of paper in the same size. Punch a hole at the center of the skinny ends of every strip of cardboard and paper. Make sure all the holes line up.

2. Trace a quarter twice on a piece of thin cardboard. Cut out the circles. Punch a hole in the center of each circle. Color these decorative circles, and let them dry if you use paint.

4. Thread the raffia or ribbon through the holes of the journal, as shown above. Tie the circles to each end.

5. Decorate the cover. Wrap the raffia ends around it.

Make Your Own Cards

Make someone's day with one of these special cards.

Pop-Up Card

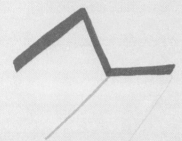

1. Fold both pieces of construction paper in half. One will be the outside of the card and one will be the inside of the card.

2. To make the cake, cut four slits along the folded edge of the inside piece. The bottom slit will be the longest, and the top slit will be the shortest.

3. Open the folded paper, then pull each crease forward and re-crease it so it pops forward instead of backward.

4. Glue the edges of the outside card to the inside card.

5. Decorate the cake layers with markers, paper candles, stickers, and anything else!

Pull-Tab Card

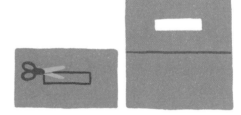

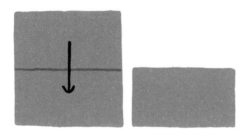

2. With a pencil, lightly draw a one-by-five-inch rectangle in the center of the top piece of the card. Cut it out carefully and erase any remaining pencil lines.

1. Fold a piece of cardstock in half from top to bottom.

Continued on next page

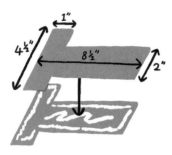

3. From the second piece of paper, cut out two T-shapes in the size shown above. Glue them together, and let them dry.

6. Make sure the pull tab is slid all the way in. Snip a small rectangular strip from cardstock and fold it like an accordion. Attach the accordion strip to both your cutout and the T-shape, as shown. Let it dry.

4. Set the T-shape inside the card, as shown. Run a thin line of glue along the edges of the entire inside of the card, except where the pull tab will exit on the right side. The T-shape should not have any glue on it. Close the card so it's glued together. Move the pull tab in and out a few times to make sure it doesn't get glued in accidentally. Let it dry completely.

7. Write PULL on the end of the tab. Pull it out as far as it will go. Then write a hidden message inside the window box.

8. Use markers or other cardstock shapes to decorate the rest of the card.

5. Cut a shape (an animal, car, or plane, for example) from cardstock and then decorate it.

Scratch-Off Card

You Need

- Cardstock
- Markers
- Clear packing tape
- Scissors
- 1 tablespoon acrylic paint
- ½ tablespoon liquid dish soap
- Paintbrush
- Glue

1. Use markers to write a message on cardstock paper.

2. Cover the message with the packing tape. Cut it out in whatever shape you'd like.

3. Mix the acrylic paint with the dish soap.

4. Paint the mixture over the tape. Let it dry. Repeat this step two more times.

5. Make a card out of another piece of cardstock. Glue the painted message inside. Decorate the card however you want.

6. Add a note that says *Scratch to Reveal!*

Fold Paper

Origami is the Japanese word for the art of folding paper into objects and shapes. Check out these six projects and get folding!

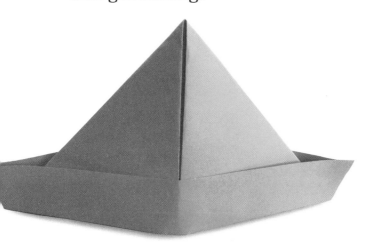

Sailor's Hat

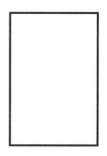
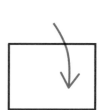

1. Fold the paper in half from top to bottom.

Drinking Cup

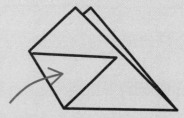

2. Fold the left corner to the right side.

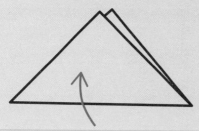

1. Fold the paper in half, corner to corner.

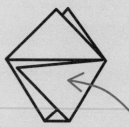

3. Fold the right corner to the left side.

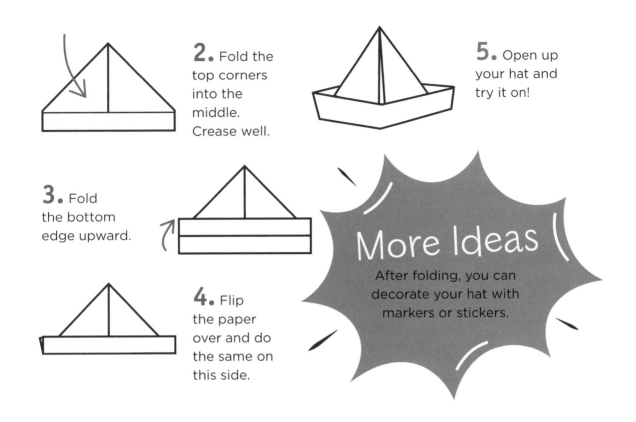

2. Fold the top corners into the middle. Crease well.

3. Fold the bottom edge upward.

4. Flip the paper over and do the same on this side.

5. Open up your hat and try it on!

More Ideas

After folding, you can decorate your hat with markers or stickers.

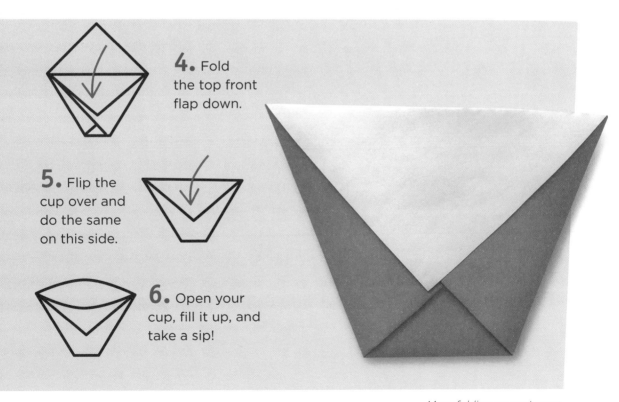

4. Fold the top front flap down.

5. Flip the cup over and do the same on this side.

6. Open your cup, fill it up, and take a sip!

More folding on next page

Bill Bow Tie

You Need

- Dollar bill or 2-by-6-inch piece of decorative paper

1. Turn the dollar facedown.

2. Fold the dollar in half, as shown, then unfold it.

3. Fold the long edges in to meet the center fold.

4. Fold the right edge over to meet the left edge.

5. Fold the two right corners to meet in the center. Crease them hard, unfold them, and then fold them in the same way to the back.

6. Unfold the corners again. Tuck them to the inside, as shown.

7. Fold the top left layer toward you and to the right along the dotted line, as shown. Then fold the remaining layer away from you and to the right so the ends of the bill meet. The folded crease should now be on your left.

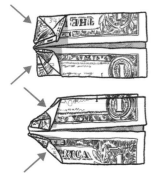

8. Fold the two left corners of the top layer forward to meet in the center. Then turn the bill over and do the same on the other side.

9. Gently separate the ends of the bill, squashing in the center as you do so. Enjoy your new bow tie!

Happy Hound

You Need

- **Square piece of paper**

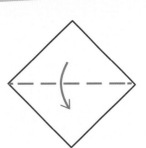

1. Fold the paper, corner to corner.

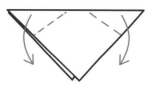

2. Fold on the two dotted lines, as shown.

3. Draw your dog's face!

More folding on next page

Secret Note

1. Write a note to a friend.

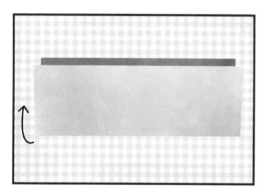

2. Fold the paper in half, from bottom to top, then fold in half the same way again.

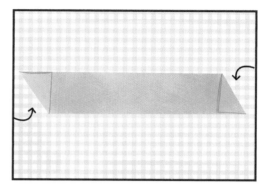

3. Fold the bottom left corner up to meet the top edge, as shown. Then fold the top right corner down to meet the bottom.

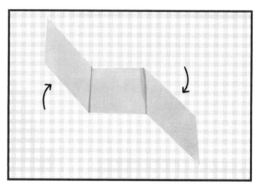

4. Fold the left-side triangle upward so the right edge of the triangle lines up with the top edge of the paper. Fold the right-side triangle downward so the left edge of the triangle lines up with the bottom edge of the paper.

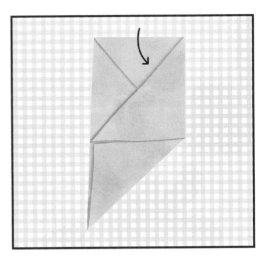

6. Fold the top triangle downward and insert it underneath the right flap.

5. Fold each side toward the center.

7. Fold the bottom triangle upward and insert it underneath the left flap.

THERE!
RE'S A SECRET NOTE.

More folding on next page

Blow-Up Balloon

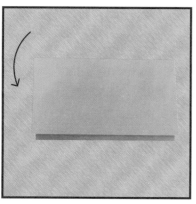

1. Fold the square paper in half from top to bottom.

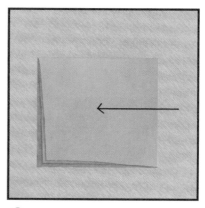

2. Fold in half the other way, from right to left.

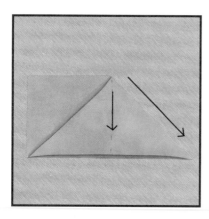

3. Lift up the front layer of the paper, then press down and to the right to create a triangle.

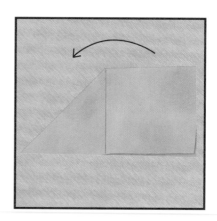

4. Flip it over, then fold just the square from right to left as if you are turning the page of a book.

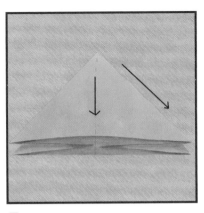

5. Repeat step 3, as in the image above.

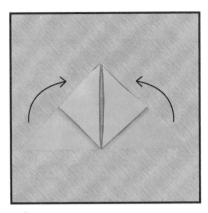

6. Fold the top layer of the bottom corners up to the center.

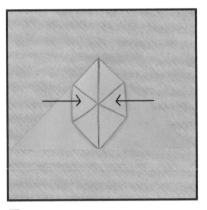

7. Fold the side corners inward to the center.

8. Fold the top-layer corners down and insert them into the pockets, as shown.

9. Flip over and repeat steps 6, 7, and 8.

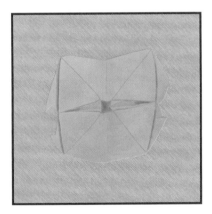

10. Slowly blow air into the opening at the bottom of the balloon. If the opening is too small, use the tip of a pen to make it a bit bigger and try again.

Paper Games

Grab a friend and get playing!

Action Dice

FOR 2 OR MORE PLAYERS

You can make this game simple or challenging. It's up to you.

You Need

- 2 small tissue boxes
- Cardstock
- Pencil or pen
- Scissors
- Markers
- Double-sided tape

1. Trace each side of both tissue boxes onto cardstock. Cut out the 12 shapes.

2. Write an action phrase onto six shapes with a marker (you can try our suggestions on the finished die or write your own). On the other six, write a number of seconds or repetitions.

3. Use the tape to attach the actions to one box and the numbers to the other.

4. To play, take turns rolling the dice and following the instructions that land faceup. The first player to complete all six actions wins.

Fukuwarai

FOR 2 OR MORE PLAYERS

Fukuwarai **(foo-koo-WAH-rye) is a Japanese game. The word means "lucky laugh."**

You Need

- 2 large pieces of paper
- Markers or colored pencils
- Scissors
- Old scarf or small towel, for a blindfold

1. One player draws the shape of a face on a piece of paper.

2. On the other piece, players draw and color two eyes, a nose, two ears, a mouth, and any other features, such as eyebrows or hair. Cut out the features.

3. Place the blank face on the floor. Blindfold a player and ask them to put all of the features onto the blank face. Help by giving directions such as "up," "down," "left," and "right." For a greater challenge, don't give any directions at all.

4. Take turns to see who makes the funniest face. Take pictures of them, if you'd like.

More Ideas

Make a bunch of different eyes, noses, mouths, eyebrows, and ears. Let the blindfolded player choose the right number from each group, or just randomly select eight or nine of them.

More games on next page

Tangram Race

FOR 2 OR MORE PLAYERS

A tangram is an ancient Chinese puzzle.

You Need

- Cardstock or poster board
- Ruler
- Pencils
- Scissors
- Markers

1. Have each player draw an eight-inch square on cardstock or poster board and cut it out.

2. On the square, use a ruler and pencil to draw three vertical lines, two inches apart, and three horizontal lines, two inches apart, as shown.

3. Use markers to draw the seven tangram shapes, or *tans*, as shown in blue. Cut them out. Each player may want to color all their tans one color.

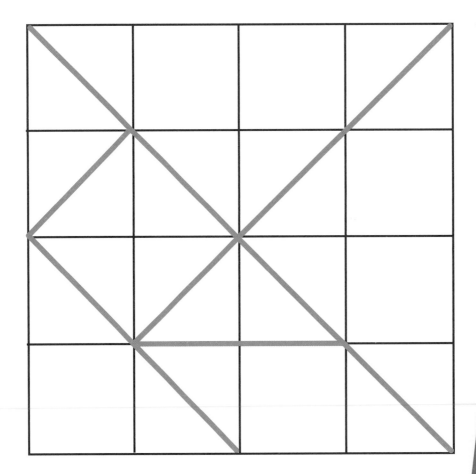

4. To start the game, one player makes a design using their tans while the other players look away.

The rules for designs are simple:
• You must use all seven tans.
• They must lie flat.
• They must touch.
• They must not overlap.

5. Once the design is finished, the other players look and then race to see who can recreate the design with their own tans the fastest.

6. The person who finishes first gets a point. If there are only two players, the player gets a point if they can recreate the design in less than 10 seconds. The player who reaches 10 points first wins.

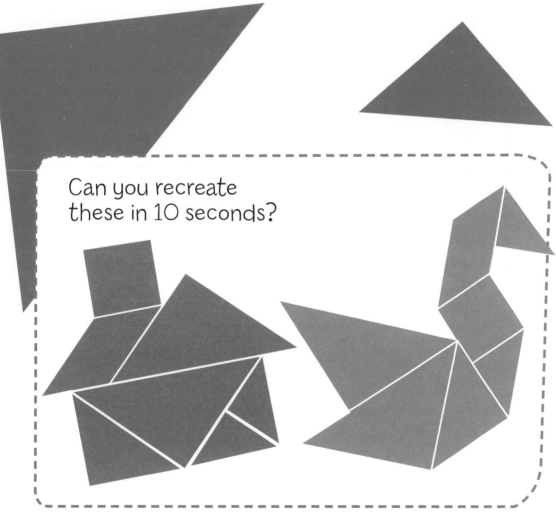

Can you recreate these in 10 seconds?

Paper Tricks

Amaze your friends—and yourself—with these tricks.

Step Through an Index Card

Using a pair of scissors and an index card, you can make a loop large enough to step into! Crazy, right?

You Need

- 3-by-5-inch index card
- Scissors

1. Fold the index card in half from left to right.

2. Starting from the folded side, cut a line that stops before the edge. Repeat near the other end, as shown.

3. Unfold the card and bend the cut pieces the opposite direction of their fold.

4. Now cut all the way along the crease.

5. Fold the card again and cut lines about a quarter-inch apart, alternating which long edge you start from. Each line should almost reach the opposite edge.

6. Gently open the card. Carefully pull it apart. Step through it and pull it apart more. Then, gently bring it up over your body and head.

More tricks on next page

Create Mind-Boggling Paper

Turn a piece of paper into an impossible shape that will mystify your friends and family.

You Need

- Pencil or pen
- Ruler
- Piece of paper
- Scissors

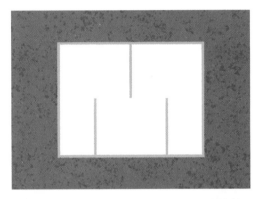

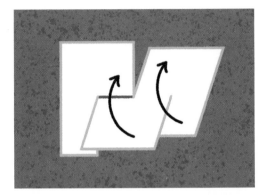

1. Draw three lines as shown above. Then cut along the lines.

2. Pick up the paper by its short sides and flip only the right side away from you. Now there will be a flap stuck up in the middle of the paper.

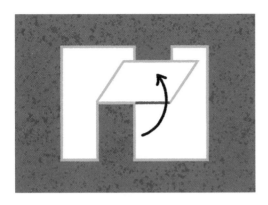

3. Lay the flap down, away from you. Crease well.

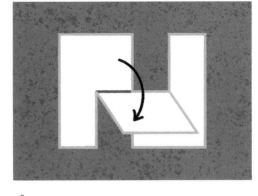

4. Now fold the flap down toward you and make a crease.

5. Pull the flap up so it stands on its own.

6. Show this impossible paper to your friends or family. Hand them a plain piece of paper and scissors—without any instructions—and challenge them to make one, too. Tell them they can make cuts and folds but can't use tape. They'll tell you it's impossible!

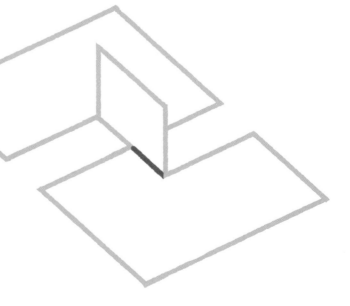

More tricks on next page

Make Super Strong Paper

Can a piece of paper hold up a tower of books? Yes, it can! This trick will show you how.

You Need

- 8½-by-11-inch piece of paper
- Scissors
- Tape
- Stack of books

1. To make six equal strips of paper for this activity, begin by folding a piece of paper in half, as shown.

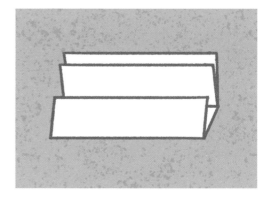

2. Now fold this new shape into thirds. First fold up from the bottom. Then fold the top edge down to meet the bottom edge.

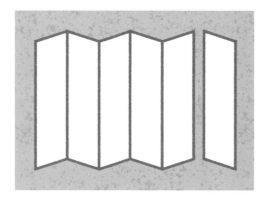

3. Unfold the paper and cut along the creases. You now have six equal strips.

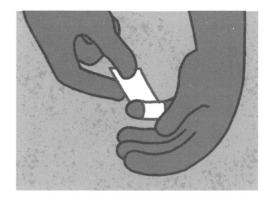

4. Pick up a strip and wrap it around a finger. Wrap it tightly—but not too tight. You'll need to slide it off.

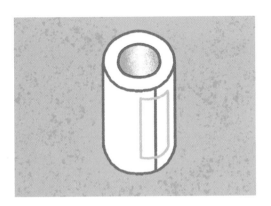

5. Slide the roll of paper off your finger, then make sure the roll is straight and tight. Tape down the flap so you have a small tube.

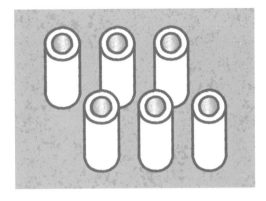

6. Do the same thing with the other strips until you have six tubes.

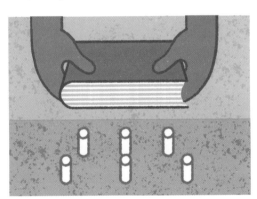

7. Spread out the tubes into two rows. Get the widest book in your stack and carefully place it on top of the tubes.

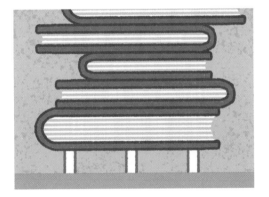

8. Carefully add more books, one at a time. See how tall your tower of books can get. That's one super strong piece of paper!

Make a Paper Tree

With simple rolling and snipping, you can turn newspaper into a forest.

1. Lay a page of the newspaper flat and begin rolling it from the bottom of the short end to the top.

2. Halfway through, place a second page of newspaper on top of the first and begin rolling it up along with the first page.

3. Repeat step 2 with a third, fourth, and fifth page of newspaper.

5. Holding the bottom of the tube tightly in one hand, put your index finger inside the tube at the top. Pull upward to reveal the fringe.

4. Holding the tube of rolled newspaper in one hand, carefully snip four slits into the top of the tube, as shown. The slits should be a bit shorter than half the tube. Make sure to cut through all the layers of paper.

6. Secure the bottom of the tube with a long piece of tape. You have a tree!

1 Last Challenge!

Make a 3-D map of your neighborhood using paper, paint, and empty containers.

THINGS TO
BUILD

Build miniature furniture with craft sticks, wooden dowels, glue, fabric, cotton balls, and other small objects.

Quick Challenges

When something you own breaks, try to figure out what is wrong with it. Then see if you can come up with a way to fix it. Have an adult help with anything electrical.

Can you build something that makes an everyday task easier? Maybe it's a holder for your pens and pencils (see page 298) or an extendable grabber to pick up items you can't reach (see page 308).

How tall can you make a stack of coins? Is one kind of coin easier to stack than others?

Stack plastic cups to make a pyramid. What other shapes can you make by stacking them?

Build a ramp out of long cardboard rolls, cereal boxes, or other large pieces of cardboard. Start it on a chair or table and connect the pieces with glue or tape.

A Confetti Cannon

All you need are a few basic supplies and you can launch confetti!

You Need

- Paper cup
- Scissors
- Plastic water bottle
- Small plastic bag
- Hole punch
- Rubber bands
- Markers or craft foam
- Confetti (choose some that's easy to clean up) or small pom-poms

1. Cut out the bottom of the cup. Cut off the cone-shaped top of the water bottle. Cut off the top of the small plastic bag.

2. Punch two holes near the bottom of the cup. Punch two holes near the neck of the cone.

Continued on next page

3. Place the cone inside the bag. Screw the lid onto the cone, outside the bottom of the bag.

4. Cut the rubber band and thread it through the holes in the cone.

5. Put the cone inside the cup, threading the rubber band through the cup's holes. Knot the ends so they're secure.

6. Pull the ends of the plastic bag over the lip of the cup. Wrap another rubber band around the lip of the cup to secure the bag. If you want, decorate the cup. Place confetti or small pom-poms in the cone.

7. Hold on to the cup with one hand (not shown) while pulling back on the bottle lid with the other. Aim the cup toward an open area and release the lid.

Change-a-Maze

This game changes every time. First make it, then challenge a friend to play.

FOR 2 OR MORE PLAYERS

You Need

- Shoebox lid
- Poster board
- Pencil or pen
- Scissors
- Ruler
- Wide straws
- Hole punch
- Metal fasteners
- Sticky notes
- Marble

1. Trace the shoebox lid onto poster board. Cut out the shape.

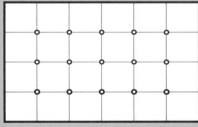

2. Draw a grid on the back of the shape, with each line two inches from the next. Poke a hole into each spot where the lines cross.

3. Cut wide straws into three-inch pieces. Punch a hole in each, one inch from one of its ends.

4. Use metal fasteners to attach the straws to the front of the poster board, as shown below.

5. Write START and FINISH on sticky notes and place them on the poster board. Put the poster board inside the lid.

6. Create a maze by rotating the straws. Place a marble on START. Give the maze to another player to solve. Once the player solves the maze, ask them to create a new one for you to solve.

Construct a House of Cards

You may not be able to live in a house of cards, but you can build one. See how long yours lasts!

1. Take a card in each hand, and lean the top edges of the cards toward each other, as shown. Gently adjust how the cards rest against each other until they stand on their own. This is the basic unit of your house.

2. Once you have one triangle, build another one next to it. The triangles should be quite close together, but they don't have to touch.

3. Build a third triangle next to the second. These three triangles are your foundation.

You Need

- Deck of old playing cards (the more worn, the better)
- Thin tablecloth or rug, to build on

Tips

- Use old cards to create friction. New cards are glossy and slick and won't work well.

- Building the house on top of a thin tablecloth or rug makes it more stable because the cards grip the surface.

- As long as a triangle seems stable, keep building, even if it's not perfect.

- Take your time, move slowly, use a light touch, and don't make any sudden movements.

- Be prepared for lots of falling cards. But if you keep trying, you will get it done.

4. Gently lay a card on top of two triangles. The card should be well balanced.

5. Gently lay a card on top of the other two triangles.

6. Now build the triangles for the next floor. Try to center the first triangle between the two triangles below it.

7. Make the second triangle. Build it slowly and gently, since it's very easy to knock over the first triangle.

8. Gently lay a card on top of the two triangles.

9. Slowly and gently build the top triangle. When it feels secure, let go. You've done it!

Did You Know

The number of triangles in the foundation (bottom floor) determines the number of possible floors. Each floor has one less triangle than the floor below it, until there's only one triangle on the top floor. Add more triangles to the foundation and see how high you can go.

Make an Electric ToothBot

Add some cardboard to an old electric toothbrush, and you'll have your own ToothBot!

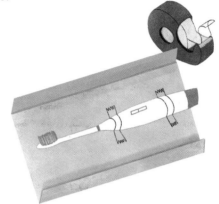

2. Tape the toothbrush to the center of the cardboard with the bristles facing away from the cardboard. Flip the cardboard over and turn on the electric toothbrush. Its vibrations will make the unit move about. Adjust the sides of the cardboard—folding them at different angles—to control the bot's movements. You can make it move straight, in a circle, or in a random motion.

1. First, make sure the batteries work in the toothbrush. Cut the cardboard into a five-by-seven-inch rectangle. It should be about the length of the toothbrush. Then fold one inch of the cardboard's long sides upward to make right angles.

3. Tape a cup to the top of the cardboard, and decorate it.

Three Ways to Play

Runaway Hoops:
With a friend, try to throw bouncy balls into the ToothBot's cup as it moves around. The first player to make three baskets wins.

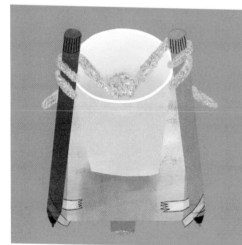

Jitter Art:
Attach markers to the cardboard with tape. Use pipe cleaners knotted to each other to tie the markers to the cup. Place a piece of paper underneath the bot, and turn it on.

Yes-or-No Bot:
Draw the words YES and NO on opposite ends of a piece of paper. Place the ToothBot in the center of the paper, ask a yes-or-no question, and turn it on. Whichever direction the ToothBot moves in is your answer.

Build Three Launchers

A catapult (CAT-uh-pult) is a device for launching things. Here are three small versions that you can make yourself.

PAPER-CLIP LAUNCH

You Need

- Paper clip

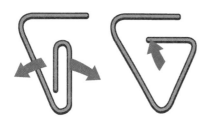

1. Unbend a paper clip so it looks like the second image above.

2. Carefully bring the ends together, latching one side under the other. This may take a few tries.

3. Allow the latched side of the paper-clip triangle to fall gently onto a hard surface. Watch it soar!

STRAW OR PAPER ROCKETS

You Need

- Paper straws
- Scissors
- Tape
- Coffee stirrer
- Lightweight paper

To make a straw rocket, cut a paper straw to the length of a finger. Cover one end with tape. Insert a coffee stirrer into the the other end and blow into the stirrer to launch your straw rocket!

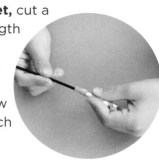

To make paper rockets, cut strips of paper and roll each strip around a straw. Close the long side and one short end of the rolled paper with tape. To launch your paper rocket, put the paper at the end of your straw and blow hard!

ULTIMATE CATAPULT

You Need

- 18 craft sticks
- Glue
- Yarn
- Ruler
- Scissors
- 2 paper clips
- Hole punch
- Small plastic cup
- Scissors
- Felt
- Stapler
- Rectangular tissue box
- Binder clip
- Low-heat glue gun or duct tape
- Jumbo straw
- Small stones or marbles
- Pencil
- Rubber bands
- Small pom-poms or balls
- Small paper or plastic bowl

Make These Pieces

Swing Arm: Glue four craft sticks together, as shown.

Frame Pieces: Glue three craft sticks together, as shown. Repeat three more times.

Yarn: Cut three nine-inch pieces.

Paper Clips: Bend two clips, as shown.

Counterweight: Punch two holes in the cup, opposite each other.

Sling: Fold a piece of felt in half and cut out an egg shape. Staple it twice, as shown. Punch a hole in each layer of felt.

Did You Know

This catapult, called a trebuchet (TREB-yoo-SHAY), uses gravity to fling objects. As gravity pulls a weight on one end of its arm toward the ground, the other end pivots upward, bringing the sling with it. The sling releases the object.

Continued on next page

Make the Catapult

1. For the base, cut off the top and short sides of the tissue box, leaving a triangle in each bottom corner.

2. Glue two frame pieces and a craft stick together, to make a frame. Repeat to make a second frame.

3. Make sure the frames are dry. Then glue them to the walls of the base, as shown.

4. Tape the bottom arm of the binder clip to the base, as shown.

5. With an adult, use a glue gun or duct tape to attach the bent paper clips and a piece of the straw to the swing arm, as shown. The paper clip that is bent outward is the finger, and the other one is the hook.

6. Tie one piece of yarn to the holes in the cup, as shown. Trim the extra yarn. Loop a paper clip around the yarn. Fill the cup with small, heavy objects, such as stones or marbles.

7. Tie a piece of yarn to each hole of the sling. Make a loop at the end of one of the pieces. Tie the end of the other piece to the paper clip at the long end of the swing arm.

8. Slide a pencil through the straw on the swing arm. Fasten the pencil to the frame using rubber bands.

How to Launch

1 Place the loop of the sling around the finger on the swing arm.

2 Place pom-poms or balls in the sling between the two layers of felt.

3 Pull the sling through the base and clamp it into the binder clip.

4 Hang the counterweight from the hook on the short end of the arm.

5 Place the bowl about six feet away. Make sure the area is clear.

6 Aim the trebuchet. (The binder clip should be on the end nearest the bowl.) Stay to the side of the trebuchet while pressing down on the binder clip to release the sling. Launch!

7 Did the pom-poms or balls land in the bowl? If not, change the angle of the sling's release by bending the finger up or down. Reload the sling, and launch again.

Build a Chain Reaction Machine

You can piece together simple machines to make a chain reaction, where one action leads to another.

1. Think about what you want your machine to do. What will its final action be? Here are some examples:

a. Catch a ball under a cup.
b. Hit a wind chime.
c. Crack an egg.
d. Close a book.

2. Brainstorm ideas for what could cause that final action. For example, a spoon could drop a ball into a cup. Then brainstorm what causes the second-to-last action, and then the one before that. Keep going until you think you've created enough workable steps to make it fun.

3. Find materials and assemble your machine, action by action. Test it, make improvements or add components, and test it again. You'll need to keep testing, reworking, and improving until you're happy with your new contraption.

Useful Rube Goldberg Materials

- Table-tennis balls, golf balls, tennis balls, marbles
- Toy vehicles
- Building toys
- Dominoes
- Small fans
- Small building blocks
- Small baskets
- Funnels
- Recyclables: egg cartons, yogurt containers, tissue boxes, bottle caps, cereal boxes, etc.

Simple Machine Supplies

Wheels: cardboard tubes, playdough, lids, plastic cups

Axles: straws, wooden dowels, toothpicks

Incline Planes: wooden blocks, door stops, toy slides, cardboard

Levers: binder clips and craft sticks, pencils and rulers

Pulleys: any kind of string with roll of tape, spools, carabiners

Adhesives: Tape and glue

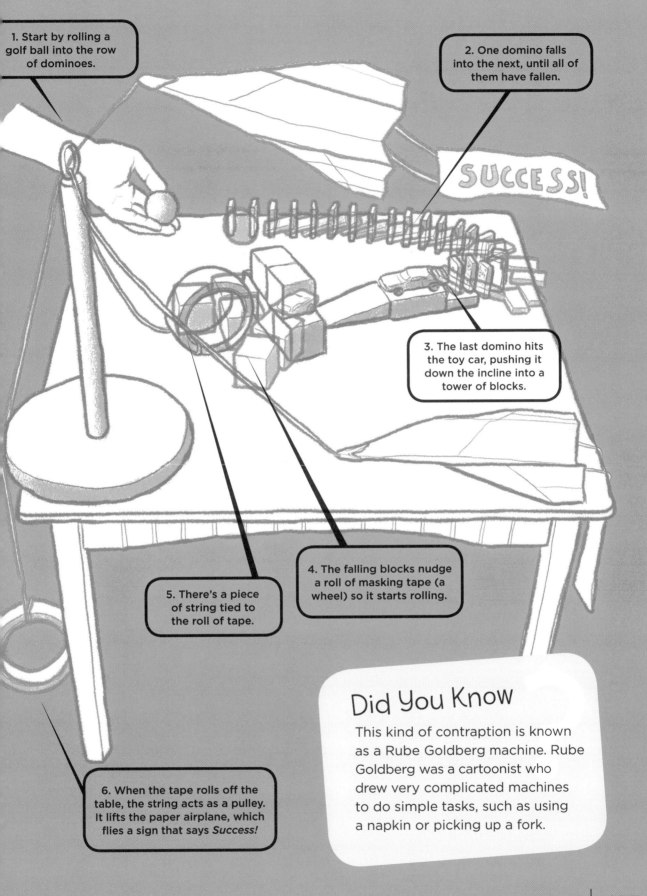

1. Start by rolling a golf ball into the row of dominoes.

2. One domino falls into the next, until all of them have fallen.

SUCCESS!

3. The last domino hits the toy car, pushing it down the incline into a tower of blocks.

4. The falling blocks nudge a roll of masking tape (a wheel) so it starts rolling.

5. There's a piece of string tied to the roll of tape.

6. When the tape rolls off the table, the string acts as a pulley. It lifts the paper airplane, which flies a sign that says *Success!*

Did You Know

This kind of contraption is known as a Rube Goldberg machine. Rube Goldberg was a cartoonist who drew very complicated machines to do simple tasks, such as using a napkin or picking up a fork.

Engineer a Flyer

The Wright brothers built the world's first powered airplane in 1903. This project is inspired by their designs.

You Need

- Poster board
- Ruler
- Pencil
- Scissors
- Glue
- Large craft stick
- 2 large paper clips

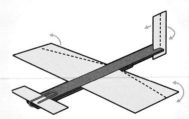

front

back

craft stick

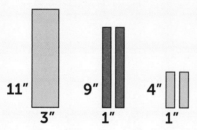

11" 3" 9" 1" 4" 1"

1. Cut out five rectangles from poster board in the sizes shown.

2. Glue the largest rectangle across the middle of a nine-inch rectangle for the wings. Glue a four-inch rectangle across the front end. Let dry.

3. Glue the second nine-inch rectangle on top of the first, with the wings sandwiched between. Glue the craft stick at the front end of the body. Slide a paper clip over the front end. Then add a second clip over the first. Let dry.

4. Make a half-inch cut in the back end. Glue the second four-inch rectangle into the slot, as shown. Let dry.

HOW TO LAUNCH

Rest your thumb on the craft stick, with your pointer and middle fingers on either side of the body, behind the wings. Throw it straight—and not too hard.

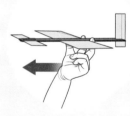

CONTROLLING YOUR FLYER

Try folding at the dotted lines to change the way it flies.

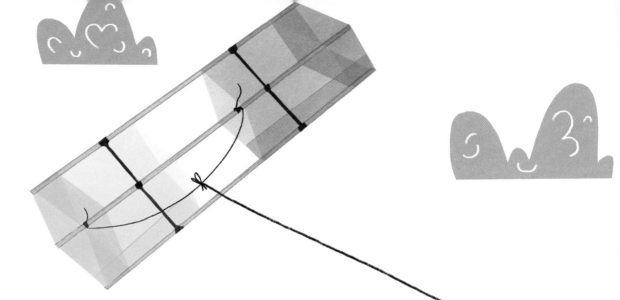

Build a Box Kite

Grab a friend or family member, gather some materials, then make your own kite!

FOR 2 BUILDERS

You Need

- Ruler
- Pencil
- 4 wooden dowels, ¼-inch diameter and 12 inches long
- 4 wooden dowels, ¼-inch diameter and 36 inches long
- 1 wooden dowel, 1-inch diameter and 12 inches long
- Floral wire or other lightweight, narrow wire
- Electrical tape or narrow duct tape
- Cellophane roll*
- Clear tape
- Kite string or light twine

*Or newspaper, wrapping paper, light plastic tablecloths, or large garbage bags

MAKE THE FRAME

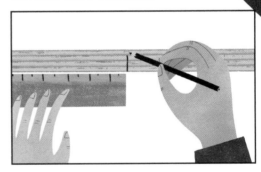

1. Mark the center of the four skinny, 12-inch dowels. Then mark 9 inches from both ends of the four 36-inch dowels.

Continued on next page

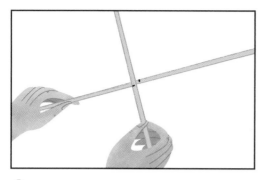

2. Take two of the marked 12-inch dowels and form an X with them by overlapping the center marks.

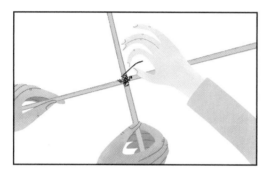

3. While one builder holds the dowels in this position, wrap a foot of floral wire tightly around the crossed dowels several times, making sure to wrap it over and under in all directions. The wire is flexible, so you don't need to knot it. Just press it firmly down.

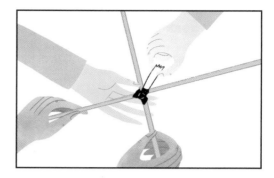

4. Tightly wrap about five inches of electrical tape over the wire. This finished piece is one of the kite's braces.

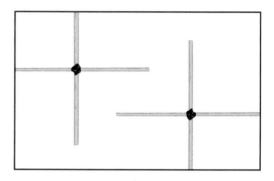

5. Repeat steps 2, 3, and 4 to make the second brace.

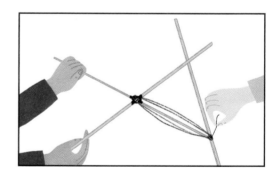

6. Have one builder take a brace and hold the tip of one of its dowels next to a 9-inch mark on a 36-inch dowel. Then wrap floral wire from the center of the brace to where the brace and dowel meet, as shown. Do this several times.

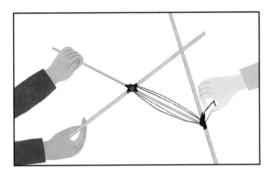

7. Tightly wrap electrical tape over the joint where the two dowels meet.

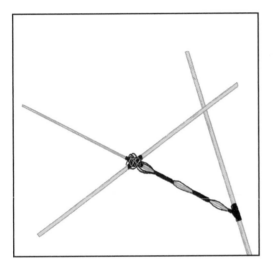

8. Take a piece of electrical tape and tape down the wire running along the brace's dowel (the spoke of the brace). This secures the wire. Use another small piece of tape to secure the wire at the center of the brace. You'll add more later.

Tip

To keep your kite as light as possible, try to use the *least* amount of tape needed to keep the kite secure.

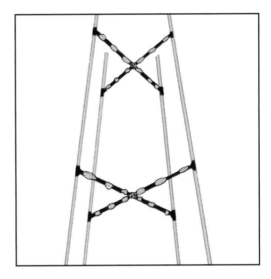

9. Repeat steps 6, 7, and 8 at the tip of each spoke in both braces, as shown.

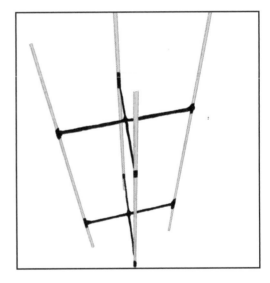

10. Wrap the center of each brace tightly with electrical tape, as shown, to completely secure the wire. The rectangular frame for your box kite is now complete!

Continued on next page

ATTACH THE CELLOPHANE

1. Cut two pieces of cellophane that are three feet long and one foot, eight inches wide.

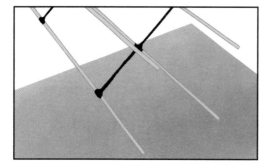

2. Lay one piece flat on your table and place the frame on top of it so that there are about four inches of cellophane beyond the dowel ends.

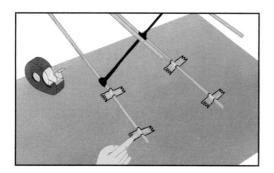

3. Tape each of the long dowels to the cellophane with clear tape—turn the kite as you go.

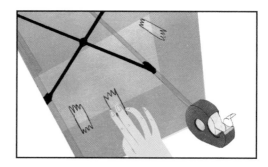

4. Fold the top of the cellophane over the tips of the dowels and inside the kite. Tape it to itself.

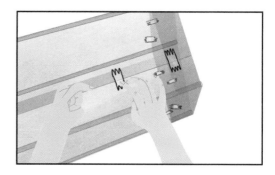

5. On the outside of the frame, tape the overlapping cellophane to itself down the side.

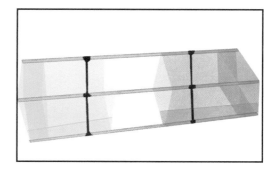

6. Repeat steps 2–5 at the other end of the kite with the second piece of cellophane, shown here in yellow.

ATTACH THE STRING

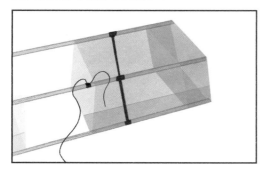

1. Cut about four feet of the kite string and tie one end of it to one long dowel on the inner edge of the cellophane, making several knots.

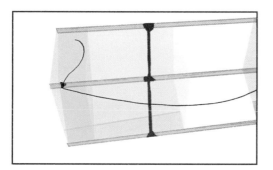

2. Attach the other end of the string to the same dowel about an inch from the outer edge of the other piece of cellophane, as shown. You will have to poke holes in the cellophane to do this.

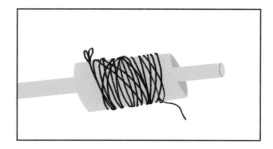

3. Take one end of the string and tie a knot around the cardboard tube. Then wrap a lot of string around the tube so your kite can fly high. Cut the string if you don't use all of it. Put the remaining dowel inside the cylinder, as shown. This is your kite reel.

4. Take the end of the string on your reel and tie it to the middle of the string attached to the kite. Fly your kite on a breezy day!

Kite Safety Tips

• Never attach anything metal to a kite.

• Fly kites in large, level, open areas. Stay away from power lines, antennae, and roads.

• Never fly a kite in a thunderstorm.

Make a Bird Feeder

Here's a way to attract birds to your home. This feeder allows several birds, such as finches, cardinals, and woodpeckers, to enjoy eating at the same time.

You Need

- Protective gloves
- 2-by-5-foot roll of ¼-inch mesh hardware cloth (steel wire)
- Micro snips
- Zip ties
- Protective eyewear
- 2 terracotta saucers, 6-inch or 8-inch
- Electric drill and ⅛-inch glass-and-tile drill bit
- Wire coat hanger
- Needle-nose pliers
- Bird seed
- Scoop

1. Wearing protective gloves, use micro snips to carefully cut a 15-by-9-inch piece of the hardware cloth. Have an adult help with anything sharp.

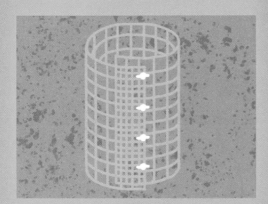

2. To make the tube, overlap the long sides of the hardware cloth a half inch. Use zip ties every two inches to keep the tube's shape. Pull the ties tight and then cut off the excess ends.

3. Wearing protective eyewear, drill a one-eighth-inch hole in the center of each saucer. Have an adult help.

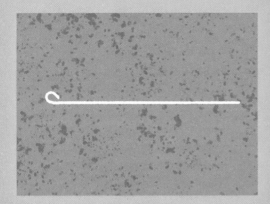

4. Unbend a wire hanger. Cut off a piece that's about 18 inches long with micro snips and recycle the rest. Make a small loop at one end with the pliers.

5. Pull the straight end of the hanger wire through a saucer from the bottom up until the saucer rests on the wire loop.

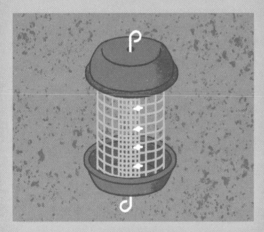

6. Put the hardware cloth onto the saucer and hold the wire up in the middle. Hold the second saucer upside down and thread the top of the wire through the saucer's hole. Then make another loop with the pliers at the top end of the wire.

7. Lift the top saucer and scoop birdseed into the feeder. Hang your bird feeder from a wire or put it over a branch.

Build a Bee House

Bees help plants survive by spreading pollen from one flower to another, and mason bees are some of the best pollinators. You can help them by building a bee house, which is a safe place for them to lay their eggs. Don't worry, mason bees generally don't sting.

You Need

- Quart-size cardboard milk carton
- Scissors
- Duct tape
- Ruler
- About 75 paper straws
- Extra-long zip ties

1. Cut off the top of the milk carton. Thoroughly wash the carton and let it dry. Cover it with duct tape.

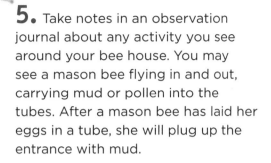

2. Cut the paper straws so they are six and a half inches long. Place them inside the bee house until it's snugly filled with straws.

3. In early spring, place your bee house outside. Look for a good spot that is near a flower garden and is at least three feet off the ground. It should get sunlight but be protected from wind and rain. A good location would be in the crook of some strong tree branches.

4. Point the opening of the house toward the morning sun and tilt it slightly down, so rain will not get inside. The eggs won't survive if the bee house swings in the wind, so tie the house securely in place with zip ties.

5. Take notes in an observation journal about any activity you see around your bee house. You may see a mason bee flying in and out, carrying mud or pollen into the tubes. After a mason bee has laid her eggs in a tube, she will plug up the entrance with mud.

6. In late June, take down the bee house very gently and put it inside a cardboard box in an unheated garage or shed. Inside the tubes, the eggs will hatch and the larvae will grow into adults.

7. When winter is almost over, put the bee house back outside, facing the sun. Over the next few weeks, the new bees will chew open the mud doors of their tubes and fly out to help pollinate the flowers.

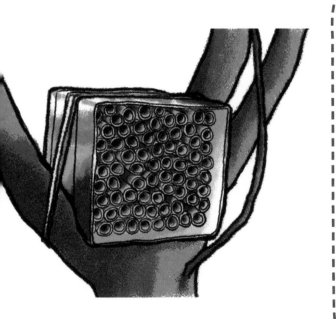

Tips

- Don't bother the bees. Mason bees rarely sting, but they may become aggressive if you disturb them.

- Mason bees need mud for the tubes, so keep a small pile of damp soil close to the bee house.

- If there are hungry birds in your garden, protect the bee eggs by wrapping some wire netting around the front of the bee house.

Create a Mechanical Card

Honey, Have a Happy Birthday!

A cam is a mechanism that changes spinning motion into straight motion. You can make your own simple cam to give as a special card.

You Need

- 2 small paper cups
- Hole punch
- Pencil
- Scissors
- Paper straw
- Glue or tape
- Quarter
- Thin cardboard
- Chenille stick
- Markers
- Cardstock

1. With the hole punch, make two holes in one small paper cup, as shown. Use a pencil to poke a hole into the bottom. Wiggle it to widen the hole. Remove the pencil. This is the base.

2. Trim off the sides of another paper cup. Cut off one-third of a paper straw. Glue the short straw piece to the bottom of the trimmed cup. This is the follower.

3. Trace a quarter onto thin cardboard. Cut it out. Punch a hole near the edge of the circle. This is the cam.

4. Fold a chenille stick in half. Push it (doubled) through the leftover piece of straw. Then bend the straw, as shown. This is the axle.

5. Place the follower inside the base with the straw sticking out of the bottom hole.

6. Push the axle through one of the cup's holes, and then through the cam, as shown.

7. Push the axle through the other side hole. Bend the chenille-stick end so the axle stays in place. Center the cam.

8. Use markers to draw animals or whatever you want on cardstock. Cut them out. Glue or tape them to the top of the follower and the base.

9. Put the cup upside down. Hold the base in one hand and turn the axle crank with the other. The follower will move up and down, and so will the shape you made!

1 Last Challenge!

Make tubes from pieces of newspaper. Tape the tubes to one another to build a skyscraper or other tall structure. See how high you can go!

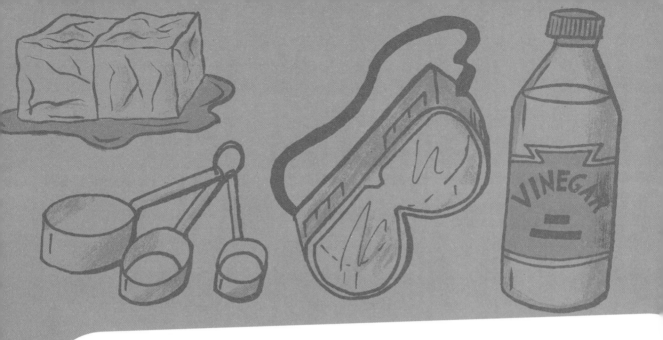

SCIENCE EXPERIMENTS
TO DO

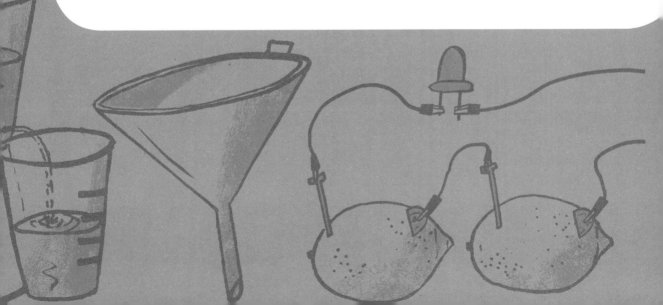

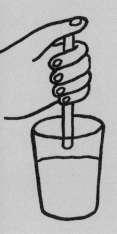

Dip a straw into a glass of water, place a finger tightly over the opening of the straw, and lift it up. Why does water stay in the straw until you lift your finger?

Ask a friend to sit with their eyes closed as you move around quietly and snap your fingers at various spots nearby. Can your friend point to where each snap came from?

Press the flat sides of two ice cubes together. Slowly count to 30, then let go of one ice cube. Why do the cubes stick together?

Put hot tap water into one glass and cold tap water into another glass. Watch as fog forms. Why does it form on different parts of each glass?

Find a few long objects, such as a spoon, a chopstick, and a ruler. Try to balance each object on your finger. Is the middle of each object its balancing point?

Put an ice cube into an empty glass and put another cube into a glass with water in it. Which cube melts faster? Why?

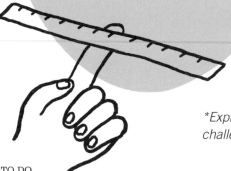

*Explanations for these challenges are on page 293.

The Disappearing Act

What do you think dissolves in water?

You Need

- Sugar, flour, cornmeal, baking soda, vegetable oil, or other basic food items
- Clear cup
- Water

Gather the food items. Which do you think would dissolve in water? To find out, stir a teaspoon of each into a cup of water. (Rinse the cup and use fresh water for each one.)

Why It Works:
The molecules of some substances, such as sugar and salt, are polar. Polar molecules easily attach to other polar molecules, like those of water. So when these substances are mixed into water, they seem to disappear. But some substances, like oil and flour, are made of nonpolar molecules, which won't attach to polar molecules. For that reason, those substances do not dissolve.

Make It Rain
Have you ever thought about why it rains?

You Need

- Nearly boiling water
- Clear glass heatproof bowl
- Any glass or metal lid that covers the bowl
- Ice cubes

1. Ask an adult to pour a few inches of the nearly boiling water into the glass bowl.

2. Place the lid upside down on the bowl.

3. Set a few ice cubes on top of the lid. Watch as water vapor condenses on the lid and "rains" back down. Gently swirl the water to see better.

Why It Works:
When water is very warm, it evaporates and becomes water vapor. Water vapor rises until it hits a cool object, such as a speck of dust high in the sky, where it cools and condenses back into a droplet. Rain occurs when water droplets join together until they're too heavy to stay up, which causes them to fall.

Here, the hot water in the bowl turns into water vapor and rises until it hits the cool lid, where water droplets form, join together, and fall.

Build a Water Microscope

You don't need a big contraption to view objects under a microscope. You can make a simple one at home.

You Need

- Large googly eye (1 inch or more)
- Scissors
- Paper cup
- Pencil
- Tape
- Spoon
- Water
- Small objects you'd like to see close up, such as parts of a flower, a slice of fruit, a shell, or a leaf

1. Carefully cut the cover off the googly eye. Take it apart. Have an adult help with anything sharp.

2. Trace the plastic eye cover onto the bottom of the cup. Then draw an upside-down U on each side of the cup. Cut along all the lines you've made, so the cup has a hole in the bottom and two open sides.

3. Cut four thin, small pieces of tape. Tape just the edges of the eye cover to the inside of the cup so the curve goes inside.

4. Spoon a little water into the eye cover so it forms a pool. Now you can put small objects under it and see them magnified. You may have to move the cup a bit to get the right spot.

Why It Works:
The pool of water on the googly eye creates a convex lens. Convex lenses are thicker in the middle and thinner around the edges. They bend the light passing through them, making the object underneath appear larger.

Freeze Your Knees

Can you lift your knees in this experiment?

Stand with your right shoulder and right foot against a wall, as shown, with your feet about eight inches apart. Try to lift up your left knee. Your knees will feel frozen and you won't be able to do it!

Why It Works: With your right foot and shoulder against the wall, you can't shift your weight onto your right leg for balance, so you can't lift your left knee. Try it without the wall and notice the difference.

Make Your Arms Float

Do you know how to make your arms float without trying?

Stand in a doorway with the backs of your hands pressed against the doorframe. Press hard outward with your hands for at least 30 seconds. Then walk out of the doorway and relax your arms at your sides. You'll feel them float back up!

Why It Works: What you notice happening is called *Kohnstamm's phenomenon*. It's named after the scientist who first noted that tightening a muscle by choice for some time will result in that muscle tightening involuntarily (not by choice) for a time afterward.

Observe Your Cat or Dog

People are not the only ones who are right- or left-handed. Some of our pets are, too!

Scientists observe that some animals can be right- or left-handed, just as most humans are. You can see for yourself with a dog or cat.

When a cat plays with toys and reaches for objects, notice which paw it uses. If your dog is trained to shake, watch to see if the dog offers one paw more often than the other. The more difficult the task is, the more likely the animal will use its preferred side.

Make a Practical Joke Cup

This cup spills all of its contents on anyone who fills it too high.

You Need

- Plastic cup
- Pushpin
- Pencil
- Bendy straw
- Scissors
- Water

1. Do this activity over a sink. Use the pushpin to make a small hole in the bottom of the plastic cup.

2. Widen the hole with a pencil until the straw can just fit through.

3. Insert the straw from beneath the cup, and pull it partway through the hole. Bend the short section of the straw so it stays down.

4. Cut off the end that sticks out of the bottom of the cup.

5. Fill the cup with different levels of water. What happens?

Why It Works:

When liquid in the cup is lower than the bend of the straw, it won't spill. As soon as liquid is higher than the bend of the straw, the filled side of the straw will spill over the bend. The straw works as a siphon as gravity pulls the rest of the liquid in the cup through it and out the hole in the bottom. A toilet bowl also has a siphon and works the same way during a flush.

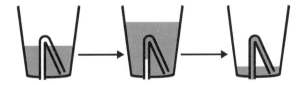

Did You Know

According to legend, this cup was invented more than 2,500 years ago by the Greek philosopher Pythagoras (peh-THAG-or-us) to teach his students moderation in life.

Construct a Water Clock

You can make a water clock like the ones ancient Egyptians used.

1. Use a pushpin to make a hole on the side of a cup, very close to the bottom. This will be the top cup.

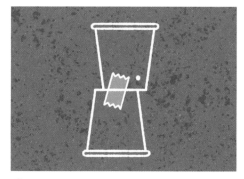

2. Tape the cup from step 1 to an upside-down cup (the base) so it overhangs the base.

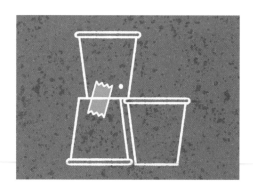

3. Place a third cup right next to the base, underneath the hole in the top cup.

4. Fill a fourth cup with water. Add food coloring if you'd like.

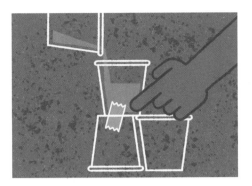

5. While covering the hole with your finger, pour water into the top cup.

6. Start a timer when you uncover the hole. Water will flow into the bottom cup.

7. When your timer reaches one minute, quickly draw a line on the bottom cup to mark the level of the water.

8. Make a line every minute. The water will flow slower as the cup empties. Stop the timer when the stream is just a drip.

9. Starting from the bottom, number each line you made on the cup. Empty the bottom cup and repeat steps 4 through 6. Check your marks against the timer. Correct them if necessary.

More Ideas

You can use your clock to measure two minutes for brushing your teeth. Put water in the top cup and brush until water in the bottom cup reaches the second line.

Homemade Ice Cream

With a lot of tossing and just a few simple ingredients, you and a friend can make your own ice cream.

FOR 2 SCIENTISTS

You Need

- 1 cup whole milk
- ¼ cup sugar
- ½ teaspoon vanilla
- 1 quart-size, zipper freezer bag
- 1 gallon-size, zipper freezer bag
- 20 cups ice
- 1 ½ cups rock salt (available in some supermarkets)
- Winter gloves (optional)

1. Put the milk, sugar, and vanilla in the quart-size freezer bag. Squeeze out the air, then zip the bag completely closed. (If it is not sealed tightly, you will end up with salty milk.)

2. Place the small bag in the large bag.

3. Pack ice almost to the top of the large bag.

4. Ask an adult to pour one cup of the rock salt on top of the ice. Zip the large bag completely closed.

5. Toss the heavy bag back and forth carefully for five minutes. It's best to do this outside in case anything drops or opens. You may also want to wear gloves because your hands will get cold.

6. Inside, open the large bag and drain out any excess water. Don't pour it on grass or other plants—salt water will kill them.

7. Have an adult add the rest of the rock salt and as much ice as will fit. Seal the bag again, then toss it back and forth for five more minutes outside.

8. Check the small bag. Do you have ice cream yet? You probably do, but if it's still runny, seal everything back up and toss it around for a few more minutes.

9. Scoop your ice cream into a bowl and add your favorite toppings: strawberries, sprinkles, whipped cream, or whatever you want. Dig in!

Why It Works:
The rock salt lowers the freezing temperature in the bag—turning the ice into super cold water. The cold water flows around the bag of milk as it is being tossed, cooling it down. When the temperature of the milk reaches its freezing point, it becomes ice cream. The more the ice cream is tossed, the smaller the ice crystals will be, making the ice cream creamier.

Test for Candy Secrets

Have you ever wondered what's in the candy you eat? With your favorite candies, water, and a few other basic items, you can discover some of the unexpected ingredients yourself.

ACID

If candy tastes sour, it contains acid. There are taste buds on your tongue for acid, and when they are stimulated, you perceive a sour taste. Most fruit-flavored candy contains citric acid, which is the sour chemical in lemons.

OIL

Many kinds of chewy candy, like taffy, are made with oil. This keeps the candy from sticking to the machinery when it's made. Oil also helps keep the candy smooth, soft, and chewy.

DYE

Candymakers often mix dyes to create certain colors.

Does it have acid?

Dissolve your candy in a half-cup of water. (WARHEADS and SweeTARTS work well.) Sprinkle in a teaspoon of baking soda. If you see bubbles, the candy water contains acid.

Why It Works:

Baking soda reacts with acid to form carbon dioxide gas. The gas makes bubbles in the water.

Does it have oil?

Dissolve your candy in a cup of hot tap water. (Starbursts or Tootsie Rolls work well.) If you see shiny puddles floating on the surface, the candy has oil. When the water cools, you may see a white, waxy layer on top, which is also oil.

Why It Works:

The kinds of oils used in these candies melt in hot water, forming the shiny puddles. In colder water, the oil can cool into a white, waxy solid. Since oil is lighter than water, it floats.

How many colors?

Cut a rectangle from a coffee filter. Wet one piece of colored candy. (Brown M&M's and purple Skittles work well.) Dab the candy onto the paper two inches from the bottom. Then stand the filter up in a half-inch of water with the colored dot above the waterline. Water will creep up the filter.

When the water reaches the top, take out the filter and see if your dye has separated into colors. (If the colors are hard to see, lay the filter on a white plate.)

Why It Works:

After the colored dye dissolves, the moving water carries it up the filter. Dyes that dissolve more quickly travel faster. Soon the dyes separate, allowing you to see each color.

Make a Lava Lamp

Be ready to "ooh" and "ahh" as you watch colorful blobs erupt and float. There are two ways to create this fascinating lamp. Try both and see which one you like better.

You Need

- Plastic cover or old vinyl tablecloth, to protect your work area
- Clear glass jar or bottle (tall and narrow works best)
- Baking soda
- Spoon
- Cooking oil (canola oil works best)
- White vinegar
- Small bowl
- Food coloring
- Flashlight or cell phone with light
- Small zipper plastic bag (large enough to hold cell phone)
- Water
- Salt

Safety Tip

Do not pour the liquid down the drain because it could cause a clog. Ask an adult to help you dispose of it.

BAKING SODA AND VINEGAR METHOD

1. Spread out the plastic cover or tablecloth. Place two or three spoonfuls of baking soda in the container.

2. Pour the oil into the container until it is about two-thirds full. Don't stir or shake the container; you want the baking soda to remain at the bottom for now.

3. Pour vinegar into the small bowl and add four drops of food coloring.

4. Slowly spoon the colored vinegar into the container. Bubbling blobs of color will move through the oil.

5. If using a cell phone light, turn it on and carefully seal the phone in the plastic bag. Place the container on the phone light. If using the flashlight, hold the flashlight under or behind the container.

6. Turn out the lights and enjoy! The chemical reaction will only last for a short while.

Why It Works:
When an acid (vinegar, which contains acetic acid) comes in contact with a base (baking soda, also known as sodium bicarbonate), a chemical reaction occurs that results in carbon dioxide and water. When carbon dioxide (a gas) is in a liquid, bubbles form. Here, because the bubbles of carbon dioxide are coated in food coloring, we can see the colored bubbles rise to the top and "pop."

Why does the vinegar sink down to the bottom of the container? The vinegar is denser than the oil.

Did You Know ?

The lava lamp first became popular in the late 1960s. A classic lava lamp is filled with liquid and a special colored wax. When the wax is at the bottom of the lamp, it is heated and becomes less dense than the liquid, causing the wax to float to the top. When the wax cools off, it becomes denser than the liquid and sinks back down.

Continued on next page

OIL AND SALT METHOD

1. Fill a container with water until it's about three-quarters full.

2. Add four drops of food coloring.

3. Pour in oil until the container is almost full. Watch as the oil floats to the top of the water.

4. When you have two distinct layers, sprinkle salt on top of the oil. You'll soon see blobs rising from the bottom.

5. If using a cell phone light, turn it on and carefully seal the phone in the plastic bag. Place the container on the phone light. If using the flashlight, hold the flashlight under or behind the container.

6. Turn out the lights and enjoy! When the blobs stop, add more salt to keep the effect going until the reaction stops.

Why It Works:
Oil is less dense than water, which is why it rises to the surface. Salt is denser than water and sinks to the bottom. When you add salt, blobs of oil become attached to the grains of salt and sink down to the water layer. As the salt dissolves in the water, the oil blobs are released and rise back to the oil layer. Adding more salt will keep the reaction going, until the water layer cannot dissolve any more salt. What do you think will happen then? Try it and see if your guess is right.

Catch a "Burp" from Soda

Why do you sometimes need to burp after drinking soda? Try this to find out.

FOR 2 SCIENTISTS

You Need

- Balloon
- 1 teaspoon salt
- Small, full bottle of seltzer or colorless soda (20 ounces or less)

1. It's best to do this outside or over a sink. It can get messy! Choose a new balloon or a used one that you know is dry inside. Its neck must be large enough to fit over the mouth of the soda bottle. Put the salt into the balloon.

2. Slowly remove the cap from the bottle. You should hear it fizzing. Have one person hold the bottle steady while the other fits the balloon onto the bottle's neck. Be sure to keep the other end of the balloon hanging down so that no salt falls into the soda yet.

3. Hold the balloon tightly in place on the bottle's neck, and lift the other end of the balloon straight up so the salt pours into the soda. You will see the "burp" inflate the balloon. Foam will go up, too. As you watch, the liquid from the foam will drain back into the bottle, and you will be left with a balloon full of gas!

Why It Works:
Adding salt to a carbonated liquid speeds up the physical change that causes the carbon dioxide to escape. In this experiment, the escaped carbon dioxide fills up the balloon. In a similar way, when you drink a carbonated liquid, the carbon dioxide gas slowly escapes into your stomach. When too much gas has built up, you burp.

Erupting Foam

Follow these simple directions to create an amazing stream of foam!

You Need

- Small plastic water bottle
- Funnel
- ½ cup 3% hydrogen peroxide
- ¼ cup liquid dish soap
- Food coloring (optional)
- ½ cup very warm water
- Small cup
- 1 packet or 2 teaspoons dry yeast
- Large baking sheet

1. Using the funnel, pour the hydrogen peroxide and dish soap into the empty bottle. Then remove the funnel and squirt in some food coloring. Swirl the bottle around to mix everything together.

2. Pour the very warm water into a small cup, then add the yeast and stir. Wait about five minutes to allow the yeast to activate.

3. Place the bottle in the middle of a baking sheet.

4. Using the funnel again, pour the yeast mixture into the bottle and quickly remove the funnel. Then step back and watch the foam come oozing out.

Why It Works:
When you add yeast to hydrogen peroxide, it breaks down into water and oxygen very quickly. But by mixing the hydrogen peroxide with dish soap first, the oxygen becomes trapped in the tiny soap bubbles and creates lots of foam.

Safety Tip
To avoid burns, don't use anything higher than 3% hydrogen peroxide.

Make a Sun Cooker

You don't need an oven or microwave to cook some foods. Instead, try cooking with sunlight!

Safety Tip
Don't use this to cook raw meat.

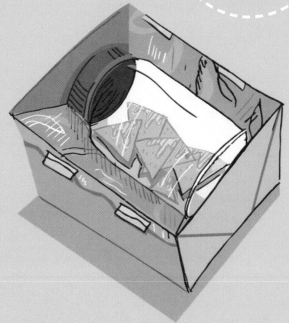

You Need

- Cardboard box
- Scissors
- Masking tape
- Foil
- Black tape or paper
- Glass jar with lid

1. Cut off the top flaps of a cardboard box. Tape foil to all the inside walls.

2. Cut a piece of foil to be as wide as the box and one-and-a-half times as long.

black tape

3. In the middle of your foil sheet, tape a three-inch-wide strip of black tape or paper that fits across the foil. Tape the foil sheet to two sides of the box so it hangs in a loose U inside the box, as shown.

4. Assemble nachos, s'mores, or other foods to cook, and put them inside a glass jar. Place the jar on its side in the solar cooker box and place the box in direct sunlight. Check the jar every 15 minutes until the food is fully cooked.

Why It Works:
The black surface absorbs light and the angled foil surface focuses the sun's rays into the glass container. This concentrated light turns into heat energy, which can't easily escape through the glass. The heat builds inside the container, warming the food.

Make a Lemon Battery

The job of a battery is to convert chemical energy into electrical energy. Lemons—with help from other materials—can do that!

You Need

- 5 lemons
- Small knife
- 5 galvanized nails, washers, or other metal household object
- 5 pennies or pieces of copper wire
- 6 short electrical wires with alligator clips (found at hardware stores)
- LED diode (3 or 5 millimeters; found in hardware and hobby stores)

1. Roll the lemons under your palm back and forth across a table. This releases the juice inside the lemons.

2. Make two small cuts on the top of a lemon, at least an inch apart. Have an adult help with anything sharp.

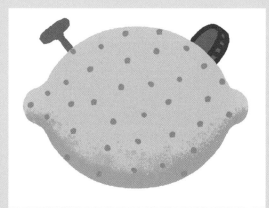

3. Insert a nail or washer into one cut and a penny or piece of copper wire into the other. Make sure they're inserted deep enough to touch the juice inside, but they should not be touching each other.

More Ideas

Try using other fruit instead of lemons, such as grapefruits or oranges. Do they work as well? Do vegetables, such as potatoes or carrots, work as well?

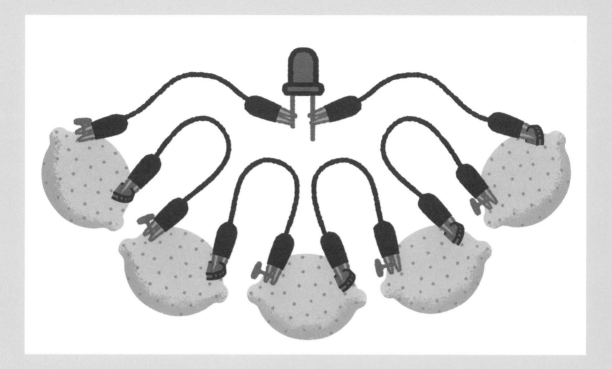

4. Repeat steps 2 and 3 with all of the lemons.

5. Line up the lemons. Make sure all of the pennies are on the right side and the nails are on the left side.

6. Using one of the electrical wires, connect the nail in the last lemon on your right to the penny in the second-to-right lemon. Repeat this with the second-to-right lemon and the one to its left. Keep going, using four wires.

7. Attach a clip of one of the last two wires to the penny on the far right lemon. Then connect that same wire's other clip to the longer leg of the LED diode. Attach the last wire to the nail on the far-left lemon and connect its other clip to the shorter leg of the diode.

8. The diode should light up! If it doesn't, make sure the pennies and nails are pushed into the lemons enough. You can also try wiggling them. Your circuit is complete.

Why It Works:
In this experiment, the nail acts as the negative terminal of a battery. It releases electrons. The copper penny or wire acts as the positive terminal, gaining electrons. The positive and negative flow of electrons through the lemon's acid changes chemical energy into electrical energy. When that energy flows through the battery, the terminals connect to the opposite ends of the LED diode and light it up.

Set Up a Circuit

Learn how to create a circuit by making either a mini cardboard tent to light up the night or a silly face with a light-up nose.

You Need

- Piece of cardboard (for tent) or a short cardboard tube (for face)
- Scissors
- LED diode (3 or 5 millimeters; found in hardware and hobby stores)
- Masking tape
- Aluminum foil
- Clear tape
- 2 AA batteries
- Rubber bands
- Markers

LIGHT-UP TENT

1. Fold the cardboard in half. Cut four notches—one on either side of the fold on both long sides.

2. Bend apart the legs of the LED diode, and place it in the center of the cardboard.

3. Press three long strips of masking tape onto aluminum foil. Then cut them out.

foil

tape

switch

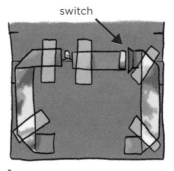

4. Fold, cut, and tape down the strips and diode using clear tape, as shown.

5. Tape the batteries together so one positive end meets a negative end.

6. Tape the ends of the batteries to the foil side of the strips. Place a rubber band around to hold them in place.

7. Fold the cardboard, wrapping a rubber band around the notches. Decorate the tent.

8. Press down on the switch (shown at top) to light the diode. If it doesn't light up, flip the direction of the diode's legs.

LIGHT-UP FACE

1. Cut the cardboard tube in half. Poke a hole through the center of one half.

2. Bend apart the legs of the LED diode and place it on top of the half-tube without a hole.

3. Press three long strips of masking tape onto aluminum foil. Then cut them out.

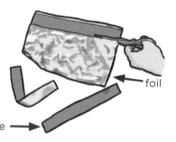

foil

tape ➡

switch ↘

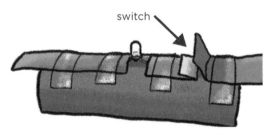

4. Fold, cut, and tape down the strips and diode using clear tape, as shown.

5. Tape the batteries together so one positive end meets a negative end.

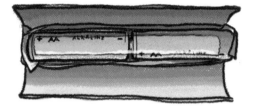

6. Tape the ends of the batteries to the foil side of the strips. Place a rubber band around them to hold them in place.

7. Press down on the switch (shown at left) to light the diode. If it doesn't light up, flip the direction of the diode's legs.

8. Put the two half-tubes together. Push the lit diode through the hole in the other tube.

Why It Works:
The LED diode lights up when an electric current passes through it, like one from a battery. The electricity moves in a circle, from the battery to the diode and back, through metal connectors called conductors. This circle of electricity is called a *circuit*.

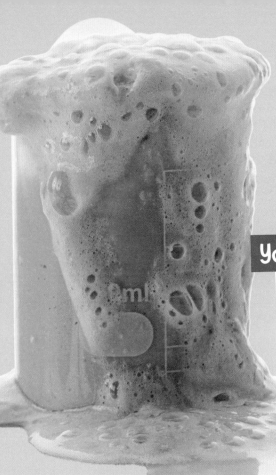

Bubbling Slime

Make slime that bubbles and flows! It's fun to watch but not safe to drink.

You Need

- 2 containers, 1 large and 1 small
- ½ cup school glue
- 2 tablespoons baking soda
- Several drops green food coloring
- ¼ cup vinegar
- 2 teaspoons contact lens solution
- Baking pan

1. Mix the glue, baking soda, and food coloring in the large container.

2. Mix the vinegar and the contact lens solution in the small container.

3. Place both containers into a baking pan. Pour the vinegar solution into the glue mixture and stir a few times. The concoction will begin to bubble.

4. If you want to play with the slime, wait for the bubbling to stop. Then mix three more tablespoons of baking soda into the slime to make it easier to handle.

Why It Works:
Vinegar reacts with the baking soda in the glue mixture to create carbon dioxide gas, which then bubbles up out of the solution. Meanwhile, the contact lens solution mixed with baking soda creates a borate ion, which helps molecules in the glue link together to form slime.

1 Last Challenge!

Using a magnet and a piece of thread, find a way to suspend a steel paper clip in midair. See explanation below.

EXPLANATIONS

6 QUICK CHALLENGES
(from top to bottom)

Straw: When your finger is on the straw, air pressure pushes up on the water from below more strongly than gravity pulls it down. When you remove your finger, air pressure pushes on the water from below and above equally. This makes gravity the stronger of the two forces, and gravity pulls the water toward Earth.

Balancing Point: Every object has a balancing point, or center of gravity, but that point isn't always in the middle. For long, straight objects such as rulers, the center of gravity is exactly in the middle. For uneven objects such as spoons, the center of gravity will be somewhere between the middle and the heavier side.

Snapping Fingers: Your friend can probably point to where you are with their eyes closed due to something called *time lag*. If the snapping occurs on their right side, it reaches their right ear before it reaches their left ear. Their brain processes the time lag, or how much time went by before the left ear heard the sound, and uses it to tell your friend that the snapping sound came from their right.

Mysterious Fog: In the challenge, we ask why fog forms on different parts of the glasses: In the hot-water glass, vapor rises from the water, touches the cool glass above the water level, and condenses into droplets. As a result, fog forms on the *inside* of the glass. In the cold-water glass, warm water vapor in the air condenses as it touches the cold glass below the water level. As a result, fog forms on the *outside* of the glass.

Make Ice-Cube Glue: When you push two ice cubes together, you create pressure between the two flat sides. Pressure melts the ice, making a thin layer of water in between. When you release the pressure, the water refreezes, "gluing" the two cubes together.

Melting Ice Cubes: The ice cube in the water should melt faster. Ice cubes melt when they are surrounded by warmer particles. Water has more particles touching the ice cube than the air does, so heat energy transfers more quickly to the ice cube through water than through air.

1 LAST CHALLENGE

To suspend a paper clip in midair, start by tying one end of the thread to the paper clip and the other end to a chair. Use the magnet to pick up the paper clip and lift it until the thread is straight. With practice, you can raise the magnet to a point where the paper clip is no longer touching the magnet, but will still be held up in the air by the magnetic pull.

(MORE) THINGS TO DO WITH
RECYCLED MATERIALS

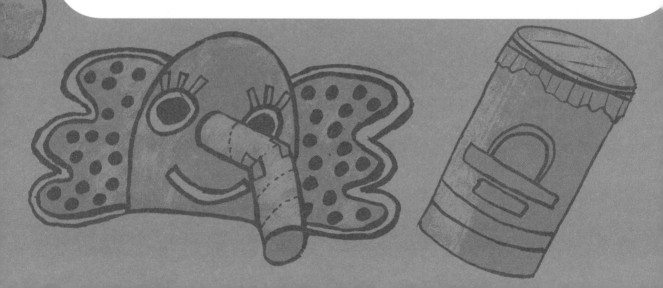

Quick Challenges

Paint and decorate an egg carton, then use it to organize a collection, small accessories, trinkets, or anything you can think of.

Set up a bowling lane, using plastic bottles or shoeboxes as bowling pins.

Create an accessory, like a hat or a bag, from recycled items.

Wash out jars and containers and fold cardboard to prepare these items for recycling.

Get a packet of seeds for small flowers or herbs. Clean out an empty yogurt container. Add some soil and plant a few seeds inside. Make sure your plants get water and sunlight. Soon you'll have a little garden.

Make a hideout for a pet using leftover cardboard boxes, scissors, and tape. Make sure they can get in and out on their own.

Reinvent Plastic Bottles

Instead of tossing your empty plastic bottles, try these new uses for them. What other creations can you make?

Watering Can

You Need

- Empty laundry detergent bottle and lid
- Permanent marker
- Electric drill and $\frac{1}{8}$- or $\frac{1}{16}$-inch drill bit

1. Rinse out the bottle and lid. Make sure all the soap is gone and there are no more bubbles.

2. Use the marker to make dots for about 10 holes on the lid. Space them out so they are about one-half inch apart.

3. Screw the lid onto the bottle. Have an adult help you drill a hole at each mark.

4. Again with an adult, drill a hole right above the handle. This will let air into the bottle so the water can flow out more easily.

5. Fill the bottle with water, then screw the lid on again. When your plants need a drink, just grasp the handle and tip the bottle over them!

More inventions on next page

Craft Organizer

You Need

- Old newspapers, to protect your work area
- Permanent marker
- 2 identical 20-ounce plastic water bottles
- Scissors
- Masking tape
- 9-inch zipper
- Low-heat glue gun

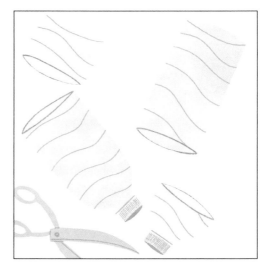

2. On each bottle, cut along the lines, then put the top parts aside.

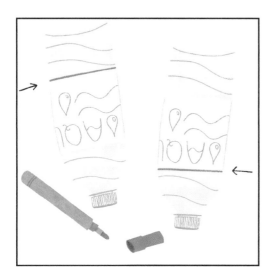

1. Cover your work surface with newspaper. On one bottle, draw a line just above the label. On the other bottle, draw a line just below the label. Peel off the labels.

3. Place the open ends of each bottle one-half inch apart. Tape the bottles together, as shown, keeping the spacing between them.

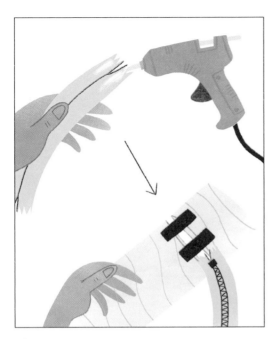

6. Continue gluing the zipper around the bottles, removing tape as you go.

4. On the back of the zipper, put some glue on the bottom tails. Have an adult help with anything hot. Let it cool slightly, then press the glued pieces to the water bottles, as shown.

7. Glue the top tails down, as shown. Fill the organizer with anything you'd like!

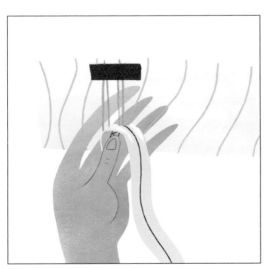

5. Near the bottom tails you just glued, put an inch of glue on either side of the material, away from the zipper's teeth. Remove more tape from the bottles, and press the piece with glue onto the bottles.

More inventions on next page

Sand Scoop

You Need

- Empty laundry detergent bottle and lid
- Rubber band
- Permanent marker
- Electric drill and $\frac{1}{8}$- or $\frac{1}{16}$-inch drill bit
- Heavy-duty scissors

3. Have an adult help you drill a hole just below the marker line.

1. Rinse out the bottle and lid. Screw the lid onto the bottle. Put the rubber band around the bottle, making a straight line from below the handle to the very bottom of the other side.

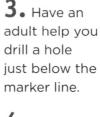

4. Starting at the hole, use scissors to cut all the way along the line. Trim any rough parts away to make the edge smooth.

2. Trace the edge of the rubber band all the way around the bottle with the marker. Take off the rubber band.

5. Use your scoop to dig deep holes in the sand, or find other ways to use it.

Tabletop Tetherball

Make your own miniature version of this classic game. To play, you'll use your fingers to flick the ball around the pole.

FOR 2 PLAYERS

You Need

- Corrugated cardboard
- Scissors
- Scrap paper
- Jumbo straw
- Yarn
- Chenille stick
- Glue
- Tape
- Pom-pom or table-tennis ball

1. Cut two circles, about four or five inches across, from the corrugated cardboard. Cover one with scrap paper. Poke a hole in the center of it.

2. Cut two slits at one end of a jumbo straw. Then, cut a piece of yarn twice as long as the straw, and a chenille stick a bit longer than the straw. Thread the yarn and chenille stick through the straw.

3. Dab glue into the hole in the circle. Push the split end of the straw through the hole. Tape the ends of the straw, chenille stick, and yarn to the underside of the circle. Glue the second cardboard circle onto the bottom of the first, covering the tape.

4. Cut a small slit in the top of the straw. Slide the yarn through it. Tape or glue the ball securely to the end of the yarn.

5. To play, try to wrap the yarn around the straw by flicking the ball with your thumb and pointer or middle finger. A player receives one point when they wrap the yarn all the way around the pole and the ball touches the pole. The player who scores five points first wins.

Handheld Game

Make a classic game that fits in your hand and takes a lot of concentration to play.

FOR 1 PLAYER

You Need

- Shallow lid from a jar, at least 3 inches across and 1/8 inch deep
- Thin cardboard
- Scrap paper
- Sharp pencil or pen
- Scissors
- Glue
- Markers
- Small round beads
- Plastic wrap or clear plastic food container
- Rubber band

1. Wash and dry a shallow jar lid. Trace around the lid twice onto thin cardboard and once onto a piece of paper. Cut out the three circles and trim them to fit inside the lid.

2. Glue the paper circle inside the lid.

3. Glue the cardboard circles to each other. When the glue has dried, draw a picture on one side of the cardboard. The picture must have several small circles in it (for example, an ice-cream cone with round sprinkles, an apple tree, or a juggler).

4. Use the point of a pen or pencil to make holes where you've put the small circles in the scene.

5. Glue the cardboard inside the lid on top of the paper, with the picture facing up.

6. Put small beads in the lid, one for each hole.

7. A plastic cover over the game will keep the beads inside the lid. You can make the cover in one of two ways: Put plastic wrap over the game, then stretch a rubber band around the lid to hold it in place. Pull the wrap tight beneath the rubber band to smooth out the wrinkles. Trim away the extra plastic wrap. Or, trace the lid onto a clear plastic food container, cut out the circle, and glue it to the rim of the lid.

8. Play the game by wiggling the lid to get all the beads in the holes.

Coach Whistle

Make a whistle with tape and leftover lids.

Tips
- Hold the whistle and blow steadily into the mouthpiece.
- Move it up and down to find the best angle for whistling.

You Need

- Scrap cardstock or thin cardboard
- Ruler
- Pencil
- Scissors
- Tape
- Low-heat glue gun
- 2 milk or jug lids of the same size
- Beads
- Yarn

1. Cut out a one-by-nine-inch strip of cardstock.

2. Cover both sides with tape. Cut a U shape in one end.

3. Use the tape or glue gun to secure a lid to both sides of the end opposite from the U.

4. Roll the lids along the strip while taping or gluing until only a quarter-inch-wide gap is left between the lids.

5. Sharply fold the strip back.

6. Fold the strip forward so that the U shape is directly over the gap, then crease the strip.

7. Tape the side edges of the strip together. Cut off the folded end.

8. Glue a bead onto the side of the whistle. Once it dries, thread a piece of yarn through it as a hanger.

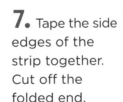

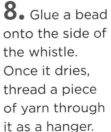

Set Up a Wormarium

For more information on earthworms, see page 75.

You can make a wormarium to watch and study earthworms. The best time to find them is after a rainstorm. When it rains, earthworms are forced from underground to the surface to keep from drowning!

You Need

- Glass jar
- Dirt
- Peat moss or sand
- Earthworms
- Water
- Black paper or old newspaper
- Tape
- Bits of lettuce, bread, and dry cereal
- Piece of light-colored mesh, like old nylon tights
- Rubber band

1. Fill your jar three-quarters full with dirt, then fill the rest with peat moss or sand. Add a little water to moisten the mixture.

2. Now you need worms: If your glass jar is quart-size, collect 3 worms. A gallon jar will house 12 worms.

3. Put the worms in their new temporary home, on top of the peat moss or sand. They will soon burrow out of sight to avoid the light.

4. Tape the black paper or newspaper around the sides of the jar. This will keep it dark.

5. Add a few small pieces of lettuce, bread, and dry cereal to the jar for the worms to eat. Cut a piece of mesh to fit over the top of the jar. Use a rubber band to keep it in place.

6. In a day or two, your worms will burrow right along the glass because no light shines through the paper. You can then remove the paper and observe some of the underground tunnels.

7. When you have finished studying the earthworms, find a spot in a yard or nearby park and let them go. They will immediately get back to work plowing, digging, and fertilizing the soil.

printing plate

Collagraph Prints

Collagraphy is a printmaking process that uses textured materials.

You Need

- Cardboard
- Pencil
- Textured shapes, like bits of old sponge, corrugated cardboard, and chenille sticks
- Glue
- Tempera paint
- Sponge
- Blank paper

1. Draw a scene on cardboard.

2. Glue textured shapes onto different parts of the scene. For example, you could cover clouds with cotton balls or water with bits of sponges. Let the shapes dry. This is the printing plate.

3. Use a sponge to dab tempera paint onto the printing plate.

4. Gently press paper onto the printing plate. Lift it off. Let it dry.

5. Repeat steps 3 and 4 to make another print.

Quill with Cardboard Tubes

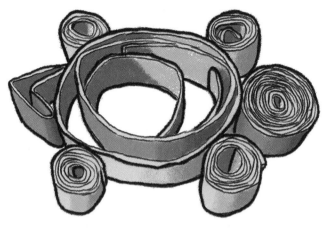

Pinch, shape, and roll cardboard tubes into creative shapes. This art form is called *quilling*.

You Need

- Old newspaper, to protect your work area
- Empty cardboard tubes
- Acrylic or tempera paint
- Paintbrushes
- Pencil
- Ruler
- Scissors
- Glue
- Paper clips
- Rubber bands

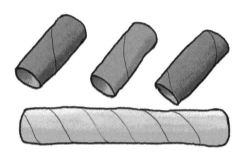

1. Cover your work surface with newspaper. Paint the outside of the cardboard tubes. Let the paint dry completely.

2. Flatten the tubes by pressing them gently. Cut each tube into half-inch pieces, using the pencil and ruler to help you measure.

3. Pinch, roll, layer, or outline and fill the pieces to make shapes. See SHAPING CARDBOARD PIECES below for how to do that.

4. After you've made shapes, use glue to make sure the shape holds. Hold the piece in place with your fingers, a paper clip, or a rubber band until the glue sets.

5. Glue your shapes together to make designs.

Shaping Cardboard Pieces

ROLL
Cut open a circle to make a long, flat strip. Roll up the strip. You can change the size of the roll by keeping it tight as you roll it to make a small shape or keeping it loose to make a larger shape. It should look like a snail shell when it's done.

Use a small dot of white glue near the end of the strip to attach it to the roll. You can wrap a small rubber band around the roll to keep it tight while the glue dries.

To make a square, start with a roll, then press on all four sides at the same time. Next, pinch the corners that form to make the shape square instead of rounded.

PINCH

Pinch one end of a circular piece to make a teardrop shape.

Pinch opposite ends to make a petal shape.

For a bow shape, pinch the middle.

OUTLINE AND FILL
Shape one piece into an outline. Fill it in with rolls, teardrops, or squares.

LAYER
Bend a piece into a small shape. Glue a second bigger shape around the first one. Keep adding layers until the shape is the size you want.

Make an Extendable Grabber

Try picking things up with this clever tool.

1. Glue the three sheets of cardboard together. After they've completely dried, draw the shapes and dots, as shown here, on the top layer. Cut out the shapes.

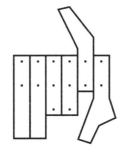

2. Punch holes in all the dots.

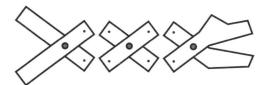

3. Set up the shapes as in the image above. Then connect the shapes together by lining up sets of holes and securing them with metal fasteners.

Mix Your Own Lip Balm

You don't need a lot of time or materials to make a soothing balm for your lips. It makes a great gift, too!

You Need

- 2 identical plastic water bottles
- Scissors
- Glue
- Scrap paper
- Coconut oil
- Small, sealable plastic bag
- ⅛ teaspoon peppermint extract
- Food coloring (optional)

For the container:

1. Cut off the neck of an empty water bottle. You might want an adult to help.

2. Glue the lid from a second bottle onto the base of the cut neck. Unscrew the original lid.

3. Glue paper onto both lids. Let dry.

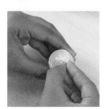

For the lip balm:

1. Put the coconut oil inside the plastic bag.

2. Add the peppermint extract and a drop of food coloring to the bag, then seal it.

3. Squeeze and rub the mixture until it's well blended.

4. Cut off a bottom corner of the bag. Squeeze the mixture into the lip-balm container. Replace the lid.

Create a Mask

Raid the recycling bin to make a unique and surprising mask.

You Need

- Recyclable materials, such as cardboard, cereal boxes, egg or berry cartons, and cardboard tubes
- Scissors
- Marker
- Sturdy twine or shoelaces
- Stapler
- Masking tape
- Low-heat glue gun (optional)
- Old newspaper, to protect your work area
- Tempera or acrylic paint
- Paintbrushes

1. Decide what kind of creature you want to make. For inspiration, think about your favorite creatures, and what unique features they have. Look for the shapes of these features—and easy-to-cut cardboard—in your recyclables.

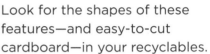

2. Create a base for your mask. Decide which type of base is best from TWO WAYS TO MAKE A BASE on the next page.

3. Add features such as eyes, ears, a nose, a mouth, a trunk, horns, or even wings! See WORKING WITH CARDBOARD AND OTHER MATERIALS on page 312 for tips. Use tape, staples, or a glue gun to attach the features. Make sure the features are all attached securely. Tape over any staples so they don't poke you. Ask an adult for help with anything hot or sharp.

4. Cover your work surface with old newspaper. Paint the mask.

For tips on painting and mixing paint colors, see page 175.

Two Ways to Make a Base

Ask a friend or family member for help making your base.

1 Cut a shape from cardboard. Be sure to leave a space for your nose to stick out. Hold the shape up to your face and make a mark on the mask in front of each ear, so the marks show the width of your head. Make small holes at the marks. Knot the ends of the twine and feed the ends through the holes to make ties. Tie the base onto your head. Ask your helper to mark where your eyes are on the mask. Take it off and cut out eye holes.

 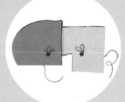  

2 Cut strips of cardboard about two inches wide. Staple them together to make a strip long enough to go around your head. Then wrap it around your head and have your helper mark where it should be cut and then stapled. Cut another piece of cardboard that's the size of your face. Have your helper hold it in front of your face and mark where your eyes and nose are. Cut out the eye holes and a hole or flap for your nose. Staple the face to the circle of cardboard.

Continued on next page

Working with Cardboard and Other Materials

JOIN SHAPES

Cut flaps on the edge of the shape you want to add. Bend the flaps, then tape them down to add the shape.

MAKE CURVES

Cut a slit in the cardboard. Overlap the edges to make a curve. Staple or tape the edges in place.

ADD DETAILS

Hair or Fur: Make fringe along the long edge of a strip of paper.

Whiskers: Use straws or twisted strips of paper.

Nose: Use a bottle cap or the bottom part of a plastic bottle.

Texture: Use masking tape to create bumps and ridges and then paint over the tape.

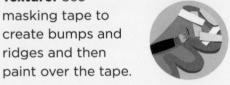

A Pinhole Camera

How does a film camera turn a big scene into a small picture? Make this cardboard camera to see it work!

You Need

- Empty cardboard cereal or oatmeal box
- Pencil
- Wax paper
- Tape or rubber band
- Blanket

1. Using a pencil, punch a hole in the center of the bottom of the box.

2. Place a piece of wax paper over the open end of the box and secure it with tape or a rubber band.

3. Sit in a dim room that has a bright object in it, such as a lamp or a window that lets in daylight. Put a blanket over your head and camera.

4. Hold the camera at arm's length, with the wax paper toward you and the punched-out hole sticking out from under the blanket. Point the camera at the bright object. On the surface of the wax paper, you will see a picture of the bright object—backward and upside down.

Did You Know

An old-style film camera uses the same principle as this pinhole camera, but does a better job since it holds a piece of film instead of wax paper. The film is coated with chemicals that are changed by light. Like the pinhole and the wax paper, when the lens of the camera lets light in, a backward, upside-down image is formed on the film.

Add sand, seashells, and blue food coloring to the water to make this lantern.

Make Ice Lanterns

Create a warm glow on a cold day with these special lights.

You Need

- Small and large plastic food storage containers, without lids
- Packing tape or duct tape
- Coins
- Water
- Add-ins, such as food coloring, beads, sand, or seashells
- Waterproof, battery-operated candle

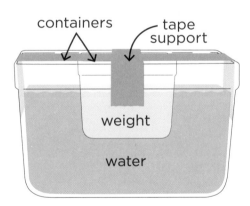

containers   tape support

weight

water

1. Use tape to suspend the small container inside the large one. Once the small container is in place, be sure there's an inch or more of space left in the large container on all sides. Place a few coins in the small container to add a little weight.

2. Pour water into the large container (not the small one) until it's an inch from the top. Set the container in the freezer. Or if temperatures are below freezing, leave it outside.

3. When the water is frozen solid, remove the small container. If it doesn't lift out easily, pour warm water into the small container to loosen it.

4. Remove the outer container. If it's stuck, ask an adult to turn it upside down (supporting the ice so it won't fall and break) and hold it under warm running water until it loosens.

5. Set the ice lantern outdoors on a surface that won't be damaged by water. By day, let sunlight glint through the lantern. At night, put a waterproof, battery-operated candle in the center. Watch it glow!

Tip

Before freezing, add opaque objects, such as small stones or evergreen sprigs, against the walls of the container to make silhouettes. Items farther in won't show as well.

More Lanterns to Try

Glowing Beads: Fill the large container partway with water. Add transparent beads, then freeze. Add more water and more beads. Continue freezing in layers.

Sunset Cooler: Pour one inch of water into the large container and add red food coloring. Then freeze it. Add more water, then mix in orange food coloring, and freeze. Repeat with yellow and then red again, or use any sunset colors.

Make a Flying Disc

In just a few minutes, you can make your own mini disc and fly it across a room!

You Need

- Scrap paper (thicker is better)
- Ruler
- Pencil
- Scissors
- Tape

3. Fold the top right corner to the bottom right.

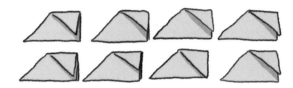

4. Fold the rest of the squares in the same way.

1. Cut the paper into eight two-inch squares.

2. Fold one square over from the top left corner to the bottom right.

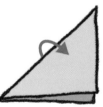

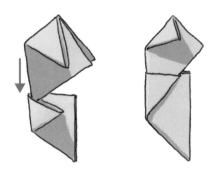

5. Push one square's point into another square's sleeve.

6. Push all the remaining squares into each other the same way until you create an eight-sided shape. Then use tape to secure the squares together.

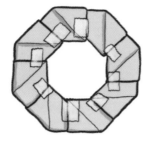

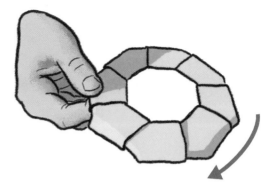

7. On the taped side, fold up the edges. The folded edge will help keep the disc aloft in flight.

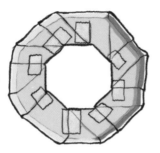

8. Hold the disc as shown above and fling it with a quick snap of your wrist. The disc should fly across the room! Practice for longer distances by adjusting the height and angle of your throw.

1 Last Challenge!

Can you make a unique costume to go with the mask you made on page 310? Use items from your recycling bin along with tape, paint, and other supplies.

DO GREAT THINGS

Quick Challenges

Surprise your mom or dad by doing a chore without being told.

Younger kids often look up to older kids. Bring joy to a little one's day by offering to play a game together.

Look for ways to be helpful and kind, like opening the door for someone or helping a classmate pick up something they've dropped. Even the smallest act of kindness can make someone's day better.

Offer to let someone else go before you when playing a game or waiting in line.

Listen and try not to interrupt when people talk to you. They will notice you care about what they have to say.

Call a friend or family member just to say hi. They might be missing you, so hearing your voice could be just what they need.

Write Sidewalk Sayings

Brighten someone's day by leaving positive messages on a sidewalk or driveway.

Your messages can be written with fancy or plain letters, and decorated with swirls, lightning bolts, hearts, or anything you'd like. First ask a parent's permission to decorate the pavement. Then grab some chalk and use one of these ideas to inspire you.

POSITIVE MESSAGE: Think of a message that will make people smile. You could share some advice, like: *Spread happiness. Be kind to everyone!* or *Always look on the bright side!* or *Make this day your best one yet!*

FUNNY MESSAGE: Write or draw something unexpected in someone's path, like *Nice shoes!* Or write *Warning: Snake!* Then draw a snake.

ENCOURAGING MESSAGE: Write a sentence to boost your readers' spirits, like *You can do it!* Your message could also make readers feel good about themselves, like *You're stronger than you think.* and *You are AWESOME!*

COLORFUL ART: You can also make people smile with just a drawing. Draw a big smiley face or a cute puppy. Or look for a crack in the sidewalk, maybe with some weeds peeking through, and make it part of your drawing.

See how to make your own pavement paint on page 183.

Find the Positive

If you are looking for a fun way to cheer up someone who's feeling blue, you can make this game. Try it on a friend, family member, or even yourself when you need a boost.

You Need

- Blank white paper
- Ruler
- Scissors
- Colored pencils or markers

2. Fold each corner in to the center. Color each triangle a different color.

1. Cut an eight-inch square from the paper. Fold the top half of the square down, then fold the right side over the left. Crease the folds, then unfold the paper.

3. Turn over the paper. Fold each of the corners in to meet at the center point. Number the eight small triangles 1 through 8.

4. Lift each flap. Under each number, write a positive message. You can try the suggestions below or come up with your own. Think about how you can personalize your messages for someone you care about.

Here are some ideas:
- You've got this!
- Stay true to yourself.
- Dream.
- You can do it.
- This is your day.
- You are great!
- Life is an adventure.
- Believe in yourself.

6. Slip your thumbs and index fingers under the colored flaps. Hold your fingers together to form a cone.

How to Use It:

1 Choose one of the four colors.

2 Spell out the chosen color, opening the cone sideways as you say the first letter, then opening the other way as you say the next letter.

3 Choose one of the four numbers showing and open the cone one way, then the other as you count to that number.

4 Again, choose one of the numbers showing. This time, lift its flap. There's your message!

5. Fold the bottom edge up to meet the top, so the numbers are on the inside. Hold the folded paper by the upper corners and push your hands toward each other.

Make a Kindness Calendar

Spreading kindness in small ways can make a big difference. Create a calendar of random acts of kindness to do throughout the year. What else can you think of?

- Surprise your friends with homemade cookies.

- Gather books to donate to a local library.

- Drop spare change into a jar throughout the year. On your birthday, give the money to your favorite charity.

- Host a movie night and let your friends pick the movie.

- Complete a chore for someone else.

- Make a colorful sign that says *Good morning!* Be the first person to wake up and tape it on the bathroom mirror.

- Offer to help a younger sibling or friend with their homework.

IN YOUR COMMUNITY

Check with a parent before getting started on these ideas.

- Shovel snow, pull weeds, or take out the garbage for a neighbor who needs help.

- Bake treats or make a flower bouquet or fruit basket for someone who is ill or has had a hard day.

- Read a book to a younger sibling, cousin, or neighbor. Try using different voices for different characters.

- Find a charitable organization that collects clothes and toys in good condition. Then ask your neighbors for donations.

- Deliver a card, drawing, or plate of cookies to your local fire, police, or ambulance station.

- Help keep your local streets or park clean by joining a cleanup day.

- Create care packages for people experiencing homelessness. Ask a parent to help you check with a local shelter or organization to find out what items are needed.

- Set up a lemonade stand and use the money you earn to buy items for the care packages.

- Go for a walk or spend time with a senior citizen who lives nearby.

- Become a volunteer at an animal shelter, food bank, nursing home, or other place that interests you. Or offer to volunteer at local events.

AT SCHOOL

■ Ask your school librarian if you can shelve books or do something else to help in the library.

■ Thank your teachers and all the great people who work at your school for being awesome.

■ Make a special effort to be kind to a new student. See more ideas on welcoming a new student on page 348.

■ Invite someone you don't know well to play or eat lunch with you.

■ Attend a school game and cheer for your team, friends, or sibling.

■ Offer to help your teacher before or after school.

■ Suggest holding a fundraiser to raise money for playground equipment or another cause.

■ Tell a joke or riddle to make a friend smile.

■ Be sure to express your appreciation with phrases like *Good job!* or *Great idea!*

■ When you're playing a game, let your opponent go first.

WEEKLY PLANNER

Monday	Tuesday	Wednesday	Thursday
DONATE BOOKS			

Friday	Saturday	Sunday	**MEMO**
	Baseball Game!	**VOLUNTEER 2–4 PM**	**Bake cookies for BAKE SALE**

Give a Homemade Brownie Mix

If you want to give a tasty gift to a chocolate lover, copy this recipe, place the ingredients into a clean jar, and decorate!

Safety Tip

Before mixing the ingredients, make sure to find out if the recipient has any food allergies.

You Need

- Index card
- Pen
- Colored pencils or markers
- 1- to $1\frac{1}{2}$-quart jar with lid
- 1 cup sugar
- $\frac{1}{3}$ cup unsweetened cocoa powder
- $\frac{1}{2}$ cup flour
- $\frac{1}{4}$ teaspoon baking powder
- $\frac{1}{4}$ teaspoon salt
- $\frac{1}{4}$ cup mini chocolate chips
- $\frac{1}{3}$ cup mini marshmallows
- $\frac{1}{4}$ cup finely chopped pecans (optional)
- Hole punch
- Ribbon or yarn

Before You Start

Copy the recipe on the next page onto your index card. Decorate it if you'd like.

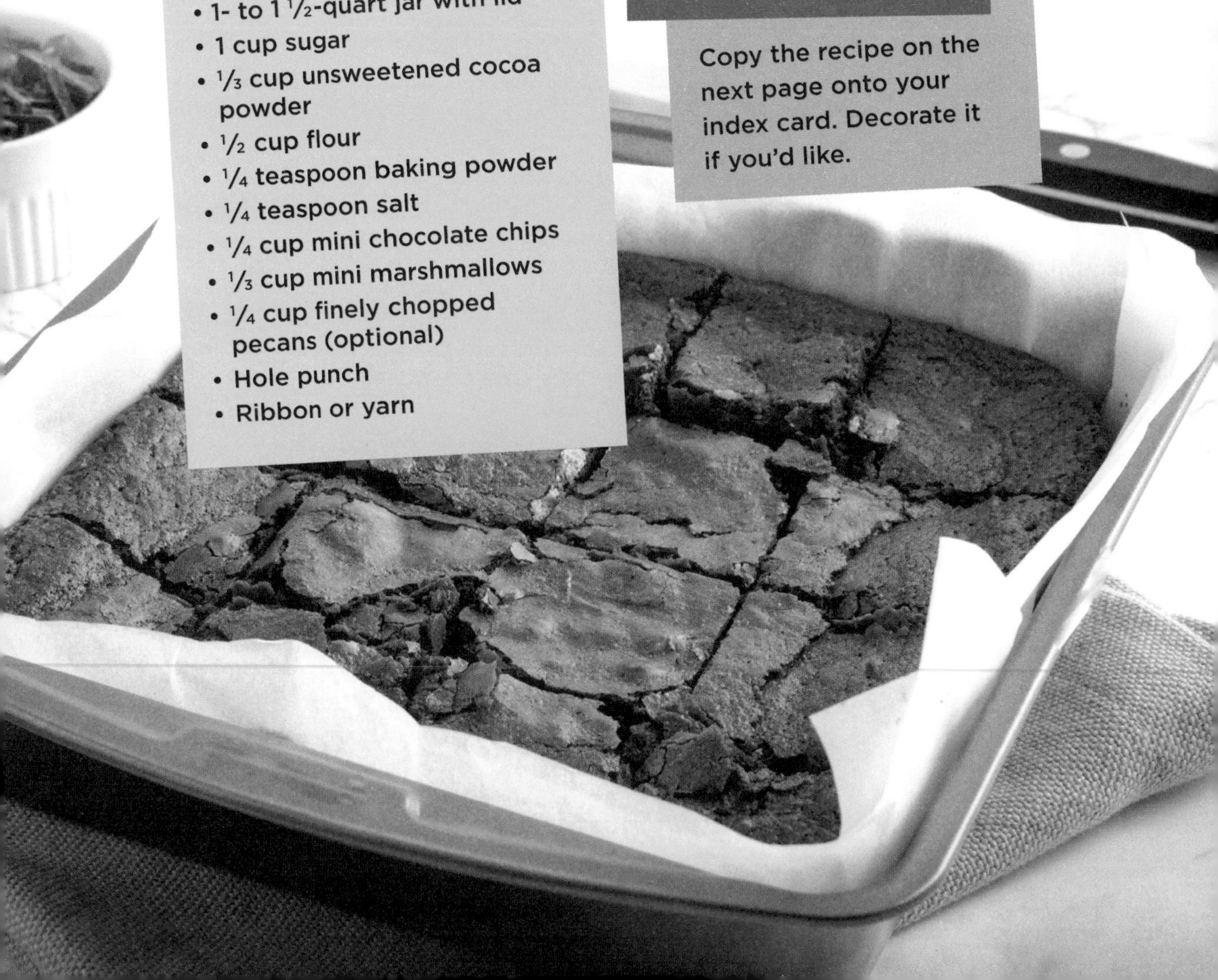

HOW TO MAKE ROCKY ROAD BROWNIES

1. With an adult, preheat the oven to 350°F. Spray a 9-inch baking pan with nonstick cooking spray.

2. Pour the contents of the jar into a large bowl. Add ½ cup of melted butter, 2 eggs, and 1 teaspoon of vanilla extract. Stir until well blended. Spread the mixture in the prepared pan.

3. Bake 20–25 minutes, or until a toothpick put in the center comes out clean.

4. Cool in the pan on a wire rack, then cut into squares. Recipe makes 16 brownies.

Fill the Jar

1 Wash your hands before starting.

2 Layer the sugar, cocoa powder, flour, baking powder, salt, chocolate chips, marshmallows, and pecan pieces in the jar.

3 Punch a hole in the corner of the index card. Thread a ribbon or yarn through the hole and tie it around the jar.

How to Make Rocky Road Brownies

Send a Care Package

Are you missing a friend who has moved away? Or do you know someone who is sick or could use some cheering up? One way to let them know you're thinking about them is to send a care package.

First think about what sorts of things the person likes. Then buy or make at least a few small gifts for them, like a book, homemade brownie mix (see page 326), small game, or something you've made from this book! Remember to protect the items with lots of crumpled newspaper or other packing material so the contents don't move around if the package is jostled.

If you would like to add personal touches to the box itself, line the inside with your favorite patterned paper, such as wrapping paper, before you pack the items.

More Ideas

You can also send care packages to people in the military overseas. For information, go to **dod.defense.gov/Resources/Community-Resources/carepackages**.

Give a Gift of the Month

If you want to give a personalized and creative gift to someone special, you could make a gift-of-the-month certificate. Start by thinking about what that person enjoys—your gift could be a monthly visit or phone call, a photo, homemade cookies, a joke, a postcard, a drawing, or something else. Spend time coming up with ideas that you can do for at least a few months of the year.

Once you've chosen the monthly gift, design a certificate for it. Come up with a name, like *Visit of the Month* or *Cookie of the Month*. Then write how long it's good for (four months, for example) and when the gift will be delivered each month (in the middle of every month, or the last week of every month, for example). Then, make sure to follow through on your gift each month!

GIFT CERTIFICATE

GOOD FOR: One postcard every month for four months

TO: GRANDMA

FROM: CHRIS

P.S. I'll send cards the first week of the month. I promise to tell you about what's new with me!

Paint Kindness Rocks

Surprising others with these rocks when they least expect it can be a great way to share kindness in your community.

You Need

- Smooth rocks, about the size of the palm of your hand
- Acrylic paint
- Paintbrushes or paint pens
- Permanent markers
- Non-toxic sealant, such as Mod Podge
- Clear spray paint

1. Before using any found rocks, make sure you are allowed to take them first. Rinse and dry the rocks to make sure they are smooth and free of dirt or sand. If you can't find any rocks, you can buy river rocks at most hardware stores.

2. Paint your rocks a solid color, a pattern, or a mix of both. Try putting polka dots or stripes on a rock, or create a decorative frame for your kind words. Just leave enough space for your message and make sure to let your paint dry completely. It also works to leave your rock unpainted, and just write the message in a bright color that contrasts with the rock's natural surface.

3. Write your message with a permanent marker.

4. Once your rock is complete, turn it over and write #*kindnessrocks* on the bottom. Then cover the entire rock with sealant. After the sealant dries, go outside to apply a coating of clear spray paint (so you don't breathe it in) to ensure your message will last in all kinds of weather. Ask an adult for help when applying the spray paint.

5. Leave your kindness rocks for others to find! Have a parent help you check if it's okay to leave the rocks in public spaces.

Here are some ideas for messages:
- Enjoy your journey.
- Smile!
- You matter.
- Rainbows rock!
- Show your true colors!
- Don't worry! Be happy!
- Hugs!
- Peace
- Breathe
- Stay kind and rock on!
- Shine on!
- Love yourself.
- You're brilliant.
- You rock!

Learn More

Get the story behind kindness rocks from **thekindnessrocksproject.com**.

Quiz Yourself: Are You a Good Listener?

One of the best ways to show that you care about someone is to really listen to what they say. Do you listen well or tune people out? Take this quiz to find out!

1. **You're playing a game on a phone when your brother comes in, crying. You:**

a Are so close to the next level . . . yes! Now for those extra points!

b Ask what's up, but keep playing. You catch some of what he says.

c Pause the game and ask your brother, "Hey, what's the matter?"

2. **Your cousin is telling you about her trip to an amusement park. You:**

a Aren't interested, so you change the subject.

b Say, "Cool," then daydream about the last time you were at a park.

c Pay attention as she talks. You can tell she's excited to share her story.

3. **Your friend seems annoyed. When you ask what's wrong, he says you've been ignoring him. You:**

a Interrupt with, "I have not!" and then talk over him as he tries to explain.

b Let him talk while you think up a reply that'll show him he's wrong.

c Explain that you didn't mean to and ask when he's felt ignored.

4. Class is about to start. Your friend hands you a video of his dog as the teacher starts talking. You:

a Hunch down and watch the video.

b Will listen to the teacher in a second. The video is funny, and it's almost over.

c Hand it back, say, "Later," and listen to the teacher.

5. In the car after school, your mom says, "When we get home, be sure to . . ." You:

a Start thinking of things you want to do at home, like play basketball.

b Only half listen. It's about chores. She'll remind you if you forget.

c Pay close attention so you don't forget what she wants you to do, and ask questions if you need to.

RESULTS

If you answered mostly *a*:
You miss a lot of what people tell you. And when you don't listen, people might think you don't care. Look people in the eye when they speak, don't interrupt, and focus on what they say. You'll see positive changes when you listen carefully to others!

If you answered mostly *b*:
You try to listen, but you easily get caught up in your own world. When you do something else while trying to listen, you can miss important information. And people usually notice when you don't give them your full attention. Try to ignore distractions and really listen.

If you answered mostly *c*:
You show that you care about what others say by listening and paying attention to them. People appreciate your consideration, and you always know what's going on.

How to Be a Good Friend

Long-lasting friendships are a treasure. They require effort and consideration of each other's feelings. Here are some tips to help your friendships grow deeper.

■ **Be willing to take turns.** People will be more likely to enjoy spending time with you if you are open to others' ideas and let them go first sometimes.

■ **Be careful not to hurt your friends' feelings** or say things that might embarrass them. But people sometimes make careless mistakes. It's important to say "I'm sorry," even if you didn't mean to make a friend feel bad.

■ **Ask your friends if they want to do something** without waiting for them to ask you first. Think about the games and activities your friends like and offer to do those things with them. It feels good to be invited and shows your friends that you enjoy spending time with them.

■ **Listen to your friends' ideas and what is interesting to them.** You don't always need to share your own opinions and experiences. Just as it makes you feel good when someone shows a genuine interest in what's important to you, your friends will feel good when you listen to what they have to say.

■ **When you disagree, try to be understanding of your friends' feelings** and points of view. Think about how you can compromise. For example, if you and a friend each want to play a different game, maybe you can play a little of both, or find something different to play that you can both agree on.

■ **Remember your friends' birthdays** and do something thoughtful for them on their special day. You could make them something from this book!

■ **Give your friends room to be who they are.** Your friends have unique personalities, likes, dislikes, and ways of doing things. Remember, you don't have to agree on everything! Some of the best friends are those who have very different ideas and opinions. What matters is that they respect each other, even when they disagree.

How to Make Up with a Friend After a Fight

Fights can happen in any relationship—sometimes you and a friend will disagree or say things that hurt each other. It's important to remember that the best way to end a disagreement is to apologize, no matter who started it.

Finding a peaceful solution can help you and your friend get back on track. See if the following suggestions can help.

■ **Remember that it's okay for friends to have their own interests, experiences, and opinions.** Most arguments start when each person wants their own way or feels they are right and the other person is wrong. But we can't insist that others feel the same way that we do. Getting along with people requires sensitivity, consideration of other people's thoughts and needs, and a willingness to cooperate and compromise.

■ **Ask your friend if they can sit down with you during a quiet time when neither of you is busy or stressed.** It's important to approach this talk with a gentle, compassionate, forgiving attitude. Remember that friendship is a two-way street and that if two people are fighting, each side shares some blame.

■ **Start the conversation by apologizing for your part in what has happened between you.** Admit it if you realize you've made a mistake. You could say, "I'm sorry for the way I acted before, and that I hurt your feelings." Express to them how much the friendship means to you and how much you would like to be friends again.

■ **Instead of insisting on your side of the story,** express sadness and sympathy that their feelings were hurt. Then you can share your own hurt feelings, but without pointing fingers or placing blame. Use "I feel" statements, such as, "I felt hurt when you didn't invite me."

■ **Even if the two of you can't quite forget that the fight happened,** maybe you can forgive each other. Holding onto angry, hurt feelings is not healthy or productive. It can take time to let go of those feelings, but clearing the air and saying you're sorry to each other can help.

■ **You might talk about ways to improve and avoid this situation in the future.** Be willing to make changes and compromise, and perhaps they will do the same. Enter this conversation ready to listen, so you can hear how your friend is really feeling.

■ **Mending a hurt friendship can take time,** so take it slow and be patient. If either of you feel that you are not ready to be friends right now, respect that decision and give each other some space. You might spend time with other friends. Continue to be friendly to this person and both of you may eventually decide that you are ready to be friends again.

■ **Remember that no person, no friendship, and no relationship is perfect.** You are human, and everyone has flaws and makes mistakes.

■ **If you are unsure about what to do after you have an argument,** it can be helpful to talk to a parent or other trusted adult about your concerns.

How to Get Along with Your Brother or Sister

Sometimes siblings have a hard time getting along. When you spend so much time together, it's normal to get on each other's nerves or be irritated by little things.

While it may be unrealistic to think that you and your siblings will never argue or disagree, there are ways that can help you fight less.

■ **Look for times when you can play, laugh, and have fun with each other.** Offer to play a game or do an activity that you both enjoy.

■ **If your sibling wants some time alone,** respect their wishes and come back another time when they are ready to play with you.

■ **If you need some alone time, that is okay, too.** You can tell your sibling kindly that you like playing with them but that you want to be alone sometimes. They may understand. You might say something like, "Right now, I'd like to be by myself. But how about we play together later? You can choose the game."

■ **If your brother or sister is annoying you,** the less you react, the less chance there will be of a fight taking place. Remaining calm shows maturity.

■ **If you feel as if you're ready to explode in anger,** silently get up and go someplace away from your brother or sister. Missing a part of a television show or something you're involved in is better than battling it out.

■ **When possible, avoid situations that tend to spark conflict,** such as certain topics, activities, or games that may lead to upset or hurt feelings. Take a break from these, at least for a while.

■ **If you have a younger sibling,** remember that a young child isn't able to act with the same maturity as an older child. You may not realize how important you are to your brother or sister, but they look up to you and are learning from you. Try to be patient and kind with them.

■ **Challenge yourself to treat your sibling as you would one of your friends.** You and your brother or sister will always love each other, and it's important to show that with kind, helpful, and loving actions. This can help build a stronger and happier relationship between you. See how to be a good friend on page 334.

■ **Ask a parent for advice** in private if there is something bothering or concerning you about a sibling. They love you and know you both very well.

How to Deal with Angry Feelings

It's natural to be angry sometimes. Frustration and anger are part of being human. Once in a while, you might even lose your temper. Here are some ways that can help you deal with angry feelings before they reach a boiling point.

■ **Try to pinpoint situations that make you angry.** Maybe you get upset more easily first thing in the morning or when you're tired and hungry. Or perhaps certain people upset you more frequently than others. Knowing what sets you off can help you understand your anger and deal with it before it bubbles over.

■ **Remember, unlike feelings, actions can be started and stopped** whenever you choose. Even when you feel angry, you can prevent yourself from saying and doing hurtful things.

■ **Try taking deep breaths when you feel your anger building,** counting to four on the inhale and eight on the exhale. As you count, think about a calm, peaceful image, such as your favorite place. Imagine every detail, including the sights, sounds, and smells. For example, if your favorite place is the beach, think about the sound of the waves lapping against the shore, and envision your toes wiggling in the sand. You can always return to this place in your mind any time you're upset.

■ **Brainstorm a list of things to do when you feel angry.** For instance, when you feel you need to "get something out," or yell, you might go outdoors and get some exercise, or use your energy to make a piece of art. Some people find it calming to write about their frustrations in a journal. You can imagine that the pages of the journal are soaking up all of your anger or stress.

■ **Talk to a parent, close family member, teacher, or other trusted adult** who would be glad to have a conversation about anything bothering you. Sometimes upset feelings are like boiling water in a covered pot—they bubble and bubble, and get hotter and hotter, until they can't be contained anymore. Sharing a concern is like lifting the cover off the pot. Heat is released and the bubbling becomes much less intense or stops entirely.

■ **Try quietly walking away from the situation** if you're feeling so angry that you can't speak nicely. Sometimes giving yourself space from what is making you upset can stop the situation from getting worse and give you time to cool down and think things through.

How to Feel Better When You're Sad or Worried

When you feel sad, worried, or anxious, it's important to remember that all feelings are okay. It's how you deal with your feelings that matters. Here are some things that you can do to feel better.

■ **It often helps to have someone listen to your thoughts and feelings.** Even though it may seem difficult, it's important to talk to a parent, close family member, or an adult you trust about the things on your mind. They care about the way you're feeling and may have ideas that will help.

■ **Try drawing or writing about your feelings in a journal or notebook.** Sometimes getting things out on paper or creating artwork can help release bad feelings.

■ **Try to see the things that cause you worry and anxiety as opportunities to learn and grow.** Many successful people have said that the challenges they faced in their lives were blessings in disguise because of what they learned. Remember that you might not feel this way right away. For example, you may feel worried about starting a new school and not knowing anyone. Try to think about how fun it can be when you *do* meet someone you like a lot. Good friends are always waiting to be found.

■ **You can make a list of the things you like about yourself**—all the activities you're good at, your special talents or strengths, and why you're a good friend. You can reread this list whenever you feel sad to remind yourself that you are very lovable!

■ **Remember to keep doing the things you enjoy**—maybe reading, drawing, participating in sports, or playing games. You might also try doing kind things for others. See some ideas on page 324. Focusing on positive things will help you feel better and enjoy life more.

■ **Remember to take care of yourself.** This can be easy to forget when you're feeling sad or full of worry. Take the time to eat a well-balanced diet, get plenty of exercise, and get enough sleep.

■ **It might also help to make a list of some things to look forward to.** Are you going anywhere exciting this summer? Are there fun things you can do outside as the days get longer? Does anyone special in your life have a birthday soon? Sometimes having things to look forward to can take your mind off whatever is bothering you.

■ **Spend 10 or 15 minutes each day letting yourself totally relax.** Go to a place that helps you feel peaceful. Or, instead of a physical place, you may choose to imagine a place you would like to be. Take a few deep breaths, and let go of any tension you are feeling. Releasing stress and tension can give you energy and make you feel more positive.

How to Help When Someone Is Sick

If you have a friend or relative who is sick, you might wonder if there is anything you can do to help.

It's kind and caring to want to show your support. Although you may not be able to visit this person right away, there are other things you can do to help them feel loved.

■ **If you can visit the person who is sick,** ask them what they'd like to do. You might offer to play their favorite board game or card game, watch television or a movie, or read aloud to them. See what they would enjoy doing with you.

■ **You might want to make a card or write a note to them.** Writing a personal, handwritten note is a thoughtful way to show your support, and they are sure to appreciate the time you put into it. Let them know that you are thinking about them and that you hope they are feeling better each day. You can find more tips on what to say in your note on page 132.

■ **If it's a friend who is sick, talk to their parents or family members** to see if they have any other good ideas. They can tell you how your friend is feeling and if there's anything you can do to make your friend happier or more comfortable.

■ **You may also ask if they'd like you to brighten their room** by putting up photos, cards, and drawings.

■ **If this is a friend from school,** you could ask your classmates to write notes to make sure your friend knows that everyone is looking forward to seeing them again.

■ **You might want to send them a care package** if it is better not to visit your friend or relative at this time. You could send magazines, puzzles, games, or books to take their mind off of being sick. See more ideas on page 328.

■ **Talk to a parent or a school counselor**—it can be scary when a good friend or loved one gets sick. Sometimes just talking to people who care about you can help you feel less upset or confused. They might have some other ideas for you as well.

How to Deal with Teasing or Bullying

It may feel like there's nothing you can do if you or someone you know is being teased or bullied. But everyone—including you—has the ability to use their voice to help put a stop to it.

Often, doing the right thing means sticking your neck out by being an *upstander*, not a *bystander*. An upstander is someone who takes action when they believe there is a problem that needs a solution. If you would like to know how you can be an upstander when you experience or see bullying, you can start with these suggestions.

IF YOU ARE BEING HURT, TEASED, OR BULLIED:

■ **Remember that you are not alone.** It is always okay to tell a parent, family member, or trusted adult about anything that is bothering you. It's not tattling to protect yourself from being hurt. They can decide if other adults, such as the school principal, counselor, or the other person's parents, should be involved to put an end to the behavior.

■ **Talk to a teacher or school counselor about what's happening.** It's their responsibility to keep students safe from bullying, but they can't help unless they know there's a problem. Ask if you can talk to them during a quiet time, either between classes or before or after school. Your parent or a family member can also talk to an adult at school.

■ **Remember that it is not a sign of weakness to refuse to fight back.** Rather, it is a sign of maturity and self-control. The easiest thing to do when someone bothers you is to react in an angry way, but fighting never settles a problem.

■ **Avoid being around this person as much as possible.** Notice where they are and try to be somewhere else. When you can't avoid them, stay calm and don't react to unkind things they may say or do.

■ **Stick with a group of friends or play near a teacher or other supervising adult.** A bully will be less likely to taunt you if there is an adult nearby who can see and hear what's going on.

■ **Try to spend time doing things you enjoy with people who care about you.** It's especially important for you to take care of yourself whenever you are feeling overwhelmed or stressed. Keep being the kind and compassionate person you are!

IF A FRIEND OR SOMEONE YOU KNOW IS BEING HURT, TEASED, OR BULLIED:

■ **Show your friend you are there for them with your words and actions.** If you hear someone saying something mean or untrue about a friend, you might say, "I don't like when you say those things about my friend. Please stop." Although you can't stop what others say or do, your reaction to a bully can let them know how you feel about their behavior. Being there for your friend may make it easier for them to deal with some of the negative feelings they could be going through.

■ **It is important to let a parent, school counselor, or teacher know what is happening if the problem continues or you feel unsafe.** Sometimes it isn't wise or safe to stand up to a bully. If kids are threatening or physically hurting each other, it often takes help from an adult to stop the behavior. If a friend asks you not to tell anyone, remember that there are times when it's okay to share something that was said to you in confidence if it feels dangerous or is really bothering you.

■ **Notice if your friend isn't acting like themselves.** Give them an extra big smile and invite them to spend time with you. Your support will help them feel like they are not alone.

How to Welcome a New Student

It can be overwhelming to start a new school. You can make it less stressful for a new student by being friendly and welcoming.

■ **A simple, friendly "Hi" is sometimes all it takes** to help someone feel better. Smiling and greeting a new student in a warm, welcoming way may help them feel at ease.

■ **Offer to give them a tour of your school.** Knowing where everything is will help them feel more comfortable.

■ **You might strike up a conversation** about what's going on in class or other things at school. Or you also could ask about their favorite things, such as books, music, sports, and hobbies, to learn more about their likes and dislikes.

■ **Listen closely to what they have to say**, and then share your own ideas.

■ **Invite them** to sit with you and your friends at lunch.

■ **Introduce them to some of your friends,** and invite them to join in an activity or game during recess or after school.

Be a Family Reporter

Have you ever wondered what it was like to be a kid when your parents or grandparents were your age? Just like you, they probably have some stories or memories that they would be happy to share. As a family reporter, you could ask them about what they did for fun, what school was like, and what their hometown was like. Choose a notebook to record your family stories so they will remain safe and you will be able to read them again in the future.

Ask your family member if they would like to be interviewed. Then think about what questions you'd like to ask, and write them down.

Here are some questions you might want to ask:

- Where did you live when you were a kid?
- What was your favorite food?
- What did you eat for breakfast?
- What was your favorite toy?
- Who were your friends growing up?
- Did you ever have a pet?
- What's something silly you did when you were a kid?
- What did you want to be when you grew up?
- Where did you go on vacation?

How to Help Take Care of the Planet

It can be hard to read and hear about environmental issues facing the planet. Habitats around the world, such as oceans and forests, are changing and being threatened due to human impact. You might wonder if you can do something to help. You can.

Wanting to learn about what contributes to environmental challenges is the best place to start. The planet needs people who are willing to work to make it cleaner. But no single person can do it all. It takes people from all over the world—learning, educating others, creating new systems and technologies to address environmental damage, and more, to help clean up the planet.

HERE ARE SOME WAYS TO HELP CREATE A CLEANER FUTURE:

■ **Start by learning more about how Earth's global climate is changing.** You can go to your school or local library and ask the librarian to help you find books and reliable online sources. As you begin finding more information, you may come across topics that interest you. You might want to learn more about a specific type of animal or species that's being affected by the planet's rising temperatures.

■ **Talk to a parent, family member, or teacher** if this is something that is really concerning you. They might have some ideas on how you can make changes in your household and school. Your teacher or principal could also help you get more kids involved in your school. You might join or help to form a club that meets regularly to talk about these issues, works on improving recycling, increases the use of environmentally friendly products, and organizes events and fundraisers. Check out more ideas on forming a club on page 20.

■ **Stop using disposable straws.** You can purchase a reusable straw to use at home or take with you to restaurants.

■ **Practice precycling.** This means buying more products that are unpackaged, reusable, or recyclable. For example, your family can decide to stop buying plastic water bottles and instead use metal ones that can last several years.

■ **Upcycle items in your house.** Instead of throwing items away, see if you can give them a brand-new use. Many of the crafts in this book can be made from items that you typically throw away. Be creative and think about what else you can turn trash into!

■ **See if there is a way to fix something that has broken** instead of buying a new one, whether it's a toy, item of clothing, or something you use around the house. Have an adult help you with bigger and more complex items. Of course, there are times when you need a professional to fix something.

Continued on next page

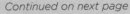

■ **Recycle as much as you can.** Talk with a parent or teacher about how you currently recycle at home or school. Are there ways to recycle items you use that currently don't get recycled?

■ **Compost food scraps.** Instead of throwing away food waste in plastic garbage bags that can linger for decades, you and your family can find out how to safely compost food in your yard, outdoor space, or community compost program. Composting reduces waste and allows food and other organic items to break down naturally.

■ **Volunteer for a park, beach, or river cleanup near you.** If you can't find one around you, talk to a parent or adult at school about organizing a local cleanup.

■ **Reduce water waste.** Remember to turn off the faucet when you brush your teeth, and check your home for leaky faucets or toilets.

More Ideas

Learn more about the planet and ways to take care of it at these sites:

**earthday.org
abagslife.com
climatekids.nasa.gov
strawfree.org**

■ **Conserve energy in your home.** Remember to close your refrigerator when you aren't putting something in it or taking something out. Always turn off lights when you're not using them. And when you're not using personal electronics, don't just turn them off. Unplug them as well.

■ **Whenever you can, walk or use public transportation** instead of asking for a ride. Check with a parent first because they may need to accompany you. Walking and using public transportation can help reduce carbon emissions because there are fewer cars on the road. If you travel by car, try to carpool.

■ **Donate old clothes and toys** rather than throwing them away. Talk to a parent first.

■ **Talk to a parent about eating foods that are grown and produced locally.** When you can, shop at your local farmers' market. Supporting local growers is a great way to help your community and can also help reduce carbon emissions.

■ **If you can, start a vegetable garden.** If you don't have enough outdoor space for one, see page 77 for how to grow a garden in a bucket.

■ **Use reusable bags** instead of the plastic bags you get at stores.

■ **Before you print something out,** think about whether or not it's really important to have on paper. If it is, print double-sided when you can.

■ **Start a collection of scrap paper** that you can use for art or school projects. You could save flyers and use the reverse sides as scrap paper. You can also hold on to wrapping paper or patterned and decorative paper that you could use again for something else.

Did You Know

According to **strawfree.org**, straws are one of the top 10 types of garbage polluting the ocean.

1 Last Challenge!

At night, think back on what happened during your day. Were there any situations in which you could have been kinder to others? For example, did you push a little to be first in line? Did you try to make something sound better than it is in order to show off?

What could you have done or said to be more thoughtful of others? Thinking about these things helps you discover what it means to be your best self wherever you go.

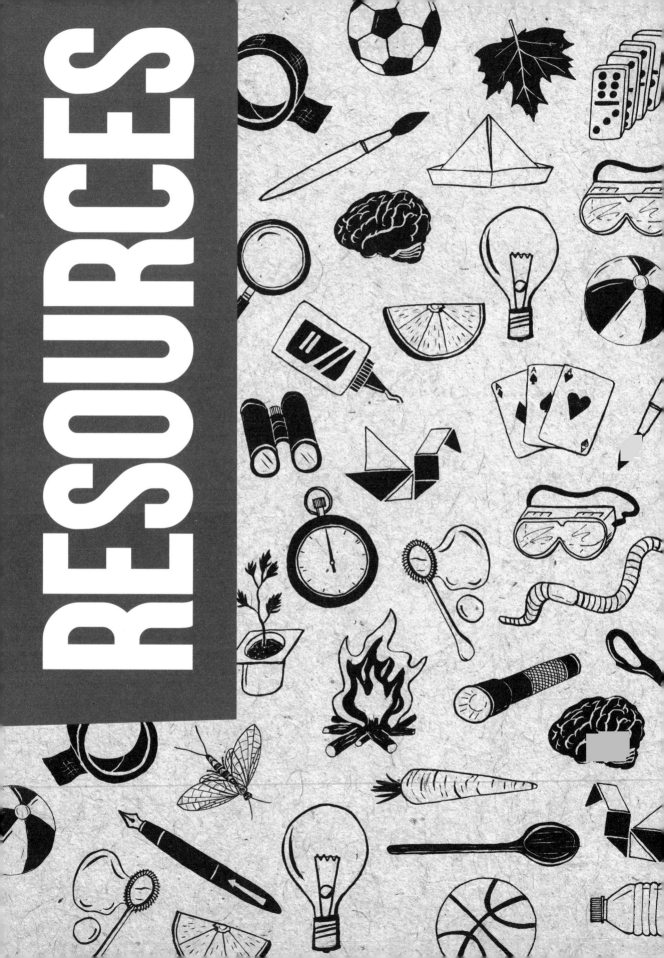

RESOURCES

Websites

For more information about taking care of the planet:

earthday.org for Earth Day details and events near you

climatekids.nasa.gov for NASA's information about climate change

strawfree.org for information on reducing plastic waste

kids.niehs.nih.gov/topics/reduce/index.htm for how you can help reduce waste

dec.ny.gov/chemical/8826.html for how to precycle

dep.pa.gov/Business/Land/Waste/Recycling/PublicResources/Pages/HouseholdBatteries.aspx for information on recycling batteries

epa.gov/rad/consumers for information on responsible appliance disposal (RAD)

For more information about trees:

treesaregood.org/funfacts for interesting facts about trees

treepeople.org/tree-benefits for some of the many benefits of trees

arborday.org/kids for games, activities, and information about trees

climatekids.nasa.gov/tree-rings for what trees tell us about climate change

For recreational areas and activities in the U.S.:

usa.gov/recreation to find a recreation area

nps.gov for locations and information about all of our National Parks

usa.gov/state-travel-and-tourism for state-by-state travel and tourism information

fs.usda.gov for locations and information about all of our National Forests

fws.gov/refuges for locations and information about all of our National Wildlife Refuges

For more information about birds:

fws.gov/birds/bird-enthusiasts/bird-watching/youth-birding.php for how to start bird watching

allaboutbirds.org for bird guides and more information

gbbc.birdcount.org for The Great Backyard Bird Count, a citizen-science project. Volunteers count birds in order to understand bird distribution and populations.

feederwatch.org for Project FeederWatch, a survey of birds that visit feeders. Volunteers contribute to this scientific study by counting birds at feeders during the winter.

Measurements and Conversions

This book uses U.S. measurements like feet, tablespoons, cups, and pounds. These charts can help you convert smaller measurements to larger ones and convert measurements to the metric system used in other parts of the world. Some conversions are approximate.

Length and Distance Measurements and Conversions

$\frac{1}{12}$ ft	1 in	2.5 cm
1 ft	12 in	30.5 cm
1 yd	3 ft	91.4 cm
$1\frac{1}{10}$ yd	$3\frac{3}{10}$ ft	1 m (100 cm)
1 mi	5280 ft	1.6 km
$\frac{3}{5}$ mi	1093 $\frac{3}{5}$ yd	1 km (1000 m)

U.S. Weight Measurements and Metric Conversions

$\frac{1}{25}$ oz	-	1 g
$\frac{1}{2}$ oz	-	14.2 g
1 oz	-	28.3 g
2 oz	$\frac{1}{8}$ lb	56.7 g
8 oz	$\frac{1}{2}$ lb	226.8 g
12 oz	$\frac{3}{4}$ lb	340.2 g
16 oz	1 lb	453.6 g
35 $\frac{3}{10}$ oz	2 $\frac{1}{5}$ lb	1 kg

U.S. Volume Measurements for Solids and Liquids

1 tbsp	3 tsp	½ fl oz
¼ c	4 tbsp	2 fl oz
½ c	8 tbsp	4 fl oz
1 c	16 tbsp	8 fl oz
1 pt	2 c	16 fl oz
1 qt	2 pt	32 fl oz
1 gal	4 qt	128 fl oz

U.S. Volume Measurements and Metric Conversions

1 tbsp	½ fl oz	14.8 ml
¼ c	2 fl oz	59.1 ml
½ c	4 fl oz	118.3 ml
1 c	8 fl oz	236.6 ml
1 pt	16 fl oz	473.2 ml
1 qt	32 fl oz	.9 l
1 $\frac{1}{10}$ qt	33 ⅘ fl oz	1 l
1 gal	128 fl oz	3.8 l

Abbreviations

c = cup
cm = centimeter
fl oz = fluid ounce
ft = foot
g = gram
gal = gallon
in = inch

kg = kilogram
km = kilometer
l = liter
lb = pound
m = meter
mi = mile
ml = milliliter

oz = ounce
pt = pint
qt = quart
tbsp = tablespoon
tsp = teaspoon
yd = yard

Kitchen Tips

Follow these safety rules when you're cooking or baking:

• **Ask an adult to help.** It's important to have an experienced adult with you to help with anything hot or sharp, or to run appliances.

• **Always tie loose hair back and roll up any loose sleeves.** If you want to protect your clothes from stains, wear an apron.

• **Wash your hands often.** Always wash them well with soap and water for at least 10 seconds before touching food. After you touch raw meat, poultry, fish, or egg products, immediately wash your hands.

• **Keep surfaces clean.** Wash your countertops or other surfaces thoroughly with warm water and soap both before and after using them.

• **Wash fruits and vegetables before cutting or eating them.** Even if a package label says it's organic, fresh, or just-picked, it's always best to give produce a good wash.

• **Wear oven mitts if you have permission to use the stove or oven.** Pots and pot handles on the stovetop can be burning hot. The same is true for pans in the oven and, sometimes, the microwave.

• **Turn pot or pan handles toward the back of the stove when you aren't holding them.** Someone walking by the stove could accidentally knock into the handle and cause the pan or hot food to fall.

• **Only use microwave-safe cookware in the microwave oven.** That means no metal, aluminum, or certain plastics should ever be in the microwave. They can melt or cause a fire.

• **If you're allowed to use a knife, follow these rules:** Never cut toward yourself, don't touch the sharp edge of the blade with your finger, and keep the hand not holding the knife away from the blade.

Other helpful hints:

How to Measure Dry Ingredients:
Using the measuring tool (cup, teaspoon, tablespoon, etc.), scoop out the dry ingredient from its package. Then use a butter knife or other straight edge to level it off over the package it came from. Or, spoon dry ingredients into your measuring tool, then level it off.

How to Measure Wet Ingredients:
Use a clear measuring cup with a pour spout. Set the cup on a flat surface and pour liquid ingredients into it. Bend down to the surface level and look at the cup straight on to see if it's at the measurement you want.

How to Knead Dough: Lightly sprinkle some flour on a clean surface, then flour your hands. Put the dough on the surface and shape it into a ball. Use the heels of your hands to push the dough down and away from you. Then fold the dough in half, taking the far end toward you and then doing the same thing with the heels of your hands. Turn the dough a quarter of the way around and do the same thing, kneading and folding. Keep going. If the dough is too sticky to handle, sprinkle a bit more flour on it. Keep kneading like this until the dough is smooth and elastic (you should be able to stretch it without it breaking), which usually takes about 10 minutes.

How to Set a Table

If you're having dessert, put the needed utensils above each plate.

Put water glasses near the upper right of each plate.

Place utensils (forks, spoons, knives) in the order they are used, from the outside in.

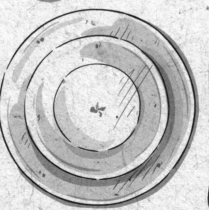

Forks are always on the left side.

Knives and spoons are always on the right side.

Napkins are on the left side of each plate.

If you're having salad first, put the needed plates or bowls on top of each larger plate.

Only use the utensils that will be needed for the meal.

United States of America Map

*The United States capital is Washington DC.

State	Abbreviation	Capital City
Alabama	AL	Montgomery
Alaska	AK	Juneau
Arizona	AZ	Phoenix
Arkansas	AR	Little Rock
California	CA	Sacramento
Colorado	CO	Denver
Connecticut	CT	Hartford
Delaware	DE	Dover
Florida	FL	Tallahassee
Georgia	GA	Atlanta
Hawaii	HI	Honolulu
Idaho	ID	Boise
Illinois	IL	Springfield
Indiana	IN	Indianapolis
Iowa	IA	Des Moines
Kansas	KS	Topeka
Kentucky	KY	Frankfort
Louisiana	LA	Baton Rouge
Maine	ME	Augusta
Maryland	MD	Annapolis
Massachusetts	MA	Boston
Michigan	MI	Lansing
Minnesota	MN	Saint Paul
Mississippi	MS	Jackson
Missouri	MO	Jefferson City

State	Abbreviation	Capital City
Montana	MT	Helena
Nebraska	NE	Lincoln
Nevada	NV	Carson City
New Hampshire	NH	Concord
New Jersey	NJ	Trenton
New Mexico	NM	Santa Fe
New York	NY	Albany
North Carolina	NC	Raleigh
North Dakota	ND	Bismarck
Ohio	OH	Columbus
Oklahoma	OK	Oklahoma City
Oregon	OR	Salem
Pennsylvania	PA	Harrisburg
Rhode Island	RI	Providence
South Carolina	SC	Columbia
South Dakota	SD	Pierre
Tennessee	TN	Nashville
Texas	TX	Austin
Utah	UT	Salt Lake City
Vermont	VT	Montpelier
Virginia	VA	Richmond
Washington	WA	Olympia
West Virginia	WV	Charleston
Wisconsin	WI	Madison
Wyoming	WY	Cheyenne

Make a First Aid Kit

When you're hiking, camping, or on any outdoor adventure, it's good to have a first aid kit with you. Here's how to make a personal kit with some basic items.

IMPORTANT: If you have a serious injury or other health problem, tell an adult immediately.

1 Get a container for your kit. Look for a sturdy container that snaps shut, like a small art supply box or lunch box. Create a large label that says *First Aid Kit*.

2 Make a list of the names and phone numbers of your family members and your family's doctors to put inside the kit. It's good to have the numbers handy in case you need to reach them quickly.

3 Stock your kit with first aid supplies.

For treating cuts and scrapes:
- Antiseptic wipes to clean out the wound
- Adhesive bandages in different sizes to cover cuts and scrapes
- Sterile gauze pads to cover large cuts and scrapes
- Small roll of first aid tape to hold a gauze pad in place
- Instant cold pack for bumps, sore muscles, and bug bites
- Travel-size bottle of hand sanitizer to clean your hands before treating a cut

For other minor injuries:
- Moleskin for blisters
- Tweezers to remove splinters

Other supplies:
- Pair of scissors to cut the moleskin, gauze, and first aid tape
- Pen and paper to write notes about what happened and what treatment you gave
- Pair of non-latex disposable gloves to wear when caring for a bleeding wound

Index

C

Camel Pose, 19
camera, pinhole, 313
camping, 58–62
Car Games, 38–39
card games
    Construct a House of
        Cards, 246–247
    Hi, King!, 10
    Race to 24, 11
    Tongues, 10–11
Card Tricks, 166–168
cards
    constructing, 216–219
    Create a Mechanical Card,
        266–267
    See also Notes and Letters
care packages, 328
cartouche, 118
cartwheels, 44
Cat Snack, 85
catapult, building, 251–253
chain reaction machine,
    254–255
Chain Tag, 53
chalk activities
    Draw a 3-D Fake Hole, 49
    Four Squares, 48
    Triangle Toss, 48
    Design T-Shirts with
        Chalk, 195
chalk maze, 44
Challah bread, 94–95
challenges, quick
    brain activities, 148
    building activities, 242
    color activities, 172
    drawing activities, 106
    great things, 320
    inside activities, 6
    kitchen activities, 82
    outside activities, 44
    paper activities, 200
    recycled activities, 296
    science activities, 270
    writing activities, 130
Change-a-Maze, 245
Character Play, 144
characters for comics, 115
checkers to go, 40

Cheesy Melts, 62
Chickadee, 68
cicadas, 73
circuits, 290–291
City, State, Country, 39
clay, sculpting, 196–197
cleaning up
    games for, 36
    tips for, 37
clock, water, 276–277
clouds, watching, 44
club, starting a, 20–21
Coach Whistle, 303
Cocoa Cooler (ice pop), 99
Coin Conundrums, 150
coin-and-cup trick, 159
Collagraph Prints, 305
color activities
    The Color Wheel, 173
    Crayon Rocks, 194
    Create Tie-Dye Patterns,
        184–187
    Design T-Shirts with
        Chalk, 195
    Make a Rainbow with
        Light, 178–179
    Make Pavement Paint, 183
    Milk and Color, 182
    Paint a Mural, 193
    Play with Paint, 174–177
    quick challenges, 172
    Sculpt Clay, 196–197
    self-portrait, 197
    Wandering Colors, 180–181
    Weird Ways to Paint,
        188–192
    See also art
Color Wheel, The, 173
Colorful Squiggles, 113
comics, drawing, 114–117
compass, for maps, 118
complementary colors, 177
Confetti Cannon, A,
    243–244
cooking
    Bake Leftover Pies, 96
    Cook Easy Lasagna, 93
    Knead Challah Bread,
        94–95
    Make a Sun Cooker, 287
    over fire, 62

See also food
costume from recycled
    things, 317
cover art, 124
Craft Organizer, 298–299
crafts
    Build a Paper Helicopter,
        202
    Coach Whistle, 303
    Collagraph Prints, 305
    Crayon Rocks, 194
    Create a Mask, 310–312
    Create a Twirling Flyer,
        203
    Create Tie-Dye Patterns,
        184–187
    Create Your Own Time
        Capsule, 37
    Design T-Shirts with
        Chalk, 195
    Fold a Napkin into
        Creative Shapes, 87–91
    Knit on Two Fingers,
        30–32
    Make a Flip Book, 122–123
    Make a Flying Disc,
        316–317
    Make a Lava Lamp,
        282–284
    Make a Papier-Mâché
        Fruit Bowl, 210
    Make a Plaster Cast of
        Animal Tracks, 78
    Make a Rainbow with
        Light, 178–179
    Make a Tool Belt with
        Tape, 22–23
    Make an Aerobatic
        Airplane, 201
    Make an Extendable
        Grabber, 308
    Make an Indoor Hanging
        Garden, 34–35
    Make Bath Fizzies, 16
    Make Checkers to Go, 40
    Make Giant Bubbles, 55
    Make Spontaneous Art, 76
    Make Your Own Books,
        212–215
    Make Your Own Cards,
        216–219

H

I

J

T

U

V

W

Y

Z

Credits

WRITERS

Alicia Anderson (98); Aubre Andrus (202, 203, 216, 217-218, 220, 224-225, 226-227, 238-239); Ana Appel (288-289); Caroline Arnold (83-84); Heather Bode (193); Helena Bogosian (196-197); Teresa Bonaddio (22-23, 30-32, 34-35, 76, 78, 107-111, 118-119, 120-121, 124, 137, 182, 184-187, 190-191); Jean G. Bowman (77); Rachel Bozek (328, 330-331, 350-353); Janice Bridgers (173, 174-177); Andrew Brisman (131, 246-247, 257-261, 282-284); Noreen Brophy (165); Mindy Burton (127); Shannon Caster (232-233); Sarah Chapman (100-101, 178-179, 180-181, 204-207, 297, 300, 306-307, 310-312); Lucy Clark Crawford (99); Marian Costello (131); Anjela Curtis (301); B. J. Deike (150); Ann Deiterich (39); Brademan Del Regno (153); Valerie Deneen (250); Teresa A. DiNicola (150-151); Karen Dobyns (228); Jed Duquette (48); Denise Etheridge (230-231); Ellen Feldman, M.D. (11); Lisa Glover (13, 40, 58-59, 62, 95, 195, 243-244, 245, 251-253, 254-255, 256, 266-267, 267, 271, 272, 275, 287, 290-291, 292, 298-299, 308, 309); Tamara C. Gureghian (8); Lisa Haag Kang (215); Christina Hackney (210); Lori Hancock (322-323); Olivia Hartman (273); Sue Heavenrich (274); Ted Heller (139, 143); Tim Hensley (47); Jannie Ho (114-117); Lois Hoffman (161); Ellen Javernick (51); Mamie Jefferson-Hill (168); Amy S. Johnson (278-279); Channing Kaiser (16); Allison Kane (86); Laurie Kane (257-261, 282-284); Joseph H. Klein (201); Chetra E. Kotzas (45-46); Josh Kropkof (160); Christian R. Küeng (209); Jean Kuhn (145, 212); Loralee Leavitt (280-281); Beverly J. Letchworth (79); Rosanne Lindsay (126); Thia Luby (18-19); Joanne Mattern (60-61, 64-67, 68-71); Beverly McLoughland (142); Carissa Monfalcone (229); Carmen Morais (10-11, 17, 20-21, 24-29, 33, 87-91, 132-136, 138, 140-142, 159, 162-163, 165, 166-167, 234-235, 236-237, 264-265, 286, 321); Susan O. Morelli (144); Francesca Nishimoto (151); Sandra K. Nissenberg, M.S., R.D. (93, 326-327); Chelsea Ottman Rak (127); Elizabeth Pagel-Hogan (188); Norene Paulson (183); Jenner Porter (36); Sharon R. Porterfield (48); Margaret Powers (79, 254-255); Rita Pray (15); Joan Reed Newman (8); Anne Renaud (273); Carrie Riggs (50-51); Kathy Robinson (7); Natalie Rompella (150); David Roper (160); Eileen Spinelli (140); Tami L. Stanton (208); Beth D. Stevens (56-57); Kimberly Stoney (122-124, 189, 192, 262-263); Mayzette E. Stover (304-305); Katherine Swarts (53); Diane Sweatman (302); Elizabeth Tevlin (12); Meg Thacher (276-277); Cy Tymony (248-249, 316-317); Christine Van Zandt (113); Rosanne Verlezza (305); Laurie S. Wallmark (38); Kristen White (219); Lois Wickstrom (270); Evelyn Witter (83); David Zinn (49)

ILLUSTRATORS

Tom Bingham (6, 22-23, 30-32, 44, 60-61, 82, 106, 120-121, 130, 140-142, 148, 159, 172, 176-177, 178-179, 200, 202, 203, 216-219, 238-239, 242, 246-247, 270, 296, 320); Hayelin Choi (12, 34-35, 47, 52, 53, 59, 77, 102-103, 112-113, 124, 139, 143, 150-151, 153, 162-163, 180-181, 184-187, 208, 209, 232-237, 243-244, 262-263, 276-277, 288-289, 304-305, 313, 336-337, 342-343, 346-347); Holli Conger (322-323); Avram Dumitrescu (24-29, 45-46, 55, 78, 83-84, 87-91, 122-124, 158, 160-161, 189, 192, 212-215, 222-223, 254-255, 264-265, 290-291, 302, 306-307, 316-317); Keith Frawley (13); Ethel Gold (220-221); David Helton (127); Jannie Ho (114-117); Tom Jay (4-5, 40, 42-43, 56-57, 80-81, 104-105, 128-129, 146-147, 170-171, 198-199, 240-241, 268-269, 294-295, 318-319, 334-335, 344-345); Gary LaCoste (86); Vicky Lommatzsch (14, 15, 36, 48-49, 54, 79, 100-101, 118-119, 126, 137, 138, 152, 166-168, 190-191, 204-207, 210, 211, 224-227, 248-249, 257-261, 271, 272, 273, 273, 282-284, 297-300, 328, 340-341, 348, 349); Robert L. Prince (250); Red Herring Design (107-111, 126, 230-231); Peter Sucheski (256); Beegee Tolpa (7, 8-9, 18-19, 45, 50-51, 58, 144-145, 154-155, 164-165, 183, 193, 229, 278-279, 285, 286, 287, 310-312, 321, 332-333, 338-339, 125)

PHOTOS

Key: SS=shutterstock, GI=GettyImages, GCAI=Guy Cali Associates, Inc., RHD=Red Herring Design

6: hchjj/SS (magnifying glass), Earlymorning project/SS (calendar); 10–11: Valentina Rusinova/SS (suits), Mixmike/GI (cards); 13: GCAI; 16: Maffi_Iren/GI; 17: elenafoxly/SS; 20–21: cosmaa/SS (heading), world of vector/SS (popcorn), IrishaDesign/SS (girl with sign); 22–23: RHD; 30–32: RHD; 37: Sanny11/GI; 38–39: zizi_mentos/SS (stopwatch), ourlifelooklikeballoon/GI (cars); 41: Mooi Design/SS; 44: zizi_mentos/SS (stopwatch), 9george/SS (clouds); 48–49: Bildagentur Zoonar GmbH/SS (triangle toss), David Zinn (fake hole); 55: khalus/GI; 56–57: New Africa/SS; 60–61: Pigdevil Photo/SS (leaf), Analgin/SS (pine needles), xpixel/SS (kindling), JIANG HONGYAN/SS (firewood); 62: GCAI; 63: Sergey Sidorov/GI (boy), AlexLinch/GI (shadows), lacuarela/SS (camera); 64–67: Zerbor/SS (willow, oak), ulumi/GI (willow leaf), Nadezhda79/SS (pine), kathykonkle/GI (pine bough), khalus/GI (tree ring), OK-SANA/SS (oak leaf), LEAF87/SS (aspen leaf), Maksym Bondarchuk/SS (aspen), Le Do/SS (maple), oleg7799/GI (maple leaf); 68–71: chas53/GI (chickadee), SkyF/GI (crow), AbbieImages/GI (blue jay), ronniechua/GI (robin), PrinPrince/GI (bluebird), Dopeyden/GI (hummingbird); 72–73: William Cho/GI (cricket), ABDESIGN/GI (firefly), Ines CarraraGI (flower fly), traveler1116/GI (cicada), 1st-ArtZone/SS (moth), Lightspring/SS (butterfly); 74–75: Aleksandar Dickov/SS (snail), knorre/GI (strider), Eric Isselee/SS (mayfly), motorolka/GI (earthworm); 76: RHD; 83–84: ben phillips/GI (grapefruit), Floortje/GI (avocado), Андрей Елкин/GI (forks), Pektoral/GI (strawberry), Andrey Elkin/GI (broccoli), Bozena_Fulawka/GI (kiwi); 85: adogslifephoto/iStock (animals), Nastco/iStock (party hats), GCAI (snacks); 88: RHD;90–91: RHD; 92: GCAI; 93: GCAI; 94–95: GCAI; 95: GCAI; 96: GCAI; 97: RHD; 98–99: GCAI; 100–101: arcimages/GI; 111: Andrey Nyunin/SS; 112–113: Martin Janecek/SS; 118–119: zak00/GI; 132: phototastic/SS (index cards), spacezerocom/SS (pencil, shavings); 133: schab/SS; 134–135: Phant/SS (pen), Vector things/SS (paper); 136: Mega Pixel/SS (pen), umesh chandra/GI (card); 148: facebook.com/okolaamicrostock/GI; 149: borisyankov/GI (pencil), stockcam/GI (paper); 150–151: TokenPhoto/GI (pennies), Fourleaflover/GI (map); 152: stockcam/GI; 173: PeterHermes Furian/GI; 174–175: vejaa/GI (bottom left), RHD (steps); 177: PeterHermesFurian/GI; 178–179: RHD; 182: RHD; 184–187: RHD (banded pillow case), CHAIWATPHOTOS/GI (blank pillow), Premyuda Yospim/GI (ice, swirl), Pink_Cactus/GI (shibori); 188: GCAI; 189–192 : RHD; 194: RHD; 195: GCAI; 196–197: GCAI; 201: RHD; 202: RHD; 203: RHD; 208: RHD; 210: GCAI; 211: RHD; 212–215: RHD; 216–219: RHD; 220–227: RHD; 228: GCAI; 238–239: RHD; 243–244: GCAI; 245: GCAI; 250–253: GCAI; 256: GCAI; 262–263: chas53/GI; 264–265: HHelene/GI; 266–267: GCAI; 272: photohampster/GI (leaves), Imo/GI (flower); 274: vitalytitov/GI (cat), GlobalP/GI (dog); 275: GCAI; 278–279: prairie_eye/GI; 280–281: GCAI; 292: GCAI; 301: GCAI; 303: GCAI; 305: GCAI; 308: GCAI; 309: GCAI; 314–315: GCAI; 324–325: Stockbyte/GI (pom-poms), OGI75/GI (coin jar); 326–327: ahirao_photo/GI (brownies), sydmsix/GI (card), GCAI (jar); 328: Roman Valiev/GI (background), oleksii arseniuk (stamp); 330–331: Elen11/GI (stroke), Susan Shadle Erb (page 330 top left and 331), Judy Tuman Burinsky (page 330 top right), GCAI (rocks); 348: vectorplusb/GI; 349: subjug/GI; 350–353: ChooChin/GI (flower), robertsrob/GI (Earth), Rawpixel/GI (girl), max-kegfire/GI (boy); 354–362: estherspoon/SS (background), kamieshkova/SS (dishes), Ataur/GI (map), Sergey Furtaev/SS (kit)